COMPLETE LINEBACKING

LOU TEPPER

Head Coach
Edinboro University

Human Kinetics

Library of Congress Cataloging-in-Publication Data

Tepper, Lou, 1945-
    Complete linebacking / Lou Tepper.
        p.   cm.
    Includes index.
    ISBN 0-88011-797-4
    1. Line play (Football)   2. Football--Defense.   3. Football-
-Coaching.   I. Title
    GV951.2.T46   1998
    796.332'23--dc21   97-37855
                                                                            CIP

ISBN-10: 0-88011-797-4

ISBN-13: 978-0-88011-797-5

Managing Editor: Coree Schutter; **Assistant Editor:** Erin Sprague; **Copyeditor:** Bob Replinger; **Proofreader:** Erin Cler; **Indexer:** Barbara E. Cohen; **Graphic Designer:** Nancy Rasmus; **Graphic Artist:** Francine Hamerski; **Photo Editor:** Boyd LaFoon; **Cover Designer:** Jody Boles; **Photographer (cover):** © John Studwell; **Photographer (interior):** Tom Roberts, unless otherwise noted; **Illustrator:** Jennifer Delmotte; **Printer:** United Graphics

Human Kinetics books are available at special discounts for bulk purchase. Special editions or book excerpts can also be created to specification. For details, contact the Special Sales Manager at Human Kinetics.

Printed in the United States of America   15   14   13   12

Human Kinetics
Web site: www.HumanKinetics.com

United States: Human Kinetics, P.O. Box 5076, Champaign, IL 61825-5076
800-747-4457
e-mail: humank@hkusa.com

Canada: Human Kinetics, 475 Devonshire Road, Unit 100, Windsor, ON N8Y 2L5
800-465-7301 (in Canada only)
e-mail: info@hkcanada.com

Europe: Human Kinetics, 107 Bradford Road, Stanningley
Leeds LS28 6AT, United Kingdom
+44 (0) 113 255 5665
e-mail: hk@hkeurope.com

Australia: Human Kinetics, 57A Price Avenue, Lower Mitcham, South Australia 5062
08 8372 0999
e-mail: info@hkaustralia.com

New Zealand: Human Kinetics, Division of Sports Distributors NZ Ltd.
P.O. Box 300 226 Albany, North Shore City, Auckland
0064 9 448 1207
e-mail: info@humankinetics.co.nz

This book is dedicated to my Lord and Savior, Jesus Christ, and my precious wife, Karen Ann Tepper.

It was June of 1965, prior to my junior year at Rutgers University, that I committed my life to Christ. Through all the pressures, joys, and pains of a college coaching career, God has given me the unusual peace he promises each of us in Philippians 4:6-7.

"Rejoice in your hope, be patient in tribulation, be constant in prayer"—this wonderful three-part verse from Romans 12:12 has been so meaningful to me. We can each enjoy hope, despite our trials. We gain the joy and patience when we enter a consistent personal relationship with our caring God.

On December 23, 1967, I made a second major commitment to Karen Ann Oleszewski, my high school sweetheart. We promised to be faithful partners for life. I have never cherished Karen more than now. She is my loving and loyal best friend. She is an amazing servant for God's gifts to us, Matthew Louis and Stacy Ann Tepper. She is my hero.

God, thank you for being so trustworthy. Thank you for the rich blessing of Karen in my life.

Contents

Part IV Techniques

Part V Teaching and Learning

Foreword

Linebacking has always been in my blood. As a youngster I would imitate the moves of NFL greats like Lawrence Taylor, who revolutionized the linebacker position with his speed, quickness, and determination. When I graduated from high school, I chose to attend the University of Illinois primarily because of its great tradition of linebackers. After all, it is the alma mater of possibly the greatest, Dick Butkus.

In my first season, Lou Tepper was the defensive coordinator as well as the linebacker coach. At the end of that year, he became the head coach. I was fortunate to play under Coach "Tep," who emphasized the fundamentals of the position. For three years straight, our linebacker corps was the finest not only in the Big Ten but also in the entire country. The training and instruction I received in college enabled me to step directly into a starting role at the professional level.

In this book, Coach shares the same techniques he used to develop some of the game's best, from the most basic to the most sophisticated ideas. He explains the tests he has developed to evaluate physical capabilities for playing the position; he tells the skills to work on during practices; and he shares the special grading system that his staff uses to measure linebacking performance.

When it comes to teaching defense—especially linebacking—Coach Tep is THE MAN. He has spent his career learning, teaching, and refining his unique approach. I am just one of many players he has helped reach the NFL. It goes to show that with hard work and the guidance of his instructions, great things can happen.

Kevin Hardy
Jacksonville Jaguars, 1995 Butkus Award Winner

Acknowledgments

To acknowledge all those who have passed on to me the knowledge presented in *Complete Linebacking* and helped present those ideas in book form would take a separate chapter. Let me recognize a few specifically and others generally.

Four head coaches hired me over a 24-year span, and each influenced me significantly. I thank Jim Root (New Hampshire, William and Mary), Bill Dooley (Virginia Tech), Bill McCartney (Colorado), and John Mackovic (Illinois) for the freedom to learn and thrive professionally.

The support staff, secretaries, and coaches at each of those institutions formed an atmosphere conducive to learning. I gained so much from many of you.

Finally, the student-athletes are the reason I am in this profession. I hope I've served you as well as you have energized my life. Thanks for the volumes you've taught me. Always remember that you can be a fierce competitor and a classy man.

The staff at Human Kinetics were accessible and professional. We both sought a quality product that would benefit players and coaches for years to come. Special thanks are in order for Ted Miller and Coree Schutter for their expertise and concern. Let's do it again sometime!

Introduction

I began developing the concept for this book decades ago, in 1968, when I entered the coaching profession. I had just finished my degree and playing career as a linebacker and defensive back at Rutgers University. As a new coach at the University of New Hampshire, I had the job of teaching linebacking to young men who were nearly my age.

To prepare, I went to every source I knew about for information. I read books, attended clinics, studied film, and talked with coaches. What I found was that the written material was limited or scheme specific; that clinic speakers provided only a few ideas, not the broad understanding of linebacking that coaches and players need; that coaches were reluctant to share information that might be passed on to an opponent. Film was helpful only to the extent that my untrained eye could analyze fundamentals and techniques. The information I wanted was either not available or not accessible.

What was lacking then and for 30 years thereafter was a comprehensive and detailed book that explained the

- qualities needed to play linebacker and the best tests to evaluate which players possess those abilities;
- fundamentals required of all linebackers, regardless of the team's scheme;
- techniques and their keys for inside and outside linebackers in specific defenses;
- ways that an offense gives clues and tips about the upcoming play before the ball is snapped; and
- effective ways to teach and learn the linebacker position in team meetings, practices, and through a grading system.

Now, *Complete Linebacking* fills the information gap for coaches and players who want a full understanding of the linebacker position. This book represents more than 30 years of knowledge that I gained from playing, studying, teaching, and coaching the position. It's the basis for instruction that has produced three Butkus Award winners and numerous NFL players.

Perhaps most important, the information in the book applies to all levels of competition and any defensive scheme. My hope is that this book will benefit you in coaching or playing football's most demanding and exciting position—linebacker.

Key to Diagrams

B	Linebacker	◖	Inside shoulder
●	Ball carrier	◗	Outside shoulder
⬭	Offensive player	◐	Head up
⬬	Keyed player	⊤	Blocking
(TE)	Tight end	⊓	Square up
(QB)	Quarterback	GL	Goal line
(WR)	Wide receiver	LOS	Line of scrimmage
(OG)	Offensive guard	▲	Cone
(RB)	Running back	⬚⬚⬚	Sled
(FB)	Fullback	▯	Long dummies (flat on ground)
(TB)	Tailback	▯	Popsicle sled
(I)	Pulling lineman	👣	Footprints
C	Cornerback	👣	Lateral crossover
ILB	Inside linebacker	◉	Plant foot
DL	Defensive lineman	•——————•	Positions aligned
DB	Defensive back	——————→	Player movement
□	Center	∿∿∿→	Shuffle, drift, backpedal
SS	Strong safety	– – – →	Jog
FS	Free safety	••••••••	Optional movement or reaction
H/C	Hook to curl	⋁⋁⋁→	Alley
H/F	Hook to force	----------⊣	Pass, pitch, toss
E	End	⌇	Pass protection
T	Tackle	——⫽→	Handoff
N	Nose tackle		

PART I
LINEBACKER PROFILE

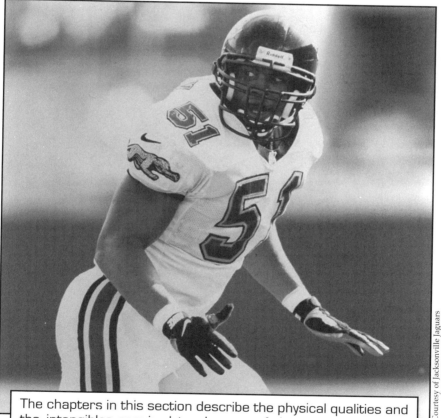

The chapters in this section describe the physical qualities and the intangibles required to play one of the most demanding positions in the world of sport. Every player, coach, and fan has a certain image of linebackers. Mobile. Strong. Tough. Dick Butkus types. Lawrence Taylor types. Actually, linebackers come in all shapes and sizes, but the ones who excel share certain attributes. Let's examine the types of physical and personality traits needed to succeed at the linebacker position.

Chapter 1

Physical Qualities

What tools does it take to play linebacker? We can probably best answer that by first identifying the fundamentals of linebacker play:

- Hit and shed
- Pursuit
- Tackling
- Coverage skills

The linebacker who can perform these fundamentals will be successful regardless of scheme. No matter what defense you devise, you will be able to use a defender who can consistently execute the ABCs.

Note that size is not a factor in three of the four fundamentals. Size has nothing to do with pursuit. A five-foot-nine, 175-pound linebacker can pursue as well as someone much larger. Tackling has little to do with bulk. Certainly a 190-pound linebacker can be an effective tackler in major college football, and smaller players can tackle well enough to man the position at the high school level. Coverage skills, whether man or zone, do not require size. Height in zone coverage is an advantage, but those of modest stature in the correct location will be very productive.

Three of the four ABCs depend mostly on movement, not size. Movement is the key to proficiency in linebacker fundamentals.

Even the hit and shed has less to do with size than most people imagine. The linebacker's base just before contact is the vital element in taking on blockers. Getting to the correct base is a product of movement and agility, not size.

The "bigger is better" mentality permeates football. Parents, players, fans, media, and yes, even coaches, have bought into this fallacy. Because linebackers must take on big blockers, the supposition is that linebackers must also be large to compete.

Let me ask a couple questions. If you were a 320-pound offensive lineman, would you fear a 240-pound linebacker? Not because of his size. Would you fear a 260-pound linebacker? No. A 320-pound lineman fears movement, not someone who weighs 60 pounds less than he does. Does that make sense? It doesn't initially to most of my first-year linebackers.

Don't get me wrong. I am not against big linebackers. I am for linebackers who can cover ground. Our rule of thumb is that a linebacker can gain weight as long as he maintains or improves his movement. Kevin Hardy, the second player taken in the 1995 NFL draft, played as a true freshman at 205 pounds. Four years later, at 240 pounds, Kevin was significantly faster. We loved his gain in movement.

Knowing what we do about the basic building blocks of linebacker play, can we test the general population to locate those most likely to have the physical qualities to play this position? Yes. We administer four diagnostic tests to every player on our squad. Each test has some implications for other positions, but these four are most meaningful in judging a linebacker's potential.

40-Yard Dash

I love to watch young players run their first dashes. I've been timing football players in this dash since 1967. The 40 in itself is not that significant. The 20-yard time might be a better indicator of linebacker speed, but after 30 years I know what a 4.81 means as opposed to a 4.68 or a 5.0.

I can still remember the excitement of seeing Melvin Martin and Jim Ryan run their dashes at the College of William and Mary. I had never coached speed like that before and quickly realized how much better it made me as a coach.

In 1980 at Virginia Tech, we recruited three student-athletes from DeMatha Catholic High School in Maryland. Derek Carter was a nationally prized defensive back. Tony Paige was a short, gritty kid that I liked as a potential linebacker. He went on to play many years

Courtesy of Dallas Cowboys

In the spring of 1988, I joined John Mackovic at the University of Illinois. We inherited a rising sophomore linebacker, who had lettered as a special-teams player in 1987 as a true freshman.

Darrick Brownlow was a brash, confident young man who packed 248 pounds on a 5-foot-10-inch frame. He announced when we first met that he would start in the fall and that he was proud of the weight he had gained since the season ended. I did my best to impress on him the importance of movement, not bulk. I could tell that Darrick was not a believer. He "listened" as many listen to the pastor in church, but it didn't change his lifestyle.

After horrible pursuit grades in spring practice, I told Darrick that if he returned at 248 pounds he would never start for me. He might play a few series, but he could never sustain the effort I would require of him. He had to streamline his body over the summer, or he wouldn't see much playing time.

Thankfully, playing was important to Darrick. Even though he didn't believe the theory initially, he *did* believe I was stubborn! Darrick returned to fall camp a svelte 224 pounds. Brownlow went on to start for three seasons, while leading the Illini in tackles all three years. Darrick was All-Big Ten three times, the league's MVP, and the 1990 Butkus runner-up. Darrick now has six years in the NFL despite his lack of NFL height.

in the NFL as an excellent blocking and pass-catching fullback. The third player from DeMatha was a six-foot-one, 220-pound guard who our staff felt might be the key to getting Derek and Tony to sign. We offered to Mike Johnson but felt his future was hazy at best.

Mike entered fall camp in Blacksburg at 16 years of age. His first 40-yard time was 4.68. Before he got back to the recorder, I had him by the arm, persuading him to play linebacker. Mike majored in architecture with an outstanding GPA. He had unusual character and the drive to be outstanding. Mike started his first professional game at 20 and was All-Pro twice. Not bad for DeMatha's third best prospect.

Speed will get my attention, but it doesn't guarantee linebacker performance. It is only harnessed speed that will translate into faster pursuit, more tackling opportunities, and better coverage. Always explore linebackers with speed, but play those who are productive.

Jingle-Jangle

I can't remember the first time we employed the jingle-jangle or how it got its name. We have used it consistently for decades, and it's a prime NFL test as well. Why? It incorporates two changes of direction within a 20-yard run. The ability to change direction is a better indicator of a linebacker's performance than his speed. I've had several linebackers who were slow in the dashes but were outstanding major college players; I've never had a linebacker with a poor change of direction perform well. Figure 1.1 illustrates how to time the jingle-jangle.

The tested athlete straddles a 5-yard line. After the timer (C2) is ready, the athlete can start on his own initiative. The clock begins on his movement. The linebacker can begin in either direction, but must sprint 5 yards and touch the line with his foot. In figure 1.1, C3 would check to see that the athlete's foot touched the first line. If he failed to touch, the attempt is aborted immediately. Then the player sprints 10 yards in the opposite direction, touching the line while C1 observes. The athlete again changes direction and sprints back through the starting point, and C2 stops his watch.

Remember these points about the jingle-jangle:

- This is a learned drill. With no experience, the athlete will post much poorer times early.

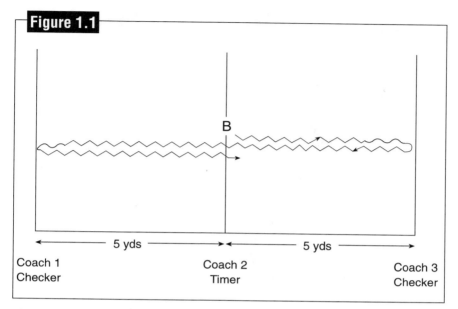

The timed jingle-jangle

- Because of the learning curve, we try to teach the drill first and then time it. Don't put a lot of stock into the initial times of this drill.
- The best jingle-jangle performances are by those who can bend low as they move and come under control at each line to push off and accelerate again.

How do we use the results? We simply subtract the jingle-jangle score from the 40-yard dash time. There are no hard-and-fast rules, but if the differential is .4 to .5 seconds the linebacker usually has the COD (change of direction) to play the position.

Barry Remington of Colorado was one of 60 linebackers invited to the 1985 NFL Combine. Barry ran the slowest timed 40-yard dash that day (5.18 seconds) and the third best jingle-jangle (4.33 seconds). The differential, an outstanding .85 seconds, was greater than I'd ever seen. It is one of the reasons Remington was so effective. He had COD!

Kevin Hardy posted the best raw jingle-jangle time for me with a 4.05, and he had the speed that Barry lacked, running a 4.61 in the 40. That .56 differential explains in part why he's an NFL millionaire.

Courtesy of University of Colorado

■ The 5-foot-11-inch Kyle Rappold transferred from a Division III college to Colorado as a walk-on. His transformation from 280 pounds to 240 pounds left a lasting impression on us about the importance of jingle-jangle testing in our program. Kyle's energy and competitiveness made him an All-Big Eight performer at Colorado.

The jingle-jangle is not just a linebacker time. I suggest that you use it to test the whole team. The times are revealing for any defensive position. A classic story unfolded at Colorado in 1984. Kyle Rappold was a Division III transfer who walked on without a scholarship. He was a 5-foot-11-inch, 280-pound offensive guard. Kyle quickly became a target of the locker-room jokers. It looked as though his career might be limited to the scout-unit offense.

That fall we tested him in the jingle-jangle. As expected, his 40 time was unimpressive. His COD time, however, turned everybody's head. It was the fastest of all the Colorado linemen. We told Kyle that if he lost weight and got serious about playing, he might have a future at nose guard.

One calendar year later, Kyle Rappold reported to fall camp in superb condition and at 245 pounds. He started all season and was eventually All-Big Eight. Without the jingle-jangle, Kyle might have remained an anonymous scout-team lineman. Since that time, we have always tested every player in this drill.

The jingle-jangle is also a strong indicator of option ability. We ran the wishbone and I-bone at Colorado and learned again that speed and COD differ. Many quarterbacks lacked 40-yard dash speed but had excellent COD and became outstanding option runners for us.

Cleans

The importance of the hang-clean or power-clean lifts in the weight room will be stressed in chapter 3. This is the third diagnostic test we would give to identify linebacker prospects.

If the linebacker has good feet and can establish a correct base before contact, the clean strength indicates his ability to explode his hips and launch his body into a blocker.

Steve Shull was such a linebacker at William and Mary. As a senior Steve was under 210 pounds. He didn't have extraordinary speed or COD but did have good control of his feet to set his base. Steve could really explode with his hips. Despite his size he shocked linemen with his hit and shed because he had such hip explosion.

Steve played six years with the Miami Dolphins and in two Super Bowls. His NFL nickname was "The Animal" because of his aggressive style.

Body Fat

The fourth diagnostic test we give prospective linebackers determines body fat. Controversy surrounds the methods used to test for body composition. The most accurate method, underwater weighing, is timely and cost prohibitive.

All other methods have their detractors, but most are inexpensive and don't use too much time. Our philosophy has been to test often and not be influenced by a single result. We look at a trend over many tests and make the players aware of how we interpret the results.

An athlete could be tested four times at 13.8, 14.5, 14.7, and 13.7. I would feel comfortable in averaging these percentages.

Another player might be tested the same four days at 22.6, 14.9, 15.1 and 14.4. I'd throw out the high score and average the others. Use common sense and don't emphasize any one result.

Before competition most quality linebackers I've had are between 10 and 15 percent fat. Again I'm interested in averages, not one raw score.

Why is body fat important? It tells a coach how long a linebacker can play hard. If a coach expects 93 percent pursuit (see chapter 4) from his linebackers over 70 snaps, plus 15 special-teams plays, their body fat better be under control.

That's why I was adamant that Darrick Brownlow lose weight in 1988. At 248 pounds, Darrick was over 20 percent body fat. It was physically impossible for him to play hard very long. I was elated when he returned at 224 the next fall. We were proud of his dramatic body-fat improvement. A coach can't count on a player with high body fat. He will always let his team down.

Frequency

How often do we test for these diagnostic results? Each varies in testing frequency.

▪ 40-yard dash: We test this least often because of potential hamstring pulls. In the fall of 1995, we lost Kevin Hardy for two weeks of practice with a deep pull. Why did we test him? It was sheer stupidity. He was fast. We knew that. What was there to gain?

Now we test the varsity only in winter conditioning, although we continue to test freshmen in the fall. Usually, we get two or three times for each player. Any player with a history of hamstring pulls is not tested.

▪ We test the jingle-jangle frequently because it takes little time and rarely causes an injury. If a groin is bothering a linebacker, we hold him out of this one.

Usually we test everyone in fall camp and again in winter conditioning. Linebackers also do this drill competitively in practice without timing (see chapter 4).

▪ Cleans are tested by our strength coach twice a year for maximum lifts. Safety is key here, and many coaches discourage testing for a one-rep maximum before fall camp. Keep them healthy!

▪ Body-fat percentage can be taken as often as the staff desire. Test every player at least four times a year, with one before fall camp and one after the season. You may choose to test particular players every two weeks to make a point to them of the seriousness of this issue.

A team doctor and the strength coach should present nutrition education to the squad on a regular schedule. Body fat is a product of sensible eating and regular exercise.

Effective linebackers can come in many shapes and sizes. Use the tests discussed in this chapter to identify players who have linebacker potential and to set goals for those who may fall short because of current physical limitations.

Chapter 2

Linebacker Intangibles

Linebackers are the glue of a defensive unit, physically and emotionally. Physically, they fill the open seams between defensive linemen inside and patrol the perimeter in conjunction with the secondary. In zone coverage linebackers provide a cohesive pass defense underneath the deep zones. In man coverage linebackers take away the early throws.

In chapter 1, we reviewed four physical tests to discover athletes with the aptitude to succeed as linebackers. The intangible qualities are more difficult to assess but are just as important, because every player in the defensive huddle will be affected by the linebackers' demeanors and personalities.

Psychological tests are available to evaluate a player's personality. I have not used these instruments but would not be opposed to exploring their use. A high school coach would often know players for years before he selected his leaders. A college coach normally has 18 months to assess how a player matches his program's values. NFL staffs have the budgets to use more costly psychological exams. Each, however, should try to determine the potential linebacker's standing in the following qualities before selecting, recruiting, or drafting at this position: character, intelligence, dependability, attitude, intensity, leadership, challenge-readiness, courage, and instincts.

Character

My father, Louis A. Tepper Sr., had an eighth-grade education and was employed as a laborer his entire life. He worked in a mill, pumped gas, and was a janitor. None of his employment was glamorous, but he was respected. His life demonstrated character. People had cheated him financially, but they couldn't take away his character. That's something unique about this quality. You can only give it away. It cannot be stolen!

Dad was not an outspoken Christian, as I have become, yet he trusted strongly that when a member of his family gave his or her word there was no backing down. Once Lou Tepper Sr. gave his word, it was his bond. One could always count on Dad's promise.

That's also a distinction I search for in linebackers. I don't want a player to give me or the team his word lightly. When a linebacker tells a coach he is going to do something, we expect him to attempt it with every fiber in his being. We want our linebackers to be trustworthy, whether it's in the view of the coaches or when he is alone.

Today's society does not value a promise as it once did. That's sad. For there to be trust between a coach and player, their words must ring of commitment. Later, the same will be true with his business and marriage partners.

I was once told that if a man were put in jail unjustly, somehow, some way, he would likely find a way to escape. If, however, a man of character entered a circle drawn in the dirt and promised he wouldn't leave, no guard would be necessary. Oh, how football teams and America need men of integrity.

Intelligence

We've never found the correlation between standardized academic test (ACT, SAT, etc.) scores and football intelligence to be as high as the correlation between grade point averages and football IQ. Those who do the work necessary to compete in the classroom are usually the ones who make the best game-plan decisions on Saturdays.

I've had some talented linebackers who were marginal students, and their limited decision-making ability often hurt the team. Intelligent linebackers put the defense in alignment and coverages that give the defense a decided edge. When a coach lacks intelligent linebackers, it really limits how well a defense can perform. A team with more than one poor student at linebacker is less able to make checks and adjustments.

Courtesy of Virginia Tech

■ Mike Johnson was one of my favorite people at Virginia Tech. He had character, intelligence, and dependability. He combined that with a great sense of humor and God-granted talent. Mike played in the pros for 10 years—mostly with the Cleveland Browns—and was All-Pro twice.

Always evaluate a linebacker's transcript closely. Find out from his teachers what he is like in class.

We want our linebackers to be active learners. I require each of my coaches to give daily tip sheets to our players. We provide the players with pencils and highlighters in their meetings. The serious linebackers add notes and highlight the tip sheets, just as the serious business student would.

Many times in my career a lesser athlete has started because he brought to the field the ability to make consistently good checks. Do not underestimate this quality when evaluating linebacker prospects.

Dependability

Find out if a young man is dependable. Ask coaches, teachers, parents, trainers, strength personnel, and others who may know him. When you meet a recruit, ask him to call or meet at a certain time. Find out if the linebacker can be counted on to follow up without constant prodding.

Because athletes love football, the coach can often change this quality in young linebackers. Why take the chance, however, if a staff doesn't need to?

Attitude

Wow, this is a key quality. It always has been, but today a young man faces so many hurdles in life that his attitude is key to his success and the success of those around him.

Bad things happen to all of us in life. Those who choose to be positive and determined in all circumstances can affect many others. During practice and games, we must endure heat, fatigue, mistakes, and worthy opponents. What profound influence a linebacker can have on the performance of his team when he chooses to be positive or optimistic in the face of adversity.

My favorite quote on attitude is the following by Chuck Swindoll:

> The longer I live, the more I realize the importance of attitude on life. Attitude, to me, is more important than facts. It is more important than the past, than education, than money, than circumstances, than failure, than successes, than what other people think or say or do. It is more important than appearance, giftedness, or skill. It will make or break a company . . . a church . . . a home. The remarkable thing is that we have a choice every day regarding the attitude we will embrace for that day. We cannot change the past . . . we cannot change the fact that people will act in a certain way. We cannot change the inevitable. The only thing we can do is play on the one string we have, and that is our attitude . . . I am convinced that life is 10 percent what happens to me and

90 percent how I react to it. And so it is with you . . . we are in charge of our *attitudes*.

I don't want a team led by linebackers who are pessimistic about the challenges that lie ahead in life, in the classroom, or on the field. In recruiting a potential linebacker, we look for enthusiasm. The linebacker corps will learn, however, that a surly individual can change. Each of us chooses our state of mind.

Intensity

How hot does his motor run? There is no motivator like a respected peer who practices and plays hard. A player who works hard in practice and pursues at 93 percent will impact the whole team if he is also a quality player. When a defensive unit has three or four athletes who are intense and admired, they can change the face of the entire season.

Top linebackers are difference makers. They raise the level of effort for the entire huddle. Their style of play will reinforce the coaches' emphasis on pursuit and give positive examples to their peers.

When I was in my early 20s and learning how to be an effective recruiter, I was given my home area of western Pennsylvania to evaluate in the spring. I had really been impressed with a young athlete who attended a high school that was a rival to my alma mater, Derry Area. He didn't show much effort, but his talents were remarkable. I decided after the dismissal bell to visit the Derry Area High School staff and get their comment on this prospect.

Bill Oleszewski, the Derry head coach (and my father-in-law) and his revered assistant, Joe Mastro, both knew the young man in question. They had seen him mature physically and knew that he had excellent talent. Both, however, questioned his desire to play.

As a recruiter, a coach wants badly for a highly rated talent and an impressive body type to be approved for a scholarship. If I had shown selected film clips, I knew my Division II football staff would have jumped at the chance for an athlete of his caliber.

Joe Mastro could see the inner turmoil I had in making this decision. He made a comment that has stuck with me whenever I have been enticed by talent without intensity. Coach Mastro said, "Lou, you can't give this kid a heart transplant." It hurt, but he was absolutely correct. Go on to the next guy.

One of the next guys happened to be Eddie Booker of Kiski Area High School. Eddie was a skinny, intense competitor who few recruited. He went on to captain the University of New Hampshire team and elevated everyone's play with his desire.

Leadership

Leadership is forced on most linebackers by the nature of their role as signal callers and communicators to the huddle and at the line of scrimmage. Because of their position, linebackers must be more vocal, and, as such, shape the defensive unit's attitude during practice and at games. Leaders are not always the most popular or talkative, but they are respected.

We have been blessed over the years with many convincing leaders. Never did we have a dominant defense without a respected leader. How did they gain that respect? They developed a set of attributes in their personalities. Some were God-given gifts; most were products of time, energy, and the desire to lead. Coaches must daily cultivate these leadership qualities in linebackers:

Hard Work

American Cardinal Gibbons said, "The higher men climb the longer their working day. Any young man with a streak of idleness in him may better make up his mind at the beginning that mediocrity will be his lot. Without immense, sustained effort he will not climb high. And even though fortune or chance were to lift him high, he would not stay there. For to keep at the top is harder almost than to get there. There are no office hours for leaders."

It's obvious to most that success begins with hard work. The seniors, captains, quarterbacks, and linebackers form the nucleus that sets the standards for the work ethic of the team. If this group does not demonstrate and demand hard work, the coach's job becomes very frustrating. When the young players see their peer commanders exerting consistent effort, they usually fall in line and that behavior becomes a habit for their careers.

I agree with the legendary Vince Lombardi when he said, "Contrary to the opinion of many people, leaders are not born. Leaders are made, and they are only made by effort and hard work."

Enthusiasm

Every great leader I have prepared at linebacker has been a hard worker. None has been lazy. Teams won't follow a player who doesn't work hard. All of our effective leaders have also been enthusiastic. Because of their position, linebackers must exhibit a genuine zeal for performing and an optimism for the future of the defensive unit.

Everyone in the huddle sees the present circumstances, to some extent, through the eyes of the signal caller. His influence can make a poor call effective or take the starch out of a superior decision by the staff. The signal caller must believe in the game plan and sell it to the huddle all week in practice and then on Saturday afternoon.

I often quote Dale Carnegie to our linebackers, beginning with fall camp and then at times of adversity during the season. Mr. Carnegie said, "Act enthusiastic and you'll be enthusiastic." I have found this statement to ring with truth. It contains a concept that I had never heard until I took his course on public speaking.

A body can actually control its mind. An athlete can be in the middle of double sessions, under a hot August sun, just trying to make it through another practice. If he follows his feelings he will lack energy, which will curtail his learning and set a slower pace for those around him.

If he will act enthusiastically by moving quickly *as if* he had energy, his mind will follow with focus and vitality. One turned-on leader can be contagious in a defensive huddle.

Showboating and trash talk are selfish enthusiasm. They are brought on by pride and desire to bring attention to oneself. They have no positive place in classy football programs.

During the modern era of football, individualism has taken a firm grasp on our society. We need to return to an age of sportsmanship. Sportsmanship has to do with manliness and respect for the opponent. A sportsman gets in the face of his teammate and jacks him up. A sportsman discourages his opponent by playing courageously until the final second.

The modern mentality of trash talk is faulty. It's rare that I have seen a competitor at the college level intimidated by someone's mouth. Almost always, the reverse is true; the competitor is inspired by the one who confronts him.

Do not confuse showboating or trash talk with genuine enthusiasm displayed by a leader to spur his squad to victory.

Purpose

No leader can succeed without a blueprint for success. A linebacker can work diligently and be eager, but he must show the troops *how* they can win. The leader must have a definite plan of action for the defensive unit to rally around.

The coaching staff designs the practice and game plans. Few people realize the hours involved in preparing a practice. Every minute is outlined and each snap is either scripted or diagrammed to ensure the exact looks for the defense.

Once practice is organized, the leaders must be prepared. They need to understand the importance of this particular day and be able to convey that to the defense. The signal callers must also have a working command of the plan by down and distance, personnel, and so on. When a linebacker can promote a call through his knowledge of the game plan, it helps endorse the coaches and sells the unit on the game plan's potential.

When the leaders can persuade the unit that this plan will stalemate their opponents, it forms a firm union in the huddle and an air of confidence at the line of scrimmage.

On inconsistent defenses, the coaches alone sell the game plan and motivate the players during practice. With leaders in concert with the staff, the results are magnified. Each practice improves and, on Saturdays, the linebacker becomes a player with a coach's ability to explain calls and make adjustments.

Cohesiveness

A leader fosters team unity. He must constantly acknowledge the importance of every member of his unit. The media and fans celebrate those who make spectacular plays, yet they seldom understand that their favorites depend on their teammates and the scheme for the opportunity to make big plays. A linebacker who leads must recognize the contributions of each of his teammates.

This attitude dilutes self-pride and promotes unity. A defense that is so tight that it operates as one heartbeat can, indeed, become special.

In Deuteronomy, God spoke to Israel about going into war. He told them that they would see armies larger than their own, but they were not to fear because God would be with them. Later, in Deuteronomy 20:8 he tells the officers to speak to the people and say, "What man is there that is fearful and fainthearted? Let him go back to his house, lest the heart of his fellows melts as his heart."

Linebackers can't be fainthearted or their teammates' hearts will falter. The leader must bring unity by showing a confident heart and promoting the value of each team member.

Ready for a Challenge

I believe that splendid linebackers love to be challenged. A common example might be with a game-plan check. Rather than give a linebacker a battery of checks and tell him that he better learn them, we would explain the reason for this group of checks and might say, "John, you can see this would be a tremendous help to us, but I think it would be unfair to expect you to recognize so much." If he agreed we would back off. Normally, the response would be, "Coach, I can do that!"

Once committed to it, he would study and be especially alert because he knew it was important. He also was aware that I'd drop the checks if he didn't master them during the week.

When we beat East Carolina in the 1994 Liberty Bowl game 30-0, our staff made Antwoine Patton, the free safety, a unanimous selection for Most Valuable Player. We had given Antwoine a "check with me" call for the huddle. It meant that, based on the formation, Antwoine would put our defense in one of eight coverages. Patton called 90 percent of the coverages that day by himself, made only one mental error, and picked off two passes.

How did he do it? First, we knew Antwoine was very intelligent (he ranked third in his high school class). Second, we knew he'd respond to the challenge. I brought him in and visually showed him the multitude of formations that East Carolina presented under Steve Logan's offense. We grouped the formations to show the obvious tendencies and then set the hook with this line: "Too bad we couldn't let you call every coverage so that I wouldn't put us in a weak call." Patton's response? "I can and want to do that, Coach!"

Patton dedicated himself to daily study. He memorized cue cards. He researched overheads in addition to the normal bowl film and tip-sheet reviews. He was on a mission to answer the challenge and performed remarkably.

In recruiting, I often challenge prospects. We emphasized the "Three Ts" at Illinois:

- **Tradition:** Illinois had a legacy of quality linebackers. Could this recruit uphold those legends?

- **Talent:** We recruited well at that position. Would the competition cause a recruit to back away or would he want to compete?
- **Training:** Nowhere would a linebacker receive such comprehensive training. Was the prospect ready for that kind of commitment?

In December 1993, we had a premier recruit visit our campus. Two of the country's top-10 football programs had already offered him scholarships. It was his final official trip, and by the time he reached our campus, he was really impressed with himself. For nearly 18 months coaches had told him how good he was. They puffed him up at every turn.

As he was leaving our campus he met with me at my office. He told me that the last university he visited had promised him that

- He would start as a freshman
- He would be All-Conference as a sophomore
- He would be All-American as a junior
- He would be on the cover of *Sports Illustrated* as a senior

He wanted to know what I'd promise him! I raised my eyebrows very high and challenged him. I told him he could earn anything, but he would be given nothing from me. I told him that most likely he'd redshirt as a freshman and learn some valuable lessons in the process. If he made postseason honors, it would be because he beat out stiff competition and got much better than he presently was. I told him we had coached three Butkus Award winners and a runner-up and never promised them anything but the best training we could provide. I challenged him to gain humility if he chose Illinois or he'd be embarrassed!

When he left my office, I knew we had little chance of getting him. That night I was shocked when he called me on the phone to apologize for his cocky attitude and beg me to sign him. He went on to tell me that he realized we were the only college that was candid and not blowing smoke at him. He responded to the challenge.

Routinely, we also challenge our linebackers with this question: "Do you want to be good or great?" The answer is obvious, and after we receive it we have license to ask a lot of our linebackers. We challenge them on their class attendance, grades, practice habits, lifting, and so on after they individually commit to be great, not good.

Courage

Another major intangible of linebackers is courage. Andrew Jackson, our seventh President, stated: "One man with courage makes a majority." How profound that is.

It is difficult to find men who, when their peers want to stray, will stand by their convictions. Defensive leaders are needed when the demands of a long practice cause fatigue or a loss of concentration. When coaches condition the team, it is encouraging to hear leaders urging the squad to strain for excellence rather than complain. One strong, respected leader can "make a majority" by using his influence.

The courageous leader is indispensable on game days when the team is not performing well. Many times in my career, our units have reversed a poor start because they refused to quit when adversity struck. This requires not only adjustments by the staff but faith and courage by the players. That bravery often emanates from their leaders on the field.

Another aspect of courage is being able to play with pain. Pain is part of playing linebacker. Few positions have such consistent high-speed contact with huge linemen and fast backs. Linebackers will invariably have bumps, contusions, and aches. Those who have low thresholds of pain won't get enough practice time. Players who can mentally block out pain can perform at a high and consistent level.

In 1990, Darrick Brownlow sustained a severe ankle sprain during a game. By Sunday, Al Martindale, our outstanding trainer, told me that Darrick's status was doubtful for the following Saturday versus Michigan State.

We always told our players that if they could not practice on Tuesday or Wednesday (our hard work days), they could not start the next game. It's been a worthwhile rule of thumb over the years. Without Tuesday or Wednesday's preparation, the starter is mentally behind. It also gives a boost to his replacement, who generally is psyched and plays well on adrenaline and the extra practice work. The team also rallies around the new guy.

The new guy replacing Darrick was Aaron Shelby, who had an impressive week of practice. Meanwhile, Darrick did nothing until our walk-through session on Friday. We had no plans to play Brownlow at all. During pregame warm-ups, Al Martindale and Darrick told me that physically he could play if we needed him.

When the game was just four plays old, Aaron Shelby went down with an injury. Michigan State had already moved across midfield. Before I was notified of Aaron's status, Darrick was on the field. In an incredible display of courage and mental preparation, Darrick made four consecutive tackles, including a fourth-down, short-yardage stop to thwart Michigan State's drive. He played with pain and dominated in a big victory.

Know the distinction between pain and an injury. Playing with an injury can create further problems for the athlete. When a trainer tells me that a player should not play, I never argue.

Instincts

Another linebacker intangible is instinct. I can't explain it, but some players have a feel for recognizing certain types of plays. Although you may drill them less than others, they have an innate ability to defend certain types of actions.

As a coach, it is important to recognize these intuitive traits. In practice, our staff knew we could not run reverses to Kevin Hardy. He was never fooled by them. Darin Schubeck, an outside linebacker at Colorado, had a knack for recognizing and single-handedly stopping screens. At Illinois, we called Eric Guenther the draw eater. On heavy draw downs, we would stunt to help other linebackers defend the draw, but not Eric.

I love college football because recruiting permits me to choose players with the intangible qualities necessary to influence a team positively. Players and coaches need to recognize the impact of these qualities on their shared goal of winning.

PART II

FUNDAMENTALS

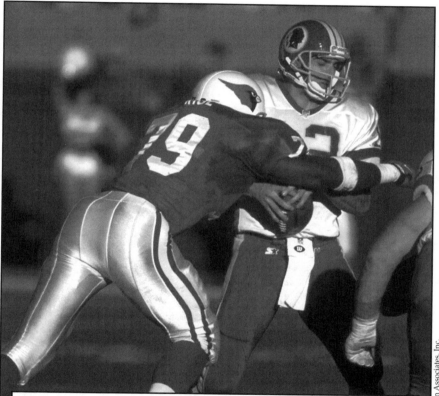

The chapters in this section describe the execution of the fundamentals—the ABCs—of linebacker play. The fundamentals form the foundation of a linebacker's entire career. A linebacker who lacks consistency in the ABCs cannot perform at an effective, competitive level any more than a house built on a fragile foundation can stand the test of time.

The ABCs are universal, meaning that these fundamentals are equally important to any defense ever created. They are not scheme specific. Players and coaches who are well grounded in the ABCs have an opportunity to distinguish themselves on the field regardless of their front or coverage calls.

Chapter 3

Hit and Shed

Taking on blockers is the basis of defensive football. It is to defense what blocking is to offense. If all the defensive players at the line of scrimmage make contact with their blockers and discard them while maintaining their position, a ball carrier would have no daylight at the line. He would face a wall of opposite-colored jerseys. Hit and shed is the act of making contact with a blocker and then discarding him while maintaining or moving to an assigned position.

Next to tackling, the hit and shed is the most important skill the linebacker must master. For the majority of players, tackling is very natural. Conversely, the hit and shed can be the most difficult fundamental for players to learn and execute.

Few high school, college, or NFL linebackers enter competition with an understanding of the concepts involved in taking on blockers. Even those who do rarely get the repetitions needed to become proficient. This is true for several reasons:

▪ The highly regarded athlete is usually able to impress the coaching staff, his teammates, and himself with spurts of impressive play, even though he may lack sound basics. He is often simply stronger and quicker than most of his opponents. This success with poor ABCs will normally cause problems for the demanding coach. When the talented, untrained linebacker becomes frustrated in mastering the new concepts, he will usually revert to his former style of play. The player must learn that only a sound hit and shed can win consistently against quality competition. If he doesn't believe it, the coach must make him a believer. Once he has confidence in the hit-and-shed concepts, he will work to make them second nature.

- Many football programs have too few coaches to give linebackers the individual attention they require.

- Most linebacker coaches at all levels, including the NFL, fail to stress the importance of proper mechanics when executing the hit and shed.

- Modern-day football has become very complex, yet we still have 24-hour days and limited practice time. Because of this, coaches have become more scheme conscious and devote less time to teaching the fundamentals.

My linebackers spend more practice time improving their hit and shed than any other single phase of the game. Rarely does a day go by, including game day, that we don't emphasize the hit and shed. We regularly stress the following concepts.

Hit-and-Shed Base

When you ask players and even most linebacker coaches to identify the keys to taking on blockers, they talk first about strength, upper-body action, or size. Few point out the importance of the player's feet, and yet that's the most critical issue when a linebacker meets a blocker. The contact surface itself is relatively unimportant. Linebackers can make good contact with their hands, shoulder, or forearm, but their effort will be in vain without a correct base.

Let's examine the three most common bases used by linebackers near the line of scrimmage.

Correct Base

When a player plants the same-side foot on the ground just before meeting the blocker with his same-side contact surface (his shoulder, forearm, or hand), he's in the strongest position to fight pressure from an opponent (see figure 3.1).

Every player and coach *must* know the feeling of power from this base. Each spring and fall we begin the first practice by demonstrating the power of this base to our linebackers. We put them in the correct base and then apply pressure to the shoulder over the planted foot. Never in 30 years have I been able to get movement on anyone in this drill. We emphasize that their weight must be over their front foot. The coach and linebacker will come away from this demonstration convinced that they possess real power in this position.

Figure 3.1

Correct base with front foot planted and same-side shoulder making contact. Hips are in excellent position to explode.

Opposite-Foot-and-Shoulder Base

The opposite-foot-and-shoulder base is perhaps the base that line-backers use most frequently. It is a terribly inefficient one (see figure 3.2A). Many coaches and players accept and use this hit-and-shed base because they don't appreciate the value of a correct base or don't know how to use a correct base consistently. With this incorrect base, an opponent who applies pressure to the contact shoulder will turn the linebacker on his up (forward) foot (see figure 3.2B).

I weigh just 180 pounds. In my career of teaching nearly 20 professional linebackers none has ever stopped me from getting movement on him. I turned each with ease. The opposite-foot-and-shoulder base renders linebackers helpless to blockers. And in chapter 4 we'll see that this base also makes pursuit more difficult.

At the University of Colorado, I would often use my son, Matthew, who was not yet a teenager, to emphasize the importance of establishing a correct hit-and-shed base to incoming freshmen. We put Barry Remington, our captain and All-Big Eight linebacker who was known for dominating much larger opponents, in the opposite-foot-and-shoulder position. The freshmen marveled as they saw little Matt turn the six-foot-four, 230-pound Remington with relative ease. This demonstration left an indelible impression on linebackers who were eager to improve.

Figure 3.2

(A) Opposite-foot- (left) and-shoulder (right) base is common, but very ineffective. (B) With pressure to the "opposite" base as shown in (A), the linebacker is turned by the blocker.

Players who are turned by offensive linemen must realize that it resulted from taking on the blocker with the opposite foot and shoulder. They shouldn't need to see it on tape. During a play on game day or in a practice drill, they should know immediately when they are caught in this base.

Strength and conditioning are important to players and coaches, and most are knowledgeable about gaining strength. But all the weightlifting linebackers do is wasted if they won't consistently sink a proper base. Better to have a correct base than to be embarrassed by a 180-pound coach or his 10-year-old son.

Pancake Base

The third base usually occurs when the young linebacker is trying to establish a correct base but fails to get his front foot planted. With only one foot for a base, he's almost always going to be moved backward (see figure 3.3).

Figure 3.3

Pancake base fails to get the front foot planted on the ground.

A player who gets pancaked before establishing a correct base needs to stick with it. He should realize that he was very close to the ideal base. He should determine whether he planted his front foot late or whether his final step was too long.

For players and coaches who don't have the resources to videotape hit-and-shed performance during practices, this method is useful. During one-on-one drills, focus on the "front" foot of the players involved. After the collision, every linebacker watching the drill should be able to say whether the participant's front foot was correct, opposite, or in the air. By focusing on this aspect of the drill everyone can see directly the importance of a correct base. This is a creative and effective way to learn even if you are able to tape practice sessions.

Pad Level

Coaches seem to have played down this fundamental since my early years in coaching. Coaches of defensive linemen and outside linebackers—players close to the line of scrimmage—still teach proper pad-level position, but this is a key fundamental for all linebackers.

If your base is correct but your pads are higher than your opponent, he will likely get movement on you. The old adage that the "low man wins" is true.

In the early 1960s it was still common to find a 200-pound linebacker playing over a 210-pound offensive guard in major college football. The guards moved quickly and contacted linebackers while still low coming out of their stances. Today, two factors have changed this dramatically:

- Offensive linemen today are gigantic in comparison to those of the 1960s. When they make contact with linebackers they are physically much higher because they are taller (most are six-foot-three to six-foot-eight) and rise more quickly from their stances.

- Linebackers play at least two yards deeper today. Because they are farther from the offensive linemen, the linemen rise higher as they leave their stances to reach the deeper-playing linebackers. We tell our inside linebackers that they are "born pad under pad."

Pad level is still important when linebackers and linemen of similar size make contact or when a linebacker is taller than an opposing lineman. That still occurs in high school but rarely in college football. Short linebackers have a true advantage in the hit and shed because they are always pad under pad on contact.

Courtesy of Miami Dolphins

■ Steve Shull was a 208-pound free agent who played six seasons for the Miami Dolphins, including two Super Bowls. His intensity and hip roll were unusual, and he was nicknamed "the Animal."

Hip Roll

One step before contact the linebacker must have his base set and his pad level lower than the blocker. Now the linebacker must launch his pads (or contact surface) into the blocker by uncoiling his hips.

The hips propel the contact surface, a fact that jumped out at me when I studied the physical conditioning results of my players after a decade of coaching. At that time, I had only four linebackers who had been in the NFL. They were not the four fastest or biggest, but as I perused the statistical data, they were the four strongest in one lift—the power clean. It dawned on me that hip roll (the

One of those four was **Craig McCurdy.** Craig came to the College of William and Mary unrecruited by many major colleges because he was a skinny six-foot-three at 185 pounds. He was an accomplished pole vaulter at Riverview High School in Oakmont, Pennsylvania, and I was attracted to his excellent movement. Craig bench pressed just over his body weight, but had an extraordinary power clean for his size. He went on to start for William and Mary as a true freshman and was drafted by the NFL, despite having marginal body weight and very limited bench-press strength.

power-clean or hang-clean action) was vital to the success of the hit and shed.

Players should work diligently in the weight room to increase their clean strength. This is the lift that will significantly improve hip roll. The cleans also require rare technique. Players should not attempt this lift without a certified strength and conditioning expert. This lift needs more athletic skill than any of the core lifts that we ask our linebackers to do.

To get maximum results from the hip explosion let's examine its relationship to the player's base:

- The player should use a compact base from which to uncoil his hips. He should set the front foot with a very small stagger (see figure 3.4).
- Players should experience the full range of movement they enjoy with their hips from a compact base. Conversely, they should take an elongated base and feel how it restricts their hip movement (see figure 3.5).
- The next concept is also key. The hips follow the path of the front foot. The front foot must point at the target, directed down the middle of the blocker (see figure 3.6), not on the edge of the opponent (see figure 3.7). We want the blocker to get the full impact of our hip explosion by directing it to the center of our opponent. We don't want a glancing blow.
- Often a linebacker will set his base correctly and have it compact but will turn his front foot at an angle (see figure 3.8). Remember, the hips follow the direction of the front foot. When

Figure 3.4

Set a short base before contact. It enhances the range of hip explosion.

Figure 3.5

A long base restricts hip roll by the linebacker.

Figure 3.6

The front foot should point down the middle of the opponent.

Figure 3.7

Here the front foot is on the edge of the blocker.

Figure 3.8

Here the front foot is turned and the hips will follow in that direction away from the opponent's midpoint.

the player places the front foot at an angle, the explosion of the hips applies only partial force to the blocker. We instruct our linebackers always to point the toe of their front foot into the crotch of the blocker. That ensures hitting the middle of the target.

Upper Body

Finally, we discuss the role of the upper body in the hit and shed. It is much less significant than anything previously mentioned, which is heresy to many linebackers and coaches. We tell our players that compared to base, pad level, and hip roll, the upper-body action is window dressing.

The upper body is the contact surface with the blocker. Years ago all linebackers made contact with shoulders or forearms. Many have since gone exclusively to hands. We actually have our outside linebackers use hands versus tight ends and a shoulder against power kick-outs by fullbacks. Our inside linebackers use hands only for cut blocks and use their shoulders for linemen and fullback isolations.

When using a shoulder, we attempt to get forearm lift over the front foot to gain separation from the blocker as our hips explode.

Simultaneously, we draw our outside hand, as if from a gunslinger's holster, to club the blocker away from the forearm.

Rarely is there a discard of an offensive lineman, while in a hole, in today's football. There is much more hit and hold ground than hit and shed. If all linebackers can hit and hold their positions while maintaining their off arms to tackle, you can play great run defense.

As a player, know that your coach can choose hands, shoulder, or forearm as a contact surface. All will be successful but only if the base, pad level, and hip roll are sound.

Approach

When a linebacker plays within one step of the line of scrimmage, he steps forward with his lead foot and establishes the base. When performing from depth, as most inside and many outside linebackers do, another dimension must be addressed—the approach.

The approach is the movement a linebacker makes toward a blocker before he sets his base. The approach distance varies depending on the depth of the linebacker and the speed of the oncoming blocker. Because of those variables, the linebacker can't measure the steps before each collision.

The linebacker should make each approach under control. Do not sprint to or attempt to sprint through an offensive lineman. The huge linemen we face today will engulf or turn a linebacker sprinting at them.

Approach under control and, just before contact, hop or skip to a correct base, get pad under pad, and explode off a stationary base. I'll describe several drills later that will reinforce the approach. Setting a correct base off an approach must be second nature to a linebacker. He will reach that point if he works it daily.

I've often asked my athletes, "If you throw a cat in the air, how does it land?" They respond, "On its feet." Then I ask, "If you throw a linebacker in the air, how does he land?" The proper response is, "With his near foot planted" or "With a correct base." This base must become a natural reaction through drills.

Hit-and-Shed Drills

Now we will discuss a sampling of drills to get proper repetitions for each of the coaching points discussed in chapter 1. A correct base will yield tremendous results, but to achieve it you must drill it so often that it becomes the only comfortable reaction to blockers. Linebackers must become like cats and always land with a correct base.

Use your imagination to create other meaningful drills to improve the areas in which your team needs work.

Air Drill

This is the first drill we use after a linebacker understands the three possible bases. The purpose is to get a high number of repetitions with a correct base. It takes little effort and produces repetitions quickly. We often see our linebackers doing this drill on their own before practice.

Put all your linebackers on a line facing you. On the command "ready hit" each steps forward with his front foot. Check to see initially that their weight is over the lead foot. Remind them that the step is a short one, so they can get good hip roll. Also check that they point the toe at the target.

Once they have the concepts get a ton of reps with the right foot and then the left by having them return to their original stance immediately after the "ready hit" command (see figure 3.9).

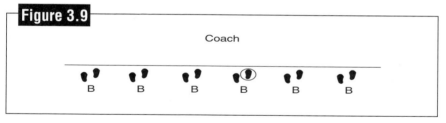

Figure 3.9

Coach

B   B   B   B   B   B

Air drill. On "ready hit" all Bs set their right-footed base repeatedly.

Sled, One-Step Drill

The purpose of the second drill is to provide limited contact one step away from a perfect base. After your players establish the correct compact base, you can emphasize hip roll.

Any sled will do, but we prefer a stationary seven-man sled. Draw five one-yard lines in front of and parallel to the sled. Seven players align one step (usually one yard) from contact, each shading a pad with his lead foot aligned in the middle of the pad.

On a "ready hit" command each of the seven linebackers steps with his lead foot and lightly touches the pad with his contact surface. The emphasis is *always* on foot placement first. Get the desired base and all else will fall into place. Practice a right-footed base and the next time up a left-footed one. Again, you can do many repetitions in a short time.

After a few times through without contact, have them explode with their hips off that base. Players should feel the power surge as the sled rocks upward off the ground (see figure 3.10).

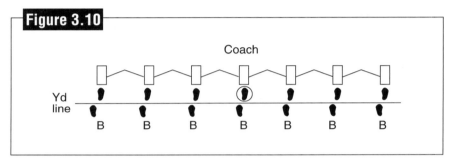

Seven-man sled, one-step drill. Bs are setting their right-footed bases here.

Sled Approach Drill

Again, any sled will work, but a stationary seven-man sled allows more players to drill. Draw lines on the field so that players will know their depths.

Back up the linebackers at various depths so that on "ready hit" they can approach and set their bases on the designated pads. Now the athlete gets to work on his particular approach. Some will skip or hop to set their bases. That's fine as long as they plant the front foot before they contact the pad. It should be bang, bang. First the foot hits the ground, and then the player makes contact with the pad. If the player makes contact with the pad first, the front foot is in the air on contact, resulting in the dreaded pancake base.

This is another drill that individual athletes can do in prepractice. It gives them great confidence in their approach to setting a base (see figure 3.11).

Figure 3.11

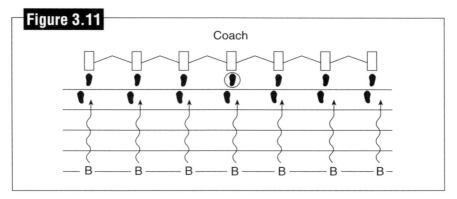

Seven-man sled approach drill. Bs are setting right-footed bases here.

Column Hit and Shed

The next drill in our progression combines an approach from either side with a live blocker. The athlete must not only react with the correct base but also adjust to a moving target.

Align the linebackers in two columns facing the challenged linebacker. The coach directs traffic behind the player being drilled. The coach calls "ready hit" and points to the column that is to block the linebacker.

When attacked from the left column, the player sets his left-footed base and explodes with his hips. He does the opposite when attacked from the right side. The coach can evaluate his base under pressure and his hip explosion. Each player should get four consecutive reps before returning to the columns (see figure 3.12).

Figure 3.12

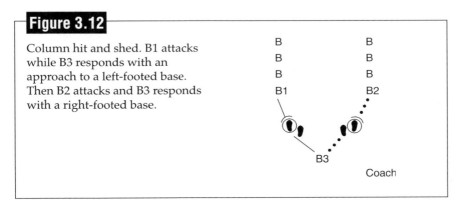

Column hit and shed. B1 attacks while B3 responds with an approach to a left-footed base. Then B2 attacks and B3 responds with a right-footed base.

Machine-Gun Drill

This is an old classic with great benefits. We use it to practice cut blocks. Usually the first blocker stays up and simulates an opponent's prime block (that is, zone block guard). The subsequent blockers attempt to cut the linebacker while he works inside-out on the running back.

We stress putting our hands on the cut blocker's helmet and shoulder pad while "running our feet." It's all right to give ground to keep your feet. Once the blocker tries to cut, he's no longer a factor—the rest of the field is yours (see figure 3.13).

Remember, that with each block (reach or cut) the inside foot (right foot in figure 3.13) is up on contact.

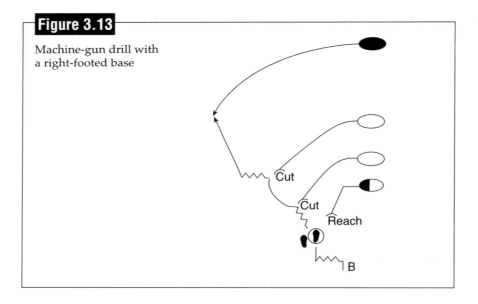

Figure 3.13

Machine-gun drill with a right-footed base

One-on-One Drill

The purpose of the drill is to identify linebackers who can execute with a proper base in a competitive setting. This drill gives inexperienced linebackers a chance to evaluate their progress under pressure.

Commonly called the Oklahoma drill, we have adapted it for linebackers that play off the line of scrimmage. I never understood why coaches put their linebackers on the nose of an offensive lineman for this drill when they never ask the linebacker to walk up that tight in a game situation.

We confine the contact with two soft bags between which the ball carrier must run. Rather than center the lineman, we make it realistic and place the lineman to one side of the opening. Now the blocker must get movement or the linebacker can make the play with his free arm (see figure 3.14).

Obviously this drill severely tests the linebacker's approach, base, and hip explosion. It's just like football. Linebackers who make plays in this drill will probably make plays on Saturday.

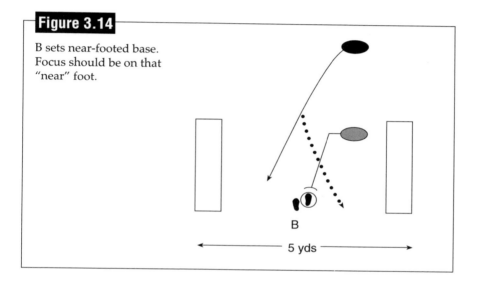

Figure 3.14

B sets near-footed base. Focus should be on that "near" foot.

B

5 yds

Bull-in-the-Ring Drill

Many coaches use this drill extensively. Although I believe it can be a solid teaching drill, I am drawn to it because of the emotion that it creates by the group dynamics. It is for that reason that I have used this drill only on game day. It is special to our players because we reserve it for that day when the intensity runs highest.

When I was at Virginia Tech, one of our starting linebackers broke his nose before a game in this drill. The drill often is a distraction for our opponents because of the crisp hitting and intensity.

Circle the linebackers and have one leader jump to the middle of the circle. He gets two hit and sheds, one with each foot. He controls the blocker by pointing to him and calling him out with "You!" The blocker comes hard and always high. The linebacker then calls out another. Repeat until all have had two live hits (see figure 3.15).

The principles of the hit and shed are widely misunderstood. Recently I read an NFL notebook for linebackers; never once were the base or feet mentioned in a presentation on taking on blockers! By digesting the information presented in this chapter and repeatedly practicing the drills, any player can increase his chances for linebacking success.

Figure 3.15

Bull-in-the-ring drill. B1 calls out B2 and sets left-footed base.

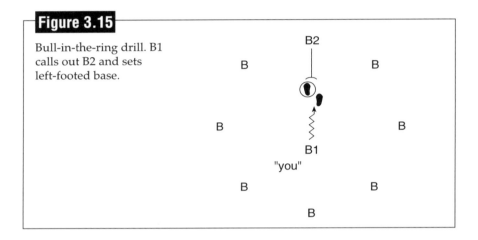

Chapter 4

Pursuit

The ultimate goal for a linebacker on each snap is to tackle the ball carrier aggressively. The most demanding phase of that process is the hit and shed. As described in chapter 3, this fundamental enables the defensive player to rid himself of potential blockers. Once free, the linebacker must get to the ball. This movement to the ball, or pursuit, is the second fundamental linebackers must master.

On the surface, pursing sounds simple and seems hardly a matter of great concern. Pursuit is not, however, unbridled running to the ball. If this were true, speed would be the only requisite for proficiency at this task. As we delve into this skill, you will discover that it requires strong discipline and proper mechanics.

Linebackers regularly employ five types of pursuit. We will discuss each one, and the chapter will end with proven drill work.

Shuffle

This is a fairly universal term in linebacker lingo. The shuffle is a controlled movement parallel to the line of scrimmage that is quite unnatural. Linebackers use it primarily from tackle to tackle when the ball is moving slowly. Usually the linebacker uses it when he is in a high-contact area.

We stress four coaching points when teaching the shuffle:

Stay Square

The football often changes direction during the course of a play, either by design or by the elusive running of an offensive back. The linebacker must be prepared to change direction with the runner quickly. Therefore we train our athletes in the high-contact area to keep their shoulders and hips parallel to the line of scrimmage while moving with a controlled shuffle.

Slide Feet

Our linebackers slide their feet when shuffling. We never permit their feet to cross when in a shuffle mode. By using the shuffle the linebacker can easily keep his shoulders and hips square (see figure 4.1).

Second, shuffling permits easy change of direction without wasted movement. Because the feet don't cross, the shuffler can change direction within one step.

The shuffle also slows down the linebacker. Why do we desire that? Why do we want to hinder his speed? Speed is certainly a desired quality, but players can use it at the wrong time. For a shuffle linebacker, all-out sprinting can be a disaster. A common mistake occurs when the backside linebacker sprints toward the initial flow and overruns the cutback runner.

We force our linebackers to memorize the completion of this adage: "The longest running plays in football . . ." and they must respond, "Break behind the backside linebacker." They hear it repeatedly during four years of their competition because it is a building block of staunch defense. The shuffle permits controlled pursuit.

Figure 4.1

Shuffle maintains square hips and shoulders. It slows the linebacker and keeps him behind the ball carrier.

Courtesy of University of Colorado

I previously mentioned **Barry Remington,** one of Colorado's all-time great inside linebackers. Barry was the classic backside protector. At the NFL Combine featuring 60 of America's best college linebackers, Barry finished last in the 40-yard dash, timed at 5.18. Impossible for a productive linebacker, you say? You didn't know Barry. In all my years I never saw backside leverage played so well. Barry's lack of speed forced him to incredible accountability on the backside. Rarely beaten by cutbacks, he was the glue in an awesome defensive structure.

In our defensive scheme, we have a linebacker position that is traditionally slow on the backside. He regularly shuffles when the ball goes away; therefore, he does not need great speed. We often joke that we chose him for his lack of speed so he had better not overrun a tailback!

Each postseason we study tape of long runs versus our defense. We've used the same scheme since 1978, and it has been very effective at Virginia Tech, Colorado, and Illinois. Still, the longest running plays each year . . . break behind the backside linebackers. Mark it down.

The final advantage of sliding the feet in crowded areas ties directly into setting a base for the hit and shed. Blockers abound in close quarters, and a linebacker must always be prepared to set his base on a threatening lineman. If running in pursuit of the ball, chances are good that the linebacker will have his feet crossed on contact or will be unable to set a correct base because of his speed of movement. The shuffle solves both problems. It slows him down, and he is always one step from a perfect base, whether he is attacked from the left or the right (see the views in figure 4.2a-b).

Figure 4.2

(A) Here the linebacker (#46) shuffles in a high contact area and sees #51 approaching to block him. (B) The linebacker responds by setting his left foot and a perfect base within one step.

Stay Low

The shuffle requires that the linebacker bend at the hips, knees, and ankles while moving. Most outstanding linebackers are flexible in those three areas. The purpose again ties into the hit-and-shed mechanics. We shuffle in a heavy-contact area so that we can set a correct base at any time. We must stay low so that we can immediately be pad under pad as discussed in chapter 3.

Maintain Vision

The final area of emphasis when teaching athletes to shuffle is peripheral vision. The linebacker must focus on the ball so he stays in correct proximity to the runner. At the same time, he must develop keen awareness to fallen bodies and active blockers in his path. You should design shuffle drills with bags or blockers to simulate the game-day traffic.

Alley

Alley pursuit begins when the shuffle cannot keep pace with the ball as it gains speed. Now we must turn our hips and run inside-out on the ball. We work our arms hard to keep our shoulders square and thus maintain control for cutbacks (see figure 4.3a-b).

Because the linebacker is running at high speed, he requires more distance between himself and the ball carrier than he requires in the shuffle. With the shuffle, we ask the defender to stay on the backside hip of the running back (see figure 4.4) where, because of his restrained movement, he can respond to cutbacks efficiently.

When the linebacker is in alley pursuit, however, we teach him to stay a full three yards inside the sprinting runner (see figure 4.5).

The defender must maintain this three-yard cushion to adjust to the tremendous open-field runners playing in great competition at all levels. When pursuing inside-out with the shuffle or alley, the linebacker's attitude should be "Please cut back, please cut back!" He should never be surprised by the cutback run. This type of attitude in early training saves many long runs that go unnoticed by most fans. Linebacker drill work must regularly provide cutback experiences to develop a mind-set on cutbacks and an understanding of the lateral distance that the linebacker must maintain against a quality runner.

The linebacker is more vulnerable to blockers in the alley because he cannot establish his base quickly. The good news is that he is now in a lower-contact area and most linemen have trouble reaching him. He may encounter cut blocks from inside, but he can easily detect them. The machine-gun drill in chapter 3 is an experience he will appreciate in the alley.

The final point in alley pursuit is our reaction to the crack-back block by a wide receiver in the alley. Often a teammate can alert the linebacker to a crack by noting the wide receiver's decreased split or a specific formation or motion. When the linebacker hears "Crack" and the block is near, he should rip his inside foot and shoulder

Figure 4.3

(A) Alley pursuit is a response to a fast-moving ball. Feet now cross for speed and the arms work hard to maintain square shoulders. (B) Alley pursuit is fast-paced. Change of direction is much more difficult than in the shuffle.

Figure 4.4

Shuffle linebacker stays on the backside hip of the ball carrier for cutback.

Figure 4.5

An alley linebacker needs three yards separation to ensure defending a cutback run.

through the topside of the wide receiver (see figure 4.6a-d). We want to intimidate the receiver and teach him he was recruited to catch balls, not mess with linebackers!

Figure 4.6

#46 feels or is alerted to the "crack-back" attempt by the wide receiver.

The linebacker turns and attacks the threat.

#46 goes "topside" the wide receiver and establishes his near foot and shoulder.

#46 rips topside the crack attempt.

Jim Ryan (William and Mary, 10 years with Denver Broncos), Mike Johnson (Virginia Tech, 10 years in the NFL and All-Pro), and Dennis Stallings (Illinois captain, 1997 draft choice of the Oilers) were probably the finest alley pursuers I have coached. Each had fine speed, but more important, they were nimble in the alley. They understood the concept of staying inside a fast-moving ball and rarely lost their feet on cut or crack blocks.

Press

This type of pursuit often separates the confident linebacker from the inexperienced one and makes the difference between solid linebackers and the elite ones.

A linebacker uses this pursuit whenever he sees an opening to the ball. Now he *presses*. He crosses the line of scrimmage to make a minus-yardage play. This type of penetration from a reading linebacker is essential for big defensive plays in the running game.

Traditionally, our scheme has not stunted linebackers a lot, yet we have often been leaders in minus-yardage plays over nearly two decades. How do we accomplish that? By giving linebackers the freedom on every play to press openings.

Although an offensive coach designs a running play to attack a particular hole, the running back has the freedom to deviate if an opening occurs elsewhere. The linebacker's key directs him to a certain area also, but if he detects an opening we teach him to press it. Most likely the running back sees it too, and we want to greet him there.

Early in my career, I believed that pressers were born. I thought this reaction was intuitive. Some, like Eddie Booker (University of New Hampshire), had it, while others did not. Eddie earned the nickname Buzzsaw because of the way he pressed running backs in open gaps as an All-Yankee Conference linebacker.

Later, I found that players could learn to react to open gaps, but it took a dedication to teaching it. In the past 20 years we have committed to drilling linebackers to press. We teach it in our ABC drills early in practice and also in our technique drills. We attempt to finish every snap with a press. Many coaches have asked me over the years, "How do you get your linebackers to stunt to the play so accurately?" Rarely are they stunting; they are reading and pressing open seams.

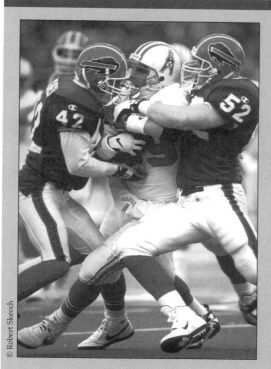

© Robert Skeoch

Dana Howard, a national recruit, committed to us at Illinois. In 1995 he went on to become the first player in school history to win the Butkus Award. We needed another linebacker to play alongside Howard, but we struck out with our next choices. With no highly rated prospects available, I had the chore of choosing from three young men who had not distinguished themselves nationally.

As I reviewed them again on tape, I charted their tackles in relation to the line of scrimmage when they were not stunting. The choice became vividly clear. **John Holecek** (#52 in above photo) was a natural presser. He didn't have the most tackles, but they were near or behind the line of scrimmage without stunting. Hardly anyone else offered John a scholarship, yet teamed with Dana Howard, the pair became the most productive tandem in Illinois history. John was All-Big Ten, captain, and was drafted by the Buffalo Bills in the fifth round. A fiery leader and competitor, he loved our system's freedom to press.

Deep Pursuit

The structure of every defense must define the deep pursuit angles that will stop long touchdown runs and passes. A long touchdown play can occur when the ball gets outside the linebacker so quickly that he cannot make the tackle for a negligible gain. Each scheme differs in that regard, but the coach must communicate and drill a deep angle of pursuit.

If the ball gets outside the linebacker he must then take a deep angle away from the line of scrimmage toward a point where he can save a touchdown. He will often use the sideline as a 12th player to pin the ball. He must anticipate the cutback near the sideline and be under control. We use our team pursuit drill, described at the end of this chapter, at least every week to reinforce this concept to our entire defensive unit.

Kevin Hardy, the 1996 winner of the Butkus Award at Illinois, was perhaps the most complete linebacker I ever taught. His attention to detail in deep pursuit was singular. He made more plays away from his initial alignment than any other outside linebacker I've had. His deep-angle pursuit was extraordinary.

Break Before the Ball

We will cover the mechanics of pursuit in the passing game separately in chapter 6, which deals with zone coverage skills.

Before the ball is thrown, however, we expect our linebackers to be in hot pursuit. Even though they may be only 10 yards deep when the ball is thrown deep downfield, we expect them to turn and sprint until the whistle.

In the early 1980s when I was at Virginia Tech, our opponent completed a long pass for what appeared to be a sure touchdown. As the receiver neared the goal line he mysteriously dropped the ball. Because Mike Johnson and two Virginia Tech teammates kept chasing, we recovered it. Conventional wisdom would ask "Why pursue like that?" The answer is that it gives you an opportunity to make big plays.

Pursuit Grade (93 Percent)

Coaches must demand the kind of effort that Mike Johnson made in the pass play just described. Bill McCartney, the head coach at Colorado in 1983, showed me that we could not only demand effort but quantify it.

The Colorado defense was bad. The Buffaloes had ranked lower than 100th (out of a possible 108) in the nation for three consecutive seasons before we arrived. Our confidence and effort were dismal, but we explained that effort had nothing to do with talent. Only a poor attitude could keep us from being the best pursuit team in America.

We told the players that we would grade every play on pursuit. If the discipline and effort were perfect they would receive a GA for "got assignment." If any part of the pursuit lacked discipline or if the effort did not continue until the whistle, they would receive an MA for "missed assignment."

A young man who pursued correctly 27 times in 30 plays would receive a pursuit grade of 90 percent. We considered that unacceptable. Only a grade of 93 percent or better would set the winning standard for linebackers. The premise is that a player who commits to that kind of effort will likely have an opportunity for one big play per game in 70 tries.

Is it worth it? Think this through. No one can guarantee it, but it's likely you'll get one big chance if you can play hard for 70 snaps. Most players feel they play hard, but few measure up to this standard. If you play both ways, it's impossible. If you are active on special teams, it is very demanding.

We sold the Colorado players on this concept: If the defensive team commits this kind of effort, the potential is there for 11 big plays each game. That's powerful stuff.

At the beginning of each week we gathered the defensive unit. We never shared with the whole unit a linebacker's technique grade, but we exposed everyone's pursuit grade. They knew each week that specific people had not given pursuit effort or discipline. They also knew that if a player earned poor grades two games in a row, we would bench him. The peer pressure became strong and effective. Colorado's ranking in total defense climbed to 81st, 17th, and then 11th by 1985.

Many players feel they can pace themselves and gear up for vital downs, but all snaps are vital. All are potential touchdowns. Those who pace their effort will miss many big-play chances.

Your best players must buy into this concept. If you permit an NFL talent to play when he is below your pursuit standards, you have no chance of having the team synergism that can make 11 average guys special. You cannot expect the team to meet your pursuit standards if you permit prima donnas to play. Have the guts to sit your undisciplined talent on the bench or ask him to play fewer plays hard. The group dynamics can be very positive.

Like everything else in football, pursuit requires practice. During the spring, grade pursuit in 7-on-7 and 9-on-7; then perhaps grade it in one team period. Let them feel the intensity and effort needed a little at a time. As they gain in mental toughness and conditioning, they may be ready for a 30-play scrimmage. By the end of fall camp it will become the only way to play.

In the years since we instituted this pursuit policy, Bill Henkel achieved the highest career pursuit grade. Fittingly, Bill was not an NFL player. He lettered four years and started on the 1990 Big Ten cochampionship squad that won the Citrus Bowl. Everyone recognized that Bill had limited ability, but his team saw his passion to play every day in his pursuit effort. He made everyone play at a higher level.

Base and Pursuit

A correct base (described early in chapter 3) is vital not only for the hit and shed but also for efficient pursuit.

When the linebacker takes on a blocker with the right foot and shoulder, it is simple for him to open his hips and push off the inside foot to a ball carrier (see figure 4.7a-d).

When a linebacker meets a blocker with an opposite-foot-and-shoulder base, described in chapter 3, the blocker turns the linebacker. The defender cannot pursue effectively because he cannot open his hips to shuffle or alley. He is often forced to spin out of the block to begin his pursuit (see figure 4.8a-d).

Pursuit Drills

Here is a sampling of drills that address the mechanics of shuffle, alley, press, and deep pursuits. We have used these base drills successfully for many years. As you understand the concepts and your needs, you will probably want to design variations.

I never use agility drills to open practice. We always call them pursuit drills so that our linebackers know that we are addressing a fundamental, not just warming up.

Cone Drills

I owe this set of drills to Bill Dooley, for whom I worked for five years at Virginia Tech. Coach Dooley had Pat Watson and me head up the winter conditioning program, and this drill became the centerpiece. Those who lacked conditioning, commitment, or discipline feared it. Everything had to be done exactly right and with maximum effort. It produced a strong peer-pressure element because if one guy screwed up the whole unit repeated the drill.

In 1988 I set up the same cone drill for John Mackovic at Illinois. We didn't know the players' names yet and were setting a tough tone for them. I made one group repeat the drill three times because one of them didn't put forth the effort. Finally, exasperated, I ejected the player from the indoor facility. Immediately, the players' reaction told me I had made a point. The young player was Jeff George, our quarterback, who two years later was the first player taken in the draft. Jeff and I always had a great relationship after that, and the team knew we had no prima donnas.

Set up the cones as shown in figure 4.9 with a ready line, a position line, and a finish line. Put three players on the ready line to start the drill. On the command "ready," in unison they rapidly move their feet. If one is slow in starting, they repeat the drill. On "position" they sprint five yards to the position line. Again, if one is late in starting or slow in moving, they repeat the drill immediately. The focus and intensity are like pregame.

Once at the position line we tell them which drill to perform and begin on the command "go." For the linebackers, in the spring or fall camp, the drill commands would usually be "shuffle" or "alley." In the winter we use the drill for players at all positions and use many variations (for example, grass drill, seat rolls, bear crawls, and so on).

For the shuffle drill the three linebackers on "go" wave back and forth with the coaches' hand directions. All must slide their feet, stay low, and change direction quickly. On the command "press" they sprint upfield to the finish line. We do the same with "alley," but it brings many groups back because players tend to anticipate a change in direction instead of going full-bore and having to strip gears to change direction.

At the finish line another coach or a graduate assistant checks the intensity of the press. He can also regularly yell "break down" before the players reach the finish line. Now all the athletes take a break-down position with feet moving rapidly in anticipation of another "press" command and the final sprint to the finish line.

Box Drills

The box drill emphasizes the shuffle, alley, and press forms of pursuit. The unique aspect of following a leader permits each player to view himself on tape in contrast to his peers.

Through most of my career I have set up our linebacker practice area near an end zone on our grass fields. Usually I have filled an

Figure 4.7

#46 takes on blocker with a correct base. The right foot is planted and in advance of the left.

Here #46 pushes off the right foot and opens his hips to the runner.

The ball carrier is moving quickly so #46 alleys inside-out.

#46 presses the runner for the tackle.

Figure 4.8

#46 meets the blocker with opposite-foot-and-shoulder base. Inside foot is back.

This base causes him to be turned by the blocker.

Now #46 is in an awkward position to pursue and must give ground or spin.

#46 may make the tackle, but it won't be for minimum yardage.

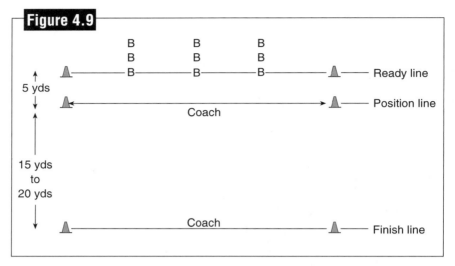

Cone drill

end zone with boxes five yards on a side. End zones are an ideal drill space because they don't get much wear and tear.

Many drills can utilize that area, and the boxes stay fresh because there are so many of them. I began using follow the leader back in the mid-1970s at William and Mary. Eddie Amos was an engaging athlete who loved to be creative leading this drill. He could start anywhere in the end zone boxes and go anywhere within them while the other linebackers followed at five-yard intervals.

When moving laterally they used a shuffle or alley. Going forward they accelerated to press, and going backward they moved in a backpedal. They used three of the major pursuit forms with some fun and freedom.

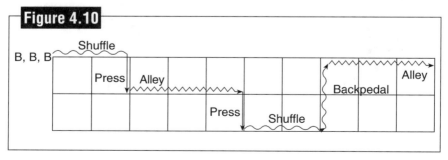

Follow the leader using end zone 5-yard squares

Coaching points are to watch the transition of the hips in going from shuffle to alley or vice versa. Players must sink the hips low during the shuffle and rise to alley (see figure 4.10).

Bag Drills

We run a series of bag drills to increase peripheral vision while focusing on the ball. This is a popular drill that is key for moving in crowded areas. We line four to five standard agility bags of various sizes to simulate fallen bodies that we must work through to press the ball.

Normally we stride through the bags to warm up. Then the linebackers shuffle through one after another, placing their hands down to feel the bags. We do the same thing at a faster pace and alley through. We work to the left and right in both movements.

We finish with a shuffle wave and an alley wave. On the waves, the coach makes the players focus on the ball while he directs them

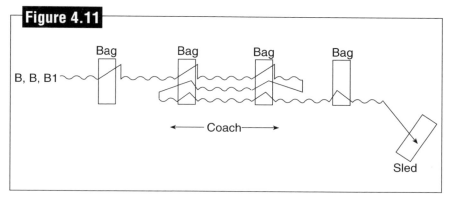

Figure 4.11

B, B, B1

Bag　　　Bag　　　Bag　　　Bag

←—— Coach ——→

Sled

Coach directs B1 on shuffle wave through bags. B1 finishes with press and a form tackle.

from side to side. Now they must feel the bags and not look directly at them. We finish each wave with a press to a form tackle on another player or a Popsicle sled (see figure 4.11). Players perform the wave drills one at a time.

Cross-Field Pursuit

I first saw a form of this drill while visiting with Jerry Sandusky in the late 1970s. Its purpose is to permit linebackers to feel the mechanics they must use in pursuit of a speedy ball carrier. Jerry used 25 yards, while we use the entire width of a football field. We have the ball carrier cut back twice during the 50-yard trip, once versus a shuffle and once versus an alley pursuit. In response to a cutback the linebacker uses a catch-and-release tackle so that the movement continues without much interruption. Obviously, a press is used on both cutbacks (see figure 4.12).

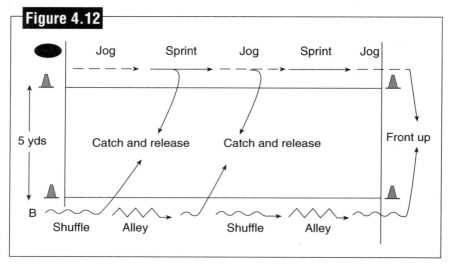

Figure 4.12

Cross-field pursuit drill

This drill allows the coach to assess the understanding each linebacker has for the pursuit concepts. Does he give three yards between himself and the ball carrier when alleying? Do his hips sink when he shuffles?

The ball carrier alternately jogs and sprints, but for no less than 10 yards in each. The linebacker shadows the ball carrier, hoping that he will cut back.

Base Push-Off

A correct base is key to both taking on a blocker and initiating pursuit. This drill combines the two so that the linebacker can experience the acceleration from a proper base. He must also adjust to the speed of the ball carrier with the appropriate reaction (shuffle or alley).

Set up a blocker over the linebacker at the appropriate depth for the linebacker's technique. Put the ball carrier in close proximity so the linebacker can set his base and then push off his inside foot to shuffle to a slow-moving runner (see figure 4.13) or alley to a fast-moving runner (see figure 4.14).

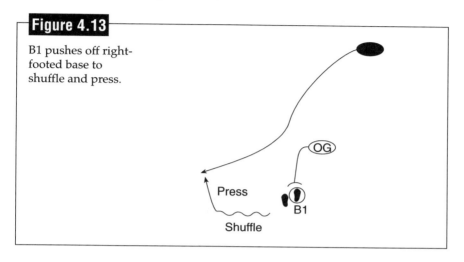

Figure 4.13

B1 pushes off right-footed base to shuffle and press.

Press

Shuffle

OG

B1

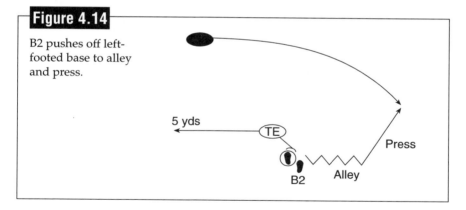

Figure 4.14

B2 pushes off left-footed base to alley and press.

5 yds

TE

Press

Alley

B2

Jingle-Jangle

We have used this diagnostic test for decades, and it is now a staple in NFL evaluations. Although we time it frequently during the year, we also use it as an alley pursuit drill with competition and no timing. The drill teaches the efficient change of direction that is vital to linebacker play.

We align two linebackers face to face, straddling a 5-yard line on the field. On the command "go" they take off on a 20-yard run with two changes of direction. At high speeds they must alley. We have them touch the lines with the nearest foot (see figure 4.15). The top performer in this drill is often a productive player.

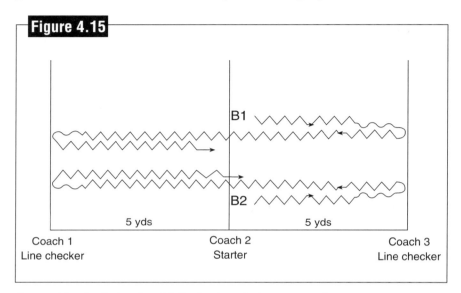

Figure 4.15

5 yds   5 yds

Coach 1   Coach 2   Coach 3
Line checker   Starter   Line checker

Competitive jingle-jangle with linebackers facing one another

Team Pursuit Drill

After instituting the 93 percent pursuit standard at Colorado in 1983, we sought team drills that would reinforce our commitment to being America's finest pursuit unit.

This drill has evolved over the years to become a staple in our practice sessions. We use it every week during the season to emphasize the discipline and effort we demand.

We spot the ball on the 10-yard line, on either hash mark or anywhere in the middle of the field. The only player needed on offense is a quarterback. Managers or coaches fill in at tight end, running back, and the two wide receivers.

The defensive unit huddles and takes a signal from the coordinator. They break the huddle and must align properly against the formation indicated by the managers and coaches. If the coaches notice any alignment errors the players repeat the drill.

The quarterback then simulates the cadence. The offense can run a draw, a pass of any type, or a perimeter run. Usually the offense emphasizes one or two plays that an opponent might use, not a host of them. The defenders respond to the play as it unfolds.

The coaching staff must have four strategically placed coaches to evaluate the drill. One stands at the goal line to evaluate the effort of those who must sprint to it to finish the drill. One stands behind the secondary to evaluate the back end and the rotation angles against the run. Each of the two others is stationed on a sideline to evaluate effort and also be the focal point of any perimeter runs. The defense must find them on those outside runs, and the coaches vary their depth from 10 to 20 yards downfield.

On a pass the rushers come hard but allow the quarterback to throw the ball. The other defenders drop, and then all 11 must break on the ball. When the ball is intercepted all 11 sprint to the goal line. If anyone misses an assignment or doesn't put forth full effort, the whole unit gets another chance. The peer pressure is strong!

On run, the quarterback fakes a toss sweep or option to either side. The running back only gives direction. The defense immediately looks to that sideline for the coach and sprints with correct cut-off angles to him. The coaches evaluate deep pursuit closely. When the players reach the coach they huddle around him with their feet chopping (see figure 4.16). If all four coaches approve of their pursuit, the sideline coach gives the players a thumbs-up sign. They

Figure 4.16

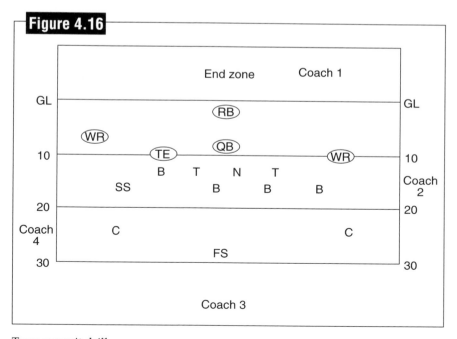

Team pursuit drill

do a grass drill and are done. If a coach finds fault with any player, the group gets a thumbs-down sign and repeats the drill. The staff should tell the unit why it must repeat the drill. The whole unit learns if the players understand their errors.

One way to vary the drill is by scrambling the quarterback. The team's reaction to a scrambler must be understood, and it is tough to reproduce in a proper setting. This is an ideal opportunity to teach a correct response that can save valuable yardage.

Double-Whistle Drill

This is another team drill we added to emphasize effort during game week. Normally we would have three or four team periods on our heavy work days, Tuesday and Wednesday. We would designate one of them as a double-whistle period. We usually chose a team period unencumbered by a lot of checks, so the thinking would be minimal.

During double whistle, the coach in charge will blow once when the ball carrier is fronted by the initial tackler. The coach will not blow the second whistle until every defensive player has surrounded the ball carrier. If any of the 11 does not sprint to the pile, the whole unit does a series of grass drills immediately. The first unit takes six consecutive snaps of double whistle, followed by the second unit's six.

Double whistle focuses on intensity during the tough part of a week's schedule. The pressure provides a good opportunity for you to survey the unit's leadership. Peer interaction will occur when the grass drills become numerous.

Pursuit becomes a habit. You must foster it during the week for it to be evident on game day. Many great pursuit drills are also tackling drills. We will look at those at the end of chapter 5.

Chapter 5

Tackling

The third fundamental is the most important and enjoyable thing that we do on defense. Players love to knock runners to the ground. Most of us who played relished the thrill of contact. Although it happened 30 years ago, I can still describe tackling Calvin Hill in the Yale Bowl and causing two fumbles to help Rutgers to an upset victory in 1966.

Tackling is the defender's trademark. All linebackers want to tackle well and generally are willing to work diligently to improve this skill.

Obviously, pursuit plays a vital role in tackling. Individually, the strong pursuer gets more opportunities to tackle. As a squad, the aggressive pursuit units often sound like "rat-a-tat-tat" before the whistle. If one defender misses a tackle, others arrive to limit the gain.

The staunchest defenses always have good pursuers and intense tacklers. To excel at defense, a unit must value those skills and vow to work on them constantly.

Most defensive coaches have similar views on this fundamental. Although coaches use many kinds of pursuit drills and some don't understand hit-and-shed concepts, most agree on the main aspects of tackling. We've stressed these linebacker coaching points.

Focus and Hat Placement

Just before contact a player's focus should be on the jersey numbers of the ball carrier. Young linebackers often concentrate on areas of the body that can deceive, for example, the head and the hips. Wherever the jersey numbers go, so will the ball carrier.

Many years ago it was standard to teach players to put their helmets in the ball carrier's chest. Since the American Football Coaches Association exposed the high risk of head and spinal cord injuries, leading with the top of the helmet has been forbidden by game rules and coaching ethics.

Never should a player use the top of the head to initiate contact. Not only is it a major health risk, it is also an unsound tackling technique because the defender's eyes must be looking toward the ground. Most coaches now teach their players to look at the jersey numbers and, just before contact, slide the forehead to the ball.

This tackling instruction produces two benefits. Players keep their eyes up so they miss fewer tackles. Also, the forehead hits the softer football and can cause a fumble.

In 1992, Illinois had a dramatic 18-16 victory over Ohio State when a young running back named Eddie George (later the 1995 Heisman winner) coughed up two goal-line fumbles created by Illinois defenders putting their hats on the ball. Jeff Arneson returned one 96 yards for an electrifying Illini touchdown.

Base

Chris Cosh played linebacker for me at Virginia Tech and gained the nickname Crash for his collisions on the field. He then coached linebackers for me at Illinois. He is one of the finest teachers I've known. Chris taught our up-front players to get shoe to shoe with the ball carrier and chest to chest in confined areas. He always wanted linebackers to tackle *through* runners, not *to* them.

The linebacker's body weight should be in advance of his base. If his weight is directly over his base he tackles with the force of his body weight only. If his weight is out in front of his base, he plays much bigger.

A great example of this was an exceptional linebacker named Ashley Lee. In 1980, as a true freshman, Ashley led Virginia Tech in tackles and to a Peach Bowl bid opposite Miami. What was so unusual? Ashley weighed 182 pounds. By his senior season he was 206 and was drafted in the seventh round. As a frosh, however, he had to have his weight well in advance of his base to tackle 200-pound running backs.

In the mid-1970s I faced a challenge I was not prepared for and have not faced since. During an evaluation meeting before spring practice, I spoke to a linebacker I'll call Rudy. Rudy had all the physical qualities to be a fine linebacker. He was, however, a terrible tackler, and I became frustrated because his play in the fall gave no indication that he would improve. His teammates ridiculed his lack of courage, even though they recognized his athletic ability.

I asked Rudy how we could help him develop as a tackler. Rudy wept and confessed that he was scared to tackle. He went on to say that he enjoyed football, but for as long as he could remember he closed his eyes and turned his head before tackling. Never before had I heard this from a player. I commended Rudy on having the boldness to admit his fear and promised him that if he wanted to overcome it, I'd try to help. He was eager but only if our sessions were private. He was embarrassed and couldn't chance that his teammates would find out.

We had closed-door sessions unlike any I've had since. I gently tapped him on the forehead while he strained to keep his eyes open. Later on, he began to wear a helmet, and I banged on it with a ruler. By spring practice, he could hit my office desk or a cinder-block wall with his protected forehead and not blink.

I couldn't believe we were doing this in Division I football, but Rudy had to overcome a deep-seated fear. What courage it took to share those feelings with his coach.

Rudy went on to start several games his senior season. He didn't have an all-star career, but he became an adequate player and regained the respect of teammates. It was one of my most gratifying experiences as a coach.

If you can't focus on the tackling target with your eyes open, you can never be a consistent tackler.

Explode Hips and Club Arms

Once the tackler sets the base, he explodes his hips and clubs his arms around the ball carrier. The physical tacklers use their hips and arms aggressively. Dana Howard, the Big Ten's all-time leading career tackler, punished ball carriers in confined areas because of the brute strength of his hips and the impact of his arms. In each of four consecutive years he logged over 100 tackles at Illinois.

Many effective tacklers lack great body control and overwhelming strength but have a tremendous resolve to tackle. They may not be classic tacklers, but the ball carriers go down. This is where grabbing cloth becomes important. Many times I've witnessed a linebacker competitively holding on to a runner's jersey until help arrives. When a defender collides with a runner, he should grab the runner's jersey.

Stripping

In the early 1980s, I visited the Denver Bronco's camp in July to see Jim Ryan, whom I had coached at William and Mary. I noticed the defense spending an inordinate amount of time practicing to dislodge the ball during their tackling drills. After practice, I asked Jim about it, and he said Dan Reaves had sold them on getting turnovers and they drilled it a lot.

That season the Broncos created a lot of fumbles and had a big turnover ratio in their favor. Was it by accident? I don't think so.

Since then we have fostered stripping in this manner:

- The initial tackler secures the runner's body.
- The next defenders look to strip the ball by punching it, raking it from behind, or ripping it from the rib cage of the runner.
- Most of our tackling drills include a second defender who works to strip the ball.
- We show on tape players in position to strip and encourage them to do so.

Simeon Rice, Rookie of the Year in the Big Ten in 1992 and Rookie of the Year in the NFL in 1996, was the finest stripper I have coached. Although he caused many fumbles while rushing the passer, Illinois fans will never forget Simeon's stripping the Michigan tailback in Ann Arbor with 42 seconds left in the game. That turnover led to an electrifying 24-21 victory—the first in Ann Arbor for Illinois in 27 years.

Recovering Fumbles

When initially teaching fumble recovery we emphasize the fetal position shown in figure 5.1.

Figure 5.1

Fetal position for fumble recovery

This is the conservative approach that we want our players to take when possession is the major concern. The player protects the ball from being taken in a pile of bodies by wrapping it with both arms and covering it with a leg. Taking the fetal position also helps prevent injuries. Too many young men lay on top of a recovered ball and expose their ribs to punishment or lay on their back and expose the ball to their opponents.

When the rules permit a defender to advance a fumble, big-play potential abounds. Through fumble drills, we determine which players we will permit to advance a fumble. To permit a slow defender with poor hands to attempt to scoop up a fumble is probably unwise.

Those we allow to advance fumbles must learn to bend and scoop without kicking the ball. The defender can best do this by keeping his feet off to the side of the ball as he gathers it into his arms.

Ball security after a fumble is identical to ball security after an interception, which we describe in detail at the end of chapter 6.

Courtesy of Virginia Tech

■ Ashley Lee was the smallest, quickest linebacker ever to play for me. He led a Peach Bowl team in tackles as a 182-pound freshman. "Lightning in a bottle," he was our first great hawk linebacker.

Missed Tackles

Keeping statistics will allow you to quantify the tackling proficiency of your players individually, as a group, and as a defense.

A variety of measurements can help you study missed tackles and reveal their frequency:

- You can simply list them on a grade sheet as, for example, 3 MTs. That would surely be significant for one scrimmage or game.

- You can develop a percentage by dividing the MTs by the number of plays. Certainly 1 MT in 73 snaps (.013) is more forgiving than 1 MT in 15 plays (.067).

- You can create a different percentage by dividing the MTs by the number of tackle opportunities. One MT for someone involved in 12 tackles is radically different from 1 MT for a linebacker involved in 2 tackles.

Denny Marcin, my assistant head coach at Illinois, introduced the tackling percentage to our staff in 1992. We kept it for the entire squad and had as a unit goal to tackle at a 90 percent rate. We also kept postcontact yards as a statistic, that revealed how much yardage the opponent gained after the first tackler made contact. Both are revealing evaluations of your team's tackling ability.

There is a proper way to miss tackles! No, this is not a trick statement. At some point all defenders will miss tackles. Running backs are good, too. The well-trained defender knows where his defensive help is.

If a player is the widest defender, such as some outside linebackers or a strong safety, he knows that his help is all inside. If he misses a tackle, he must at least turn the play inside to his buddies. To allow the ball outside shows a real lack of discipline or understanding and likely gives up a long gainer.

With inside defenders, the opposite is true. They should force the ball wide. When an inside linebacker misses a tackle, it's with inside leverage. He should never permit the runner to cross his face to the inside. Drill this daily.

Frequency

We practice tackling daily, yet 90 percent of tackling is desire. We teach the 10 percent, but the rest comes from the heart and repetition. Usually, he who wants to tackle, tackles.

We do less live tackling than I did early in my career. Now a tackling drill may be for form only, without putting the runner to the ground except for the final repetition. We put more attention on form tackles in group drills (that is, 7-on-7, 9-on-7, or team) where we can closely approximate real situations.

We want our defense to have an attitude that no one should ever be able to run through them. Thus, in all group periods we demand that the defense front up against the offensive players. It gives both sides valuable work that drills cannot easily simulate. By way of example, I've witnessed 7-on-7 drills where the defenders could not touch the receivers. What kind of message does that send?

Our wide receivers know they better secure the ball and prepare to make the defense miss. Our defenders always stay high but seek to front up and strip. Without taking bodies to the ground, we use most of the types of tackles seen on game day, which creates a gamelike feeling.

Tackling Drills

The day before the game is the only day that we don't plan tackling in our practices. The following drills prepare defenders for tackling by working on shuffle and alley pursuit, using the sideline to pin runners, and practicing special-teams tackles and goal-line swarming.

When your schedule includes open dates or your team has postseason practices, defensive players should tackle during every practice. You can reduce hitting but not tackling. It doesn't take long to get rusty.

Confined Tackling Drill

This simple drill works on three distinct types of tackles in confined areas with the ball moving slowly and the linebacker using the shuffle in pursuit. Align the cones in a five-yard square with a linebacker facing the running back slightly to the runner's inside (see figure 5.2).

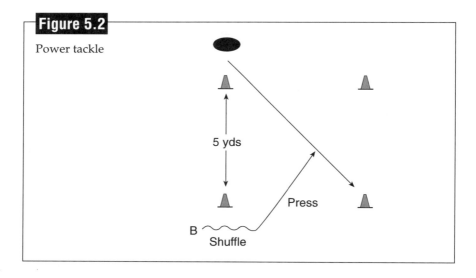

Figure 5.2

Power tackle

5 yds

Press

B

Shuffle

The first type of tackle is with the ball carrier running at a 45-degree angle much as he might on a power play. The linebacker shuffles and presses. Usually each athlete will get three or four heavy-hitting tackles without putting the ball carrier to the ground. On the final repetition we would typically go live.

The ball carrier should take turns both left and right. A stripper can be placed at any side of the square, but he doesn't take action until the initial linebacker makes contact with the ball carrier.

The second tackle in this series is the cutback. The ball carrier runs at the same 45-degree angle but cuts back to the linebacker's backside shoulder. The linebacker must not overrun the ball carrier. This forces him to stay on the ball carrier's backside hip (see figure 5.3). A stripper can be included.

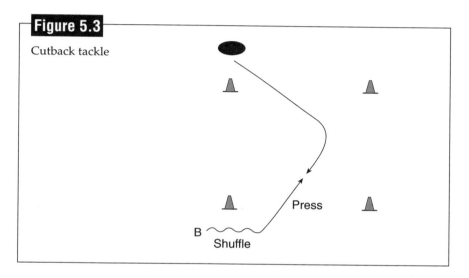

Figure 5.3

Cutback tackle

Press

B
Shuffle

The final drill in a confined area is the short-yardage or spin tackle. The ball carrier runs at a 45-degree angle, but on contact he spins away from the linebacker (see figure 5.4). The tackler must use a wide base and club his arms around the ball carrier. If the tackler's base is narrow, the spinning ball carrier will cause the linebacker to spin and lose the chance to thwart the first-down attempt. The spinning action will also break the arm hold on the runner if the linebacker does not forcefully club him. Spinning is prevalent on short-yardage downs, and linebackers must be ready to counter with a wide base and a vicelike grasp.

Eye-Opener

Bill Dooley, head coach at Virginia Tech, required every position coach on defense to open each full-padded practice with this drill. It was his way of emphasizing tackling. Besides being an excellent way

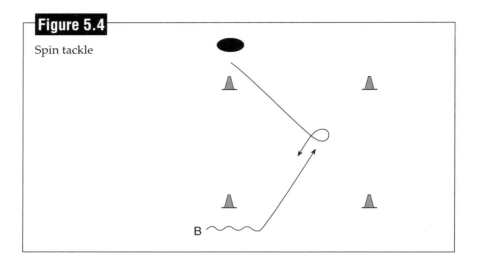

Figure 5.4

Spin tackle

to work the front seven on the shuffle and press, the drill helps develop unit pride.

Place flat-bottom bags parallel to one another but staggered. Use four at each drill site to simulate holes for a running back to attack. The linebacker always aligns behind the ball carrier and stays on his backside hip to prevent any cutback. He shuffles behind the ball carrier but presses as the ball carrier declares his open gap. The bags are staggered to permit the linebacker to press upfield (see figure 5.5).

The ball carrier can run through any of the gaps. Hard, crisp collisions result, although the tackler doesn't take the ball carrier to the ground. Again, you can add a stripper after the initial linebacker makes contact.

Alley Tackling

This is a physically exhausting drill that stresses option responsibilities within a scheme. The drill can involve two to four linebackers but requires only a small supply of quarterbacks and running backs.

Place the ball on a hash mark with a cone on the opposite hash to represent the defender with pitch (contain) responsibility versus the option. Place another cone on the line of scrimmage at the sideline nearest the ball (see figure 5.6).

The coach stands behind the linebackers and controls the offense with a direction of the option and whom he wants with the ball. The offense can execute the option to the field or into the boundary.

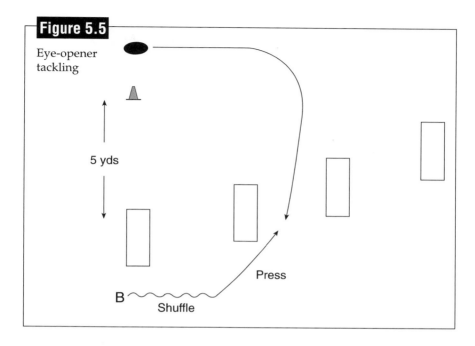

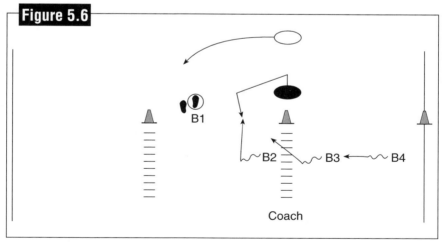

QB cuts back to test backside leverage.

The linebackers respond with proper pursuit mechanics, option responsibilities, and 93 percent effort. In figure 5.6 the offense runs the option to the field, and the quarterback cuts back. The drill does not end until all four linebackers reach the pile.

Linebacker B1 slow plays the quarterback in our scheme with outside leverage. B2 and B3 shuffle with inside leverage and press the quarterback. When B2 secures the quarterback, B3 should attempt to strip. B4 has backside leverage to defend the reverse.

When the quarterback pitches out (see figure 5.7) our outside linebacker (B1) can learn to force the pitch properly and then work on his alley pursuit. The same is true for the frontside inside linebacker (B2), who now leaves his shuffle to alley. B3 shuffles until the pitch, whereupon he must not only move faster, as B2 does in the alley, but also determine his deeper angle. B4 must leave his leverage pursuit for deep pursuit.

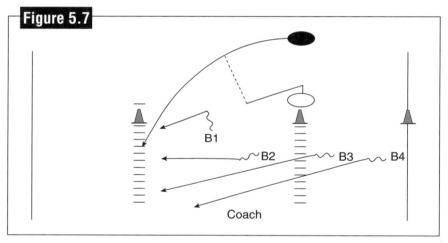

Figure 5.7

Pitch to the wide side forces alley and deep pursuit.

The control of this drill by the coach can be exceptional. If B1 makes the tackle on the pitch and the coach wants to emphasize deep pursuit, he just tells B1 to "MT" (miss tackle) so that the others must adjust on the run.

Players hate this drill because it involves so much running. Although the drill will condition your athletes, its real purpose is to teach alley and deep-angle pursuit. The tackling can be live, but it usually is not. Obviously, the backs should run the option both ways, and both backs should carry the ball. After four snaps, a new set of linebackers replaces the original group. This is an excellent drill to get on tape for tackling, pursuit, and option discipline.

Sideline Tackling

Outside linebackers need to work this drill more than other line-backers because they make more tackles near the boundary.

We want them to pin the runner to the sideline by getting their hats across the bow or by simply putting their helmets on the ball, that runners universally carry in their outside arm. We want each of our defenders to have most of his body between the ball carrier and the goal line, not just an arm.

We practice this drill in slow motion first with a pole-vault pad adjacent to a sideline. We put the tacklers one step from contact. On command from their coach, they slide their helmets across the runner's body to the ball while uncoiling their hips and clubbing their arms as described earlier in this chapter (see figure 5.8a-d).

They continue with more separation and force until they make live tackles into the pad. You can do this drill with only helmets and shoulder pads.

Later, be sure to include a cutback element to practice staying under control while approaching the sideline collision. At Illinois in 1988, Indiana had a 20-15 lead with 2:06 left in the game. Bill Mallory had his quarterback run a naked bootleg that caught us completely by surprise. The quarterback seemed to be running out of bounds after a significant gain when he elected to cut back into the field of play. Our defender, Chris Green, put his hat on the ball, popped it into the air, and our drop linebacker Julyon Brown caught it. We marched to a touchdown with only :26 seconds on the clock and had a 21-20 upset win.

Inside and In-Front Drill

This has become a staple among our tackling drills because line-backers are so involved in punt and kickoff coverage. We use this drill every week for our special-teams players. It reinforces two basic concepts for coverage lanes:

- keep the ball to your inside and
- keep the ball in front of you.

We align two columns of tacklers about 20 yards from a ball carrier. The cover guys sprint to the runner, who waits until they come under control (break down) with their inside feet up and their bodies square.

Figure 5.8

The sideline tackle drill can begin just a few steps from contact.

Have body not just an arm in front of the runner. The helmet should aim at the ball.

On contact, club with arms, grab jersey, and unleash the hips into the runner.

The pad absorbs the fall so enough repetitions can be gotten.

   Once the tacklers break down, the runner sprints left or right and keeps changing direction. The ball carrier wants to get outside either of the coverage linebackers.
   Meanwhile, the defenders simply keep the ball carrier inside and in front. We tell them that if the ball carrier is "even (head up) he's leaving." As the runner works back and forth, the defenders will finally front him up. The next two coverage guys then repeat the drill with a fresh ball carrier (see figure 5.9).

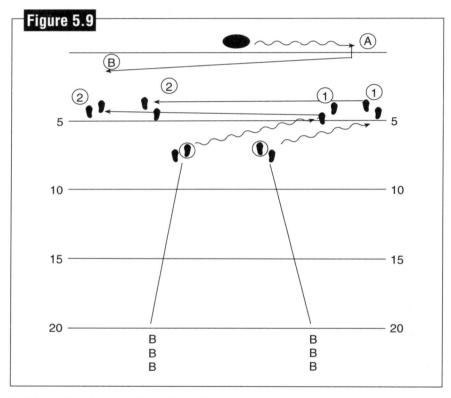

Figure 5.9

Inside and in-front drill. As the ball carrier gets into position A, the linebackers should be in position 1 with inside feet up. As the runner moves to position B, the linebackers should respond to position 2, keeping the runner inside and front.

   After they break down, the linebackers use the shuffle, alley, and press to maintain the ball carrier to their inside. This is an impressive drill for young special-teams participants to witness.

Circuit Tackling

My first experience with this drill was watching my dear friend Fisher DeBerry run one like it at the Air Force Academy. The drill provides three or four tackling experiences through individual station work. Assign a coach to each drill. The defense divides into groups and rotates through the three or four stations every few minutes. Station 1 might be the eye-opener, station 2 the sideline tackle, station 3 the popsicle tackle, and station 4 goal-line tackling (see figure 5.10).

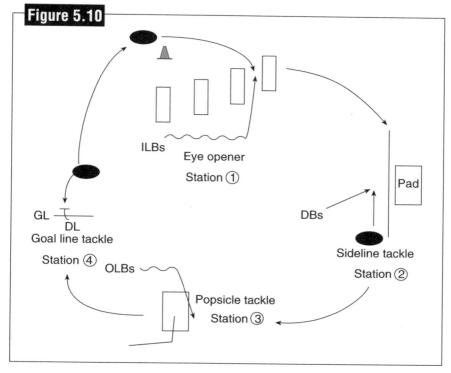

Figure 5.10

Circuit tackling

The concept here is to do three or four specific tackling drills with a lot of repetition in 10 minutes. The types of drills are endless. Tailor them to emphasize specific defensive needs.

Goal-Line Tackling

Linebackers often do not take the correct position in a goal-line defense. The ball is a foot from the goal line, and percentages are that the tailback is going to get the ball and attempt to jump over the line of scrimmage to get into the end zone.

The linebackers have studied the scouting report and adjust by

a. getting tighter to the ball
b. running forward before the snap
c. none of the above

The answer is c, none of the above, but linebackers usually crowd the ball when a tailback is going to sky toward the end zone. When linebackers crowd the line they cannot press the ball. Defensive linemen often are knocked backward; if that happens the linebackers have no chance to gain momentum.

Linebackers should gain depth. They should align at least four yards deep in this situation. On the snap they should press the tailback and then leap to meet him in the air with their shoulder pads. The tailback will drop straight to earth.

It's a concept that your players need to experience in spring ball and fall camp. Once a linebacker understands it he will have a chance to stop the great ones on the goal line.

Drill this by building a wall of pads or a small high-jump pad on the goal line. As a tailback skies, two linebackers come from proper depth, jump with their heads up, and meet the tailback with their shoulder pads (see figure 5.11).

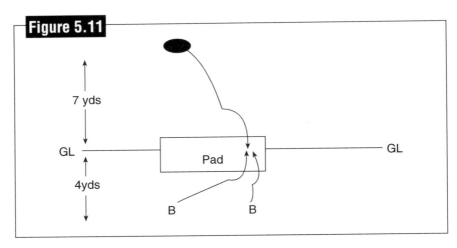

Figure 5.11

7 yds

GL

4yds

Pad

GL

B   B

Goal-line sky tackling

Tempo Tackling

Ironically, an offensive coach introduced our Colorado staff to this drill. Steve Logan, later the head coach at East Carolina, was our running back coach at Colorado. We were looking for a team period that would be up-tempo to get the players moving and excited.

We broke this nine-minute period into three segments, but I will describe here in detail only the final two minutes. We began with four minutes of individual movement drills for everyone on the squad. On defense this took the form of individual pursuit drills. The next three minutes were unit drills. The offense did some form of team time-up or specific plays versus the air. The defense ran three minutes of the team pursuit drill explained in chapter 4.

When the air horn blew for the final two minutes, the whole team except the offensive line ran to designated spots at midfield. There we had three tackling stations, all running the same tackling drill, with high intensity but with no one going to the ground (see figure 5.12).

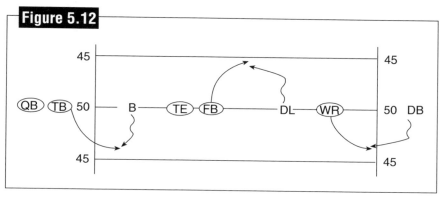

Figure 5.12

Tempo tackling. Defenders shuffle and press.

The ball carriers immediately run with the ball protected in their outside arm to one 45-yard line or the other. They cannot cut back but try to stay in bounds by putting their near shoulder into the defender.

Meanwhile, the defender shuffles and presses as explained earlier in the confined tackling drill. We want heavy contact but no takedowns. This is also a strong sideline tackling experience for defenders.

Tempo tackling becomes a positive experience for both units if the coaches are emphatic about its importance. Tempo tackling brings a shot of adrenaline to practice. It also gives the offense and defense a time to work together, which may rarely occur on the college level.

Conduct this drill at a rapid pace. As soon as one ball carrier goes, the next is up and running. This may be the running backs' longest two minutes in practice. The defenders get the benefit of many tackling experiences with quality competition.

During the season we did this drill once per week against either the offense or the scout squad. In the spring the first units nearly always faced each other.

An excellent defensive team must be strong tacklers. To reach that goal, players must understand and regularly practice the common tackles. The tackling edge can be lost quickly, so emphasize it nearly every day. Develop a group attitude that will not permit an opponent to run through team members!

Chapter 6

Zone Coverage Skills

Coverage skills are the fourth fundamental of linebacking. At higher levels of play, this ABC becomes increasingly important. The college player spends much more time than he did in high school practicing this fundamental because university teams throw effectively. It is not uncommon for some linebackers to play only on heavy run downs, replaced by specialized pass-down defenders on long-yardage situations. At the NFL level the passing game becomes even more important. An aspiring player learns to defend against the passing game, or he will be a part-time contributor. Today's football demands excellence in this area.

The earlier the defender knows that the offense is passing, the more effective he will be. At times, it is obvious by down and distance, or formation tendencies. Linebackers need help when it is not so clear. That is when keys can be helpful.

Once the key tells a linebacker that the offense will pass, it is his responsibility to communicate this clearly to his teammates. To be useful, a defender's key and his interpretation of it must be reliable. We do not permit all players to be communicators of a run-pass key. Defenders must earn this status by consistently making the correct signal. Usually we designate only two or three communicators who can yell "pass" or its coded word. This signal will activate the whole defense—the drops into zones and the pass rush up front. The run-pass key can also change the defensive call if a designated player recognizes it before the snap. After the snap the correct signal can eliminate the confusion of play-action passes.

Retreat

A linebacker in zone coverage retreats in one of two popular ways. Either can be effective as long as the linebacker understands the purpose and limitations of each.

What is the purpose of this retreat? Once we recognize pass, we want depth, with vision on the quarterback, and we want to be at the desired coverage angle. Let's examine the two popular forms of retreat and how they compare in reaching the goals of an effective drop.

Crossover

With the crossover the linebacker opens his hips on a pass key at the prescribed angle and crosses his inside leg over the outside leg as he gains depth. The athlete keeps his head on a swivel so he has a view of the passer and the receiving threats.

It was Darrick Brownlow, the three-time All-Big Ten linebacker, who said, "When I drop on pass, I keep my inside eye on the quarterback and my outside eye on the receiver." Few of us have that kind of eye control, but the thought is on target. We want to gain depth while observing both the thrower and receiver.

The crossover allows the linebacker to run fast while seeing the necessary zone codes to interpret his path. It also permits the athlete to gain width easily by simply leading his outside foot at the proper angle (see figure 6.1).

The advantage of the crossover is that the defender can retreat quickly and maintain vision of the passing game. The disadvantage

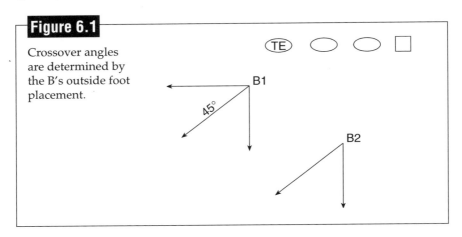

Figure 6.1

Crossover angles are determined by the B's outside foot placement.

is that if the ball is thrown while the defender is crossing over, he can intercept it only if it is thrown in the direction of his flow. He cannot play balls thrown to his inside or in front of him when he is in a full-speed retreat to the outside.

Backpedal

The backpedal is executed by running backward with hips and shoulders parallel to the line of scrimmage. It is most efficient when the body is bent at knees, hips, and ankles with the shoulders leaning forward over the toes. Most linebackers lean backward when backpedaling, which creates an awkward movement with less potential to change direction.

The backpedal gives excellent vision on the quarterback and allows a three-way break (left, right, or forward) on any thrown ball. The disadvantage is that it does not cover as much ground as the crossover and doesn't expand (gain width) easily.

Pull-Up

No matter how a linebacker retreats, it is my firm opinion that when the quarterback stops his drop and sets to throw, the linebacker must pull up. Pulling up means to be square to the offensive line in a bent football position, focused on the quarterback and ready to break on the first indication of the throw. This pull-up position gives the defender the necessary base for the three-way break.

Any movement in a crossover or backpedal retreat *after* the quarterback sets up constitutes *drift*. A linebacker who is drifting cannot make a play on a throw unless the quarterback throws it in the direction of his drift. Drift eliminates the three-way break, and thus the coach and player must eliminate drift.

Figure 6.2 shows two linebackers who retreated on the threat of pass. B1 squared up when the quarterback stopped to throw. He will read the quarterback for his three-way break. B2 is still moving when the quarterback sets up. Because he is drifting, he will not be able to break effectively on an inside or underneath throw.

Is drift ever permissible? Yes! We teach that there are three specific times when it's OK to drift:

▪ On third down and more than 15, we teach the linebackers to leave the huddle calling "drift" to remind the undercoverage *not* to pull up with the quarterback. We cross over for depth, and

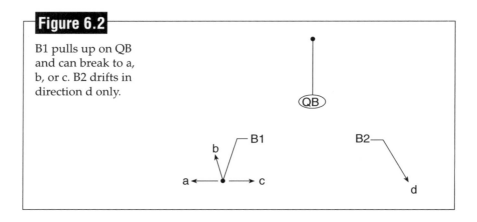

Figure 6.2

B1 pulls up on QB and can break to a, b, or c. B2 drifts in direction d only.

when the quarterback sets up, we square up and drift in a backpedal. We do this to force the quarterback to throw the ball underneath us. But we never drift deeper than the first-down marker.

▪ As a rule, we teach our inside linebackers to drift when they get a drag route coming toward them. For most teams the drag is part of a high-low route, and we want to defend the deeper part of that route in our drop. Figure 6.3 shows one of football's productive routes. The quarterback keys the linebacker (B1). If the linebacker jumps the drag, the quarterback throws over him to the wide receiver's square-in. When the linebacker sees drag, he should drift to force the shorter throw to the tight end, that can be defended by an outside linebacker (B2).

▪ The third drift situation occurs with less than 30 seconds remaining in one of the halves. When the opponent cannot score with a completion of a shorter route, we tag the term *deep* to the coverage (for example, cover 4 deep). This again alerts the undercoverage that when the quarterback sets, they are to continue to backpedal, getting under the intermediate routes. This forces the quarterback to throw too deep or to throw a dump-off to a short receiver who cannot advance the ball far enough in the time remaining (see figure 6.4).

Break Before the Ball

We use the phrase *break before the ball* to encourage our linebackers in a pulled-up position to read the quarterback and break toward the receiver *before* the ball is thrown.

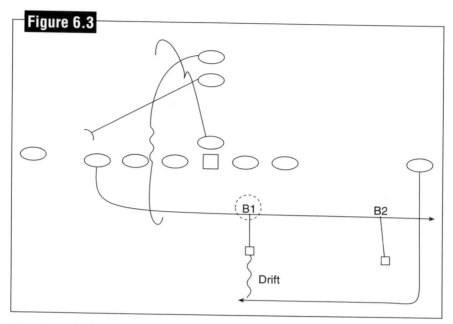

B1 drifts on TE's drag under SE's square-in pattern.

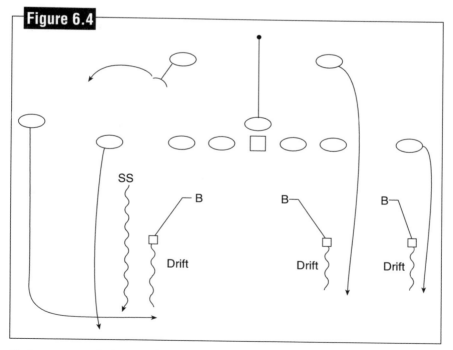

Undercoverage drifting with 30 seconds or less in the half

As linebackers study quarterbacks, it's amazing how they can get a feel for the direction of the ball and the timing of the release before the ball leaves the passer's hand. We call this feel *getting an indication*. Sometimes it comes from the quarterback's lead hand or front foot, but usually it is from his eyes.

Linebackers who can get an early indication can really cover some ground. I have a classic film clip of Barry Remington (Colorado) pulled up in coverage alongside a companion linebacker—a player who could better him in the 40-yard dash by a half second. Remington broke before the ball was thrown and crossed his buddy's zone to make the tackle. How did he do it? He pulled up with a purpose, a focus, and an anticipation that he would make a play.

Zone defenders should see the ball and make plays on it. Mike Johnson (Virginia Tech) had five interceptions in one season. A linebacker can't do that without a strong retreat, a timely pull-up, and ability to break before the throw.

Drop-Back Passes

In the next segments, we will discuss zone coverage and how it relates to the basic concepts employed by most schemes when defending pocket passes.

First, we will describe some fundamental inside linebacker zones and then do the same with the outside players.

Hook to Curl (H/C)

This ancient double-zone responsibility makes up the base of much linebacker coverage. When I began coaching in 1967, this was the major responsibility for inside linebackers in a three-deep zone. A decade later, overshifted coverages began to give some relief to the inside linebacker in an attempt to restrict the width of his drops. Now some clubs are beginning to revive the three-deep concept. Hook-to-curl zone duties will probably have a major place in linebacker play for years to come.

When we give the linebacker hook to curl, we ask him to defend the hook when it is threatened and expand to the curl when no one occupies the hook. When we assign hook to curl (H/C) in any zone coverage, we do not want a linebacker to run to an area and hold his hands in the air. After recognizing pocket pass, the linebacker begins to retreat toward the hook (see figure 6.5).

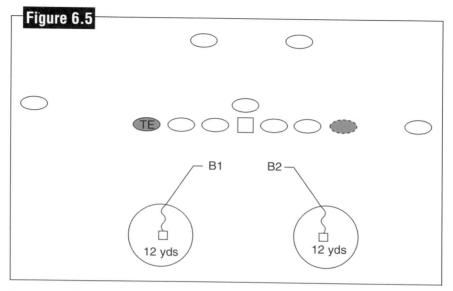

B's drop-to-hook areas are usually 12 yards deep.

We describe the hook as an area 12 yards deep from the tight end (B1 in figure 6.5) or where the tight end would have aligned had there been one (B2 in figure 6.5).

As the linebacker retreats he must see the quarterback and read his key receiver. The key receiver in an H/C responsibility is a tight end, if there is one, or the second eligible receiver to a split end side (see figure 6.6).

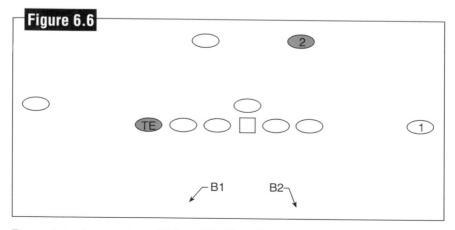

Determining key receivers. B1 keys TE. B2, with no TE, keys #2.

When the key receiver blocks, our scouting report will determine how we respond. Generally, if he sits, we sit. In anticipation of a delay or screen, the linebacker should slide to the middle of the formation (see figure 6.7).

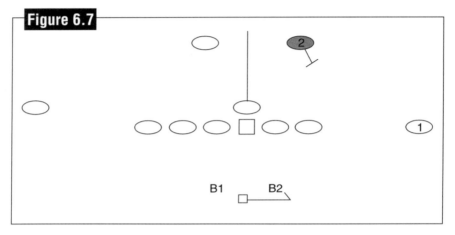

Figure 6.7

B2 slides to the middle when his key receiver blocks.

Against teams that do not run delays in this fashion, we will have B2 expand immediately to the curl when the key receiver blocks. Each week we study this reaction for the best response.

When the key receiver releases vertically, we protect the hook by keeping inside leverage on him. When the quarterback sets up, we want the linebacker to keep hands on the receiver, who is now behind him. The key receiver may be out of sight but never out of feel (see figure 6.8).

Remember, it is entirely legal to collide with receivers as long as the ball has not been thrown and the receiver is in front of the linebacker. In 30 years, I can remember only one penalty for hitting a receiver at the same depth as the defender. Chopping a receiver is unsound and illegal.

When the key receiver streaks down the field, the linebacker should widen to bump him and slow his progress to the deep zone. Because the key receiver does not slow down to make a cut, realize that he may be trying to run the linebacker deep and bring a wide receiver shallow underneath. This has become a popular route in the 1990s. Train the linebacker to sneak a peek at the wide receiver when the key receiver tries to clear out vertically (see figure 6.9).

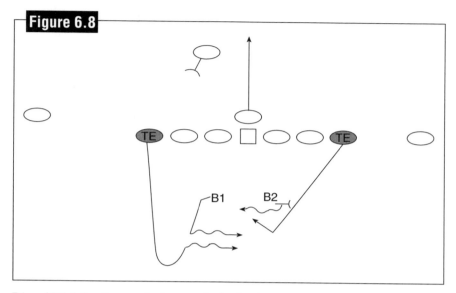

B1 and B2 defending vertical routes in the hook area

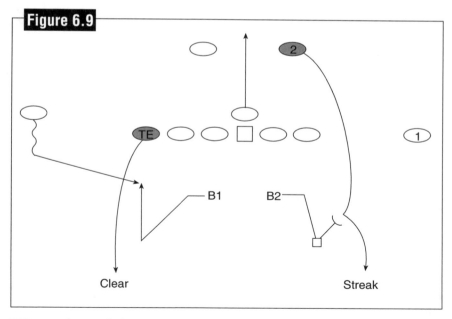

B2 bumps the streak. B1 recognizes clear route and breaks up on shallow WR pattern.

When the key receivers swing or release into the flat (nonvertical routes), the linebacker should not widen with them. Although key receivers direct the linebacker's drop, this is not man-to-man coverage. The defender should gain depth and width while looking for the curl of the outside receiver. Always keep the receiver outside the linebacker's drop. If the quarterback is going to throw, force him to throw the longer pattern outside the linebacker (see figure 6.10).

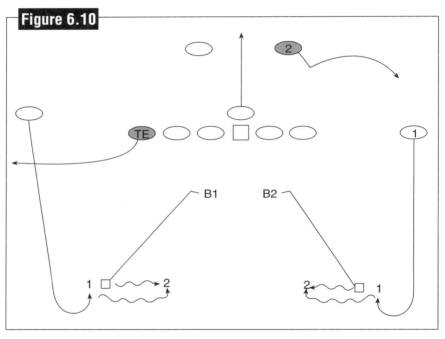

Figure 6.10

B1 responds to TE's flat route, while B2 reacts identically to #2's swing pattern.

Remember, once the curl receiver is in position #1 (figure 6.10) and sees the linebacker approaching to take away that passing lane, he will begin to slide inside to position #2. The linebacker must anticipate this movement and counter by opening his hips inside and shuffling with him. This is the linebacker's most difficult zone challenge because it pits him against a wide receiver in space.

When the key receiver releases on a drag pattern (see figure 6.11), the linebacker should yell "drag" or "crossing" to the opposite linebacker. He should treat this as a nonvertical and accelerate toward the curl. When a drag comes to a linebacker, he should drift once the quarterback sets up, anticipating the high-low concept described earlier in figure 6.3.

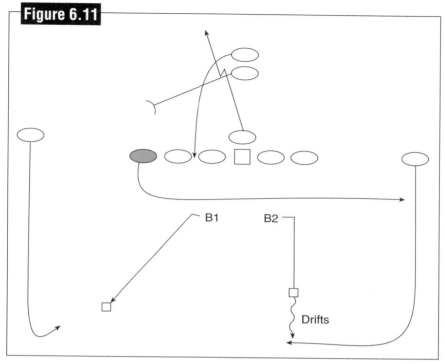

Figure 6.11

B1 expands to the curl on the TE's nonvertical and calls "drag" to B2, who drifts on the drag.

Hook to Force (H/F)

At Virginia Tech in 1978, our defensive staff began to experiment with linebacker play toward an overshifted coverage. Bill Dooley loved the coverage. Steve Bernstein, an excellent secondary coach, and I coordinated the play of his alley/curl free safety and my eagle linebacker.

The advantages for a linebacker were exciting. Because the defensive backs had flat and curl, the linebacker had a restricted drop. He never had to expand to the curl. This suited less athletic or inexperienced linebackers. Because they didn't need to sprint to a wide zone, they could really sit on draws, whereas an H/C linebacker had to make a quick decision and then get on his horse to defend a curl route.

Essentially, the hook-to-force linebacker has to defend a 5-yard-by-12-yard box from the alignment of a tight end to the center of the formation (see figure 6.12).

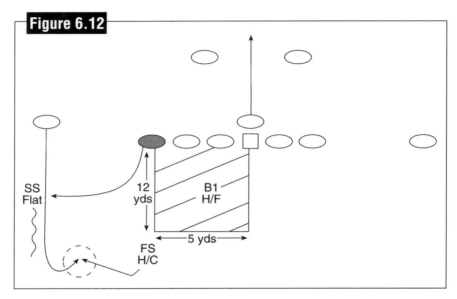

B1 has H/F and is responsible for his 5 yard × 12 yard box.

After the linebacker recognizes pocket pass, he begins to read the tight end to his side. Against a twins formation (see figure 6.13) the linebacker would key #3. Regardless of the read, the linebacker never has curl when he has a hook-to-force duty.

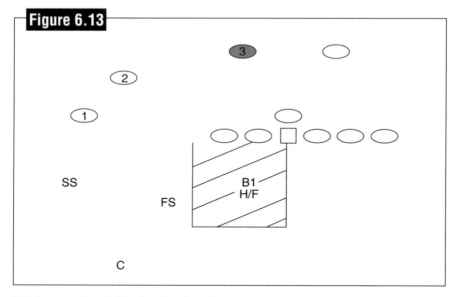

B1's key receiver is #3 when hook to force versus twins.

When the key receiver releases vertically, the defender should keep inside leverage on him. The linebacker can slide inside all the way to the middle of the formation. He can stop the tight end center route by collapsing inside with it (see figure 6.14).

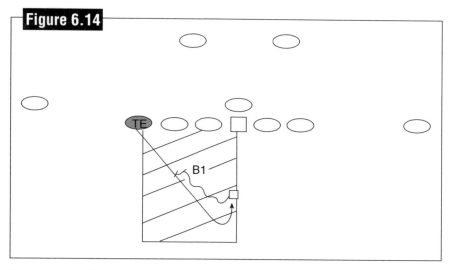

Figure 6.14

Hook-to-force B1 must defend his box and stay inside and in front of the TE.

When the key receiver runs a nonvertical route as in figure 6.12, the linebacker gets no wider than the frontside hook.

We developed a short-drop concept later at Colorado in the early 1980s. Now against certain formations, we tell our restricted dropper to get no depth at all versus drop-back pass. He defends the middle of his box and jumps any threat passing through the box.

This idea becomes an effective tool with delays, middle screens, shallow routes by wide receivers, and draws. Knowing down and distance is also critical. Even a short dropper would gain depth on third and more than 10, and he would drift on third and more than 15.

Flat

The final underneath zone that we will consider is commonly called the flat area. Usually, linebackers are responsible for most of the underneath zones (that is, zones in which receivers run shorter routes). Figure 6.15 illustrates for our linebackers the relationship of these zones to each other and to the football field.

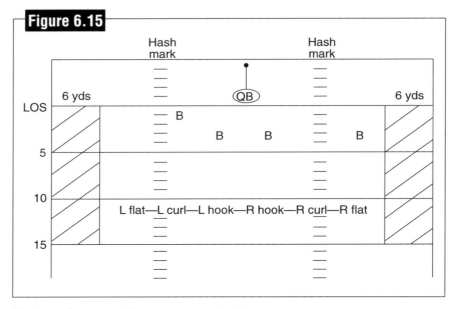

Underneath zones with remote areas shaded

Defenders can best cover the six zones in figure 6.15 if they get to the center of their zones and break on the indication of the quarterback, as outlined in the earlier discussion of hook-and-curl responsibilities.

The flat areas differ in that the shaded portions are farthest from the passer. Both time and the sideline aid the flat defender in these remote areas. The ball must be in the air a long time and the passer must throw accurately for it to reach the flat in bounds.

As a base concept, our outside linebacker with flat duty knows that he need not enter the remote area until the throw is indicated by the quarterback. The flat defender need not be closer than six yards to the sideline on a pocket pass.

When the linebacker's key tells him drop-back pass and the ball is in the middle of the field, he should turn at a 45-degree angle to his outside, run to a point 12 yards deep and 2 yards inside the widest receiver, and pull up with the quarterback's set (see figure 6.16).

B3 never wants to be closer than six yards from the boundary and always maintains inside leverage on the wide receiver to force the longer throw.

In Figure 6.16, another outside linebacker concept is apparent. B3 hangs in the curl, even though it is not his zone, to bide time for B2

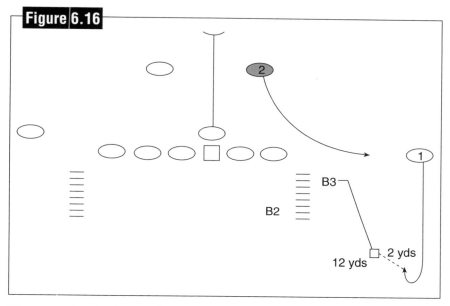

Figure 6.16

B3 opens to his flat drop with ball in middle of the field.

to make the longer trip to the curl. When #2 crosses B3's face, B3 widens and leaves B2 to cover the curl alone. This is a basic thought that all flat defenders must recognize. As flat defenders gain experience they learn how long they can hold the curl. With long-yardage situations, let the #2 receiver gain width if he cannot make the first down. Against one Big Ten opponent, we declined to defend the flat against a 260-pound fullback who averaged one catch in four games. Our outside linebackers squeezed the curl, forcing the quarterback to throw to him. He dropped the pass.

Outside linebackers also frequently get two receivers in their flat zones. We instruct them to get to the deepest part of their zone and break on the shorter route (see figure 6.17).

Now B3 retreats and either sees the wide receiver running an out or pulls up and breaks to the wide receiver before the quarterback's throw. In either case the passer has these thoughts:

- If I underthrow the wide receiver, the linebacker can score on an interception.
- If I overthrow in the remote area, the receiver may catch the ball out of bounds.
- My safe throw is to the shorter #2 receiver.

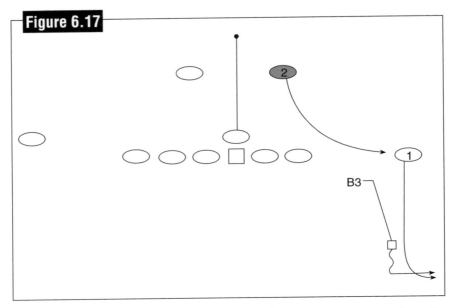

Figure 6.17

B3 defends the deepest part of his flat zone with two receivers in it to force the shorter throw.

The defender must keep his eyes glued on the quarterback and react to his throw. Force the shorter toss and then make the receiver pay the price on contact. Remember, there is a reason the flat defender is called an *outside* linebacker: All his help is on the inside. He must tackle with his helmet on the outside edge of the receiver.

When the ball is on the hash mark in high school and college football, the outside linebacker into the boundary enjoys a narrower area to defend. Now when he recognizes the pocket pass, little or no width is necessary due to the proximity of the widest receiver. Outside linebackers often use the backpedal exclusively here so they don't get into the remote area (see figure 6.18).

The initial depth of all our zone undercoverage depends on the drop of the quarterback. On a short three-step drop, we pull up quickly and immediately break for the nearest outside receiver. With the popular five-step drop, we expect our undercoverage to get 10 to 12 yards deep. On the classic seven-step drop, all the linebackers should have excellent depth. Obviously, the route depth is tied to the depth of the quarterback's drop.

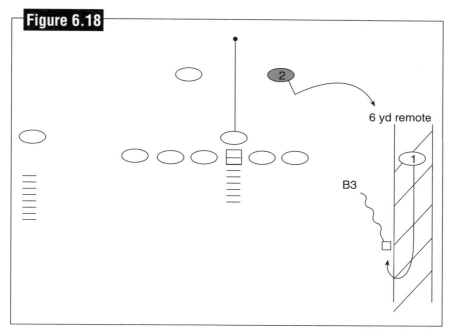

Figure 6.18

6 yd remote

B3

B3 backpedals with the ball on the hash. He doesn't need width when so close to the shaded remote area.

Action Passes

Action passes comprise a varied group of passes that move the quarterback from the pocket. Sprints, rollouts, play actions with width, bootlegs, and so on are all part of this grouping.

When addressing these passes, we attempt to give our linebackers consistent and easy-to-follow rules. Basically, the zone rules define just two reactions—one for pocket passes and one for action passes—not one for every different pass type.

Three-Deep Zone

In figure 6.19, the passer gains width to throw. With a sprint pass (position 1, figure 6.19) the linebackers move in concert and flow to the curl, frontside hook, and backside hook. They give up the remote backside flat. The linebacking corps does not read key receivers as they did versus pocket passes. Now the passing field is reduced because of quarterback's movement. The corps keys only the quarterback. When he sets up, they square up ready to break before the ball.

Figure 6.19

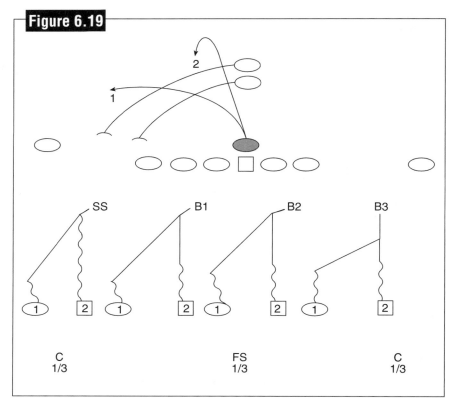

The LB corps must respond in concert to the QB's action path.

When the quarterback sets up with less width in position 2 (in figure 6.19), the linebackers work for width, but all pull up sooner, just as the quarterback does. Now the zones are more balanced, like those defending pocket passes.

The coach must make rules for contain of the quarterback when he threatens the corner. In a three-deep zone structure, we instruct our linebackers to stay in coverage until the quarterback crosses the line of scrimmage. They will be tempted to void a zone to attack the quarterback. When they do, a veteran quarterback will simply throw to the voided area. Be ready for this when playing a heavy action-pass team.

Two-Deep Zone

In figure 6.20 the typical two-deep zone adds a frontside curl defender from the secondary. Now the frontside linebacker (B1) has a hook-to-force restricted drop. Because the free safety takes away the

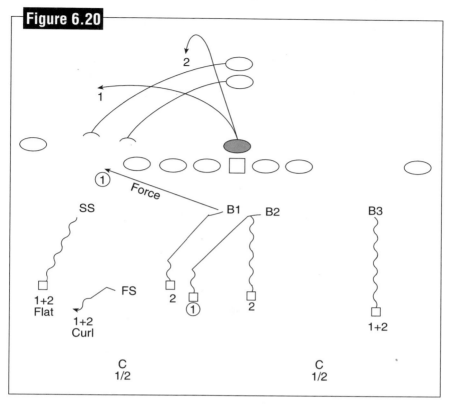

The LB corps reaction to action pass with a two-deep zone

curl in figure 6.20 and B2 will work to the opposite hook with sprint away, B1 is free to force the quarterback immediately.

Back in the late 1970s the sprint-pass action was very popular, and our H/F linebackers got many pressures and sacks forcing this action. Today we rarely see the quarterback on the corner except for bootleg. The reaction should be the same, however, if the H/F linebacker has a key to recognize the bootleg early.

Another variation with two-deep coverage concerns the outside linebacker, B3. B3 now has only a halves player inside him rather than a three-deep corner behind him as we saw in figure 6.19. With action away, he cannot collapse as far inside as he could with a three-deep zone. He must keep proximity on the split receiver to his side and have depth for a potential throwback.

Action passes are easy to respond to if keys are accurate. Flowing with the action is correct and also very natural. The undercoverage

Courtesy of University of Colorado

■ Dan McMillen was our first lanky, rush linebacker. A tremendous coverage player on special teams, he could run fast and do it all game long. A relentless pass rusher, his success altered our ideas about what body type we sought for the position.

must work in concert so that no pickets are missing in the action-pass fence. The entire defense must understand contain responsibility against a running quarterback.

Zone Coverage Drills

This section discusses some of the drills that we have used to improve our linebackers' zone coverage. We begin with a drill that focuses on movement mechanics and end with drills that most linebackers live for—ball drills that have them making the big play.

Line Drills

The purpose of the zone coverage line drills is to work on the mechanics of the two basic forms of linebacker retreats.

Align three players facing the coach with their backs to the sideline of a field. They should space themselves 10 yards apart and key the ball that the coach is holding. When the coach pushes the ball toward them, all three lean forward and backpedal down their lines. The coach checks each for bend in the ankles, knees, and hips. Weight should be forward and arms working vigorously.

When the coach brings the ball to his shoulder level as if to throw, all three should pull up. If the coach pushes the ball toward them while in this broken-down position, they should drift or continue to backpedal until the quarterback (coach) sets up. When the instructor gives an indication to throw, the linebackers must all break in that direction (see figure 6.21).

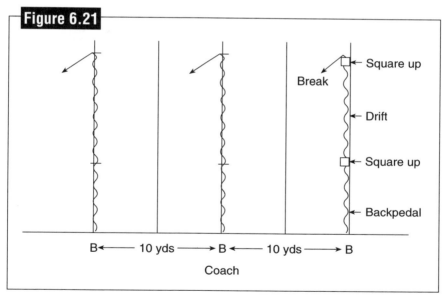

Figure 6.21

Square up
Break
Drift
Square up
Backpedal

B ◀—— 10 yds ——▶ B ◀—— 10 yds ——▶ B

Coach

Backpedal line drill

This drill will provide repetitions at backpedal mechanics, force the linebackers to focus on the quarterback for their pull ups, and prepare them to break on the desired indicator of the opponent's quarterback.

You can use the same drill alignment to work on crossover mechanics. The linebackers backpedal as before when the coach pushes the ball toward them. When the coach points the ball to the left or right, the three respond by crossing over in that direction directly down the line. This is a 90-degree turn that many coaches use when moving down zone landmarks (that is, hashes, field numbers, and so on). The drill forces the players to keep their vision on the coach while in their crossovers. To flip his hips to the opposite side, the linebacker must jerk around his elbow nearest the ball and open his hips in that direction. If the athlete can stay on the line while flipping his hips, he has good mechanics and hip flexibility. As before, when the coach sets up and indicates a throw, the player must pull up and break (see figure 6.22).

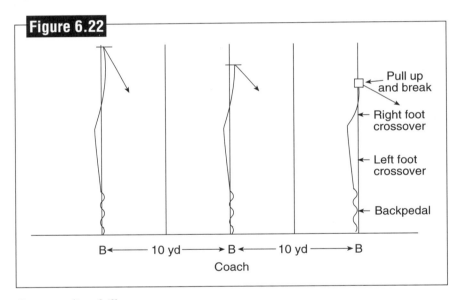

Figure 6.22

Crossover line drill

Remember, the reason for the crossover is speed in the retreat. We must be able to get depth with vision so a linebacker can pull up and be square to the quarterback for a three-way break.

Bag 45s

Although coaches often ask linebackers to cross over vertically (90 degrees), they more frequently require that linebackers open at a comfortable 45 degrees when retreating to most receiving threats.

As they open, the linebackers must see the quarterback and, peripherally, the receivers. They must also be prepared to change direction
on action passes. This drill addresses those issues.

In figure 6.23, two linebackers are facing the coach with their backs
to a row of three or four agility bags spaced five yards apart.

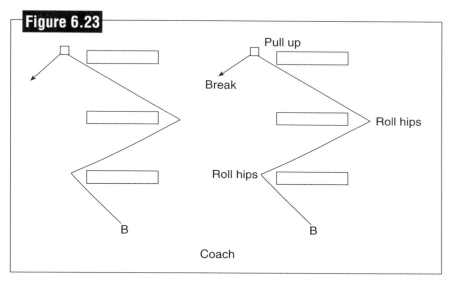

Figure 6.23

Pull up

Break

Roll hips

Roll hips

B   B

Coach

Bag 45s

The coach directs them through this minefield by pointing the
ball left or right. The linebackers respond by crossing over at 45-
degree angles and training their vision on the coach (quarterback)
while peripherally seeing the bags.

At any point, the coach can set up to throw, so the two participants must focus on him. Once the defenders pull up, they are glued
visually to the quarterback for their break on the ball. The coach can
throw the ball and have the athletes sprint back to him with it.

Cover-Ground Drill

The intent of this drill is to demonstrate how much ground a player
can cover from a pulled-up position.

Place a linebacker in a squared position as if he had retreated and
already pulled up with the quarterback. This drill should make apparent that the quarterback is set up 7 to 9 yards deep and the linebacker is pulled up 10 to 12 yards downfield.

Then place three receivers 5 yards away on either side and in front of him. Have the quarterback throw to one of the receivers. The linebacker should break on the indication and easily cover 5 yards to the intended receiver. This is also a good opportunity to provide tips on intercepting, breaking up passes, and stripping receivers.

Place the receivers farther away each time the linebacker has success. It will give the coach and the athlete an appreciation of the ground the defender can cover when he breaks before the throw (see figure 6.24).

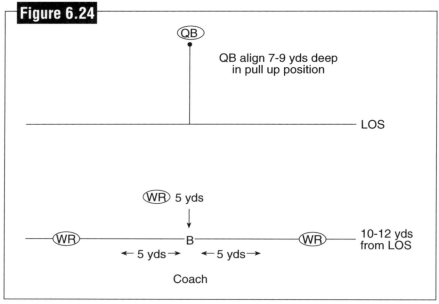

Figure 6.24

Cover-ground drill

Drop-Versus-Air Drill

We use this drill early in the teaching progression of coverages in fall camp and spring practice. It permits the coach to view all his linebackers as they respond to various coverage rules, ball placements, or pass types (three-step, five-step, seven-step, or action). We also use it as a final review once the game plan is in to solidify assignments and test understanding.

Have the coach play quarterback and give the linebackers the huddle call. On the snap, the quarterback demonstrates the pass type and, knowing the coverage and field position, the linebackers respond to him.

I like to have all the linebackers work at once with the units lined up behind one another. Any mistake in the drops jumps out at the entire group (see figure 6.25).

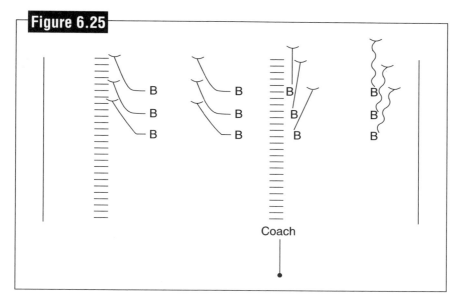

Figure 6.25

Drop-versus-air drill

7-on-7 Drill

This drill is so universal that I will not describe it but will instead talk about our emphasis for this indispensable part of practice. This is our finest pass-teaching period if we organize and script it well.

We have our defensive units alternate, with each taking only four to six plays in succession. More than that cuts down on the intensity of the pursuit we require (93 percent; see chapter 4). For this reason, I dislike the habits often formed in summer 7-on-7 leagues. Players take too many consecutive repetitions and cannot build proper pursuit routines.

We have found several variations of 7-on-7 to be beneficial:

- Work two half-coverage drills. Take a snap with the frontside of a coverage followed by a snap of the backside. Now you can direct reps to a limited number of routes that the opponent runs specific to those coverage shells. Both sides of a coverage get equal work.

- Employ only an undercoverage drill without the deep-zone people involved. Here, you can give a large number of reps to attacking high-low routes, delays, screens, and so on that are more specific for linebackers.

Our 7-on-7s rarely involve anything but pocket passes. The players know that every call is a pass in 7-on-7. It is much more effective to work on play action, bootlegs, screens, trick passes, and so on in a team setting where run is an equal possibility. Plan one quarterback scramble in each 20-minute pass skeleton. It gives the defense experience in defending the deep zones when time permits an offense to freelance and lengthen routes.

Ball Drills

All my former linebackers over three decades are probably chuckling as they see this section heading. I will admit that few linebacker coaches ever spend enough time in this area, but if they do, they are probably neglecting something significant. Usually, I did ball drills in a five-minute period twice per week during the season. In spring training and fall camp we allotted more time to it but never as much as the linebackers desired or needed.

Ball drills can make practice more fun and competitive. For years we took our team to a movie theater Friday night before games. My wife, Karen, would make popcorn for the movie and put it in bags for the winners of that week's ball drills. The competition for those cheap bags of popcorn was fun and intense!

We ran our drills on a break from a pulled-up position. Linebackers would break on my throwing motion, and each player would catch with two hands going left, then right. The next time through the linebackers would catch with one hand to increase concentration and hand-eye skills. The third time I would throw the ball slightly behind them to simulate a poorly thrown ball on their break (see figure 6.26). The throws can be as short as five yards to get more repetitions and to save an old arm.

We called the final trip through this drill "distraction." Now players partnered up, and a teammate distracted the interceptor verbally and physically as he broke on my throw. The distracter could hit the linebacker anywhere but on the arms as he broke to the ball. This drill forced concentration.

Another item to address is ball security. Because linebackers carry the football so little they are vulnerable to fumbling. Make sure they

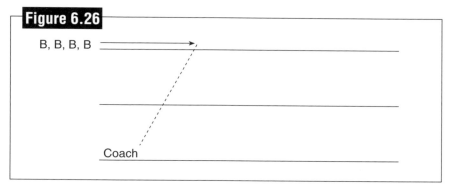

Break-down-the-line ball drills

put the ball away and feel the five pressure points securing the ball (fingers, palm, forearm, elbow, and ribs). Never permit reckless handling of the ball. An interception on third down fumbled back to an opponent for a first and 10 is a traumatic setback.

Linebackers need to be aware that after an interception they should *never* switch the ball from one arm to the other. We don't have enough experience doing that at high speeds. Just before contact they should cover the ball with two hands.

Wide receivers are today doing a much better job of stripping linebackers of the ball. They have more speed and can strip from behind successfully. We teach our linebackers that a wide receiver is always closing on him from behind. They should never be surprised by a strip attempt from the rear.

Chapter 7

Man Coverage Skills

Man-to-man coverage skills are another part of the fourth fundamental of linebacker play. The principles of zone and man coverage are distinctly different. Nearly all defensive schemes employ both man and zone coverages to some extent, but most use one or the other as their foundation. Few teams use both equally well.

Man Coverage Advantages

Man-to-man coverage has several advantages over zone coverage. It can provide tighter coverage, reduce the opponent's completion rate, and permit increased pressure by the pass rush.

Tighter Coverage

On the snap, the casual fan can easily detect man-to-man coverage by linebackers. In zone, the linebacker retreats when he recognizes pass, as described in chapter 6. In man, the linebacker's first steps are forward in reaction to the pocket pass.

This forward movement toward the receiver makes man coverage tighter than zone. Defenders closely guard short routes by receivers in man coverage. The same route against a zone defense will have linebackers breaking from depth to it.

This is why man coverage is popular on third and short or medium down and distance. A four-yard gain is acceptable to a defense on third and six, but not on third and three. Tighter coverage is required, and teams often choose a form of man coverage.

In the red zone (usually inside the 20-yard line), the goal line is nearer and the defense must give ground grudgingly. Here, too, defenses often call upon man-to-man for tighter coverage.

Lower Completion Percentage

Completion percentages logically go down when defenders are in closer proximity to receivers. It takes a more accurate pass when there is less room between the target and the linebacker.

More Pressure

A man-to-man coverage unit does not necessarily employ more pass rushers than a zone defense, though that is typically the case. Even if the number of rushers is identical, well-executed man coverage can force the quarterback to throw early. The longer he holds the ball, the better the chance of pass-rush pressure. Heavy man coverage teams normally create more hurried passes and sacks.

Man Coverage Disadvantages

Man coverage has drawbacks. Although it usually permits fewer completions, longer gains often result. Interceptions are less likely. Man coverage is susceptible to isolation tactics by the offense, and blitz coverage is problematic.

Isolation on Poorer Defenders

In man coverage, defenders can find themselves without much help, and that can lead to mismatches. Most offenses seek to work a superior athlete in space on a linebacker in man coverage.

A 235-pound linebacker who runs 4.8 seconds in 40 yards may feel comfortable in zone coverage when he breaks on a skilled 200-pound running back who sprints 4.5 in 40 yards. The same defender alone in man coverage can get real nervous before the snap.

Longer Gains

Typically, man-to-man coverage teams give up fewer completions but longer gains. When a defender is beaten in zone coverage, his teammates are all in pursuit to limit the gain because they all, ideally, see the quarterback throw the ball. But in man coverage, many defenders never see the quarterback release the ball because they are glued visually to their man. Often little help is breaking on the throw. The pressure is squarely on the linebacker to cover and make the tackle without an error. A heavy man-to-man team needs outstanding athletes at the linebacker positions.

Fewer Interceptions

Although man defenses generally force a lower completion percentage, they usually have decidedly fewer interceptions than zone clubs because their defenders have their eyes focused on receivers, not the ball.

Scrambling Quarterbacks

For the same reason, scrambling quarterbacks can give headaches to man-to-man defenses. This is particularly true for defenses that use man-under with two-deep zone. Now there are just four pass rushers, and the undercoverage has potentially turned its back to run downfield with receivers. If the quarterback gets past the front four, he can run a long way before a defender reacts back to the ball.

Confusion Factor

This can be just as large a factor in zone coverage, but the outcome is worse in man-to-man. If confusion results because a linebacker doesn't identify his man properly or because the offense shifts or uses motion, an offensive player could be free. That's not good. If a linebacker makes a mistake in zone, he always has help deep to limit the gain.

An offense often plots to confuse a man coverage linebacker by some kind of play action that would present a conflict between his run and pass responsibilities (see figure 7.1).

Figure 7.1 presents a linebacker (B2) with man responsibility for the first back out to his side of the formation. That same linebacker, however, must be part of the run defense should the tailback be given the ball on the counter play rather than the bootleg off the counter. The linebacker's key and discipline will be tested severely.

Disguise Can Be Difficult

Most quarterbacks can easily detect blitz coverages from man in today's long-yardage formations. Because it is difficult to disguise the blitz, quarterbacks can make effective checks. The opening moments of Super Bowl XXXI provided an excellent example. Brett Favre of Green Bay recognized a blitz coverage on the second play

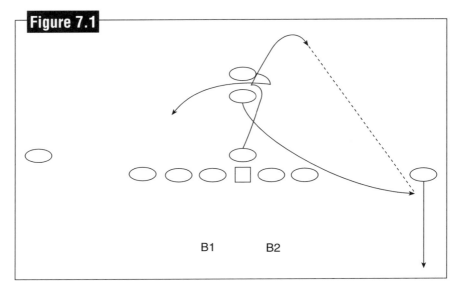

B2 has a potential conflict in rules.

of the Packers' first possession. Favre audibled to maximum protection and completed a 54-yard post route for an early 7-0 lead. The defensive back expected pressure, but received no such help and was beaten on the inside move to the post.

Zone coverage pressure would possibly void a zone or exert less stress on the passer, but it would have given more deep-zone help to the defensive back.

Many Forms of Man

Teams have been very successful as primarily zone or man defenses. Both have strengths and weaknesses that each staff must evaluate.

Coaches should teach what their staff knows best and then make variations according to the talent available. The strength of our multiple-reduction scheme over many years has been our rich experience in it. To change abruptly to an unfamiliar defense, even if it were schematically better, would give up decades of knowledge.

At the same time, man coverage units have much flexibility and can use many forms of coverage. An inside linebacker with marginal man skills can become a zone player who helps the other man players with short crossing routes. Crossing routes are a common strategy for offenses versus man teams. Figure 7.2 illustrates a way

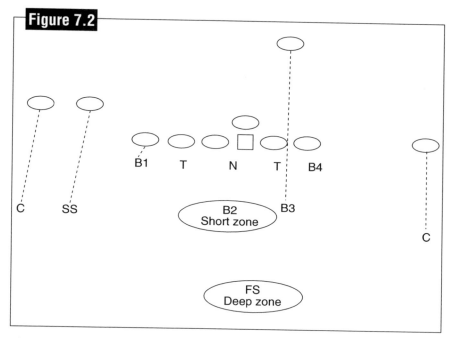

Figure 7.2

This man double-free coverage allows a linebacker with poor man coverage skills (B2) to play in man coverage without being exploited.

both to eliminate the strain on that linebacker (B2) and to stop those types of crossing patterns.

Often we have had a man coverage linebacker with excellent man coverage technique but limited speed. We give him man-to-man duties into the boundary but rarely to the field where a receiver can outdistance him.

We try to recruit outside linebackers who can match up effectively with tight ends and running backs in man coverage. It is not unusual for us to put our outside linebackers in man-to-man on a wide receiver when he has deep-zone help behind him. Our drop linebackers have been particularly adept at this form of coverage. With lesser athletes, a staff can substitute a better coverage guy in an obvious pass down.

Man Coverage Mechanics

Once the players clearly understand the scheme's man-to-man rules and can confidently identify their man responsibility, it is time to learn the mechanics of this coverage.

We can categorize all pass routes into three broad groups. There will be an occasional deviation, but correct responses to these three basic patterns will serve linebackers well.

Inside Routes

The concept that the linebacker must understand here is simple. The easiest pass to complete is the short throw. Inside breaking routes are close to the quarterback and, therefore, are high-percentage throws.

 The priority for a man-to-man linebacker is to *deny all inside breaking patterns*. We usually have the linebacker align inside the receiver before the snap. Occasionally, we will have a linebacker jump inside a receiver at the snap. We rarely have him outside his receiver unless he has inside zone help as B1 has from B2 in figure 7.2.

On the snap of the ball, if our key indicates a running play our linebackers defend the run. When his key tells him pass, he presses or moves forward to engage the receiver. We teach the linebacker to deny the inside path by attacking the receiver with his outside foot and hand. When the defender makes contact with his outside hand to the receiver's chest, he will always maintain inside leverage and halt the inside break of the receiver.

 If the linebacker does not press the receiver or if the receiver gets head up, a good athlete is likely to beat the defender inside.

Figure 7.3 shows three examples of linebackers in man coverage denying inside paths of a running back (B1), tight end (B2), and wide receiver (B3). For the quarterback these are the shortest throws. The linebacker must defend these with discipline. The defender should

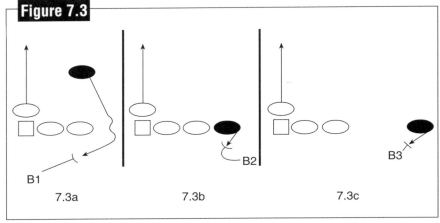

Figure 7.3

B1   7.3a   7.3b   B2   7.3c   B3

Linebackers must deny the inside breaking routes from all these alignments.

always thwart this type of route first by positioning the body inside and being physical on contact.

Once he makes contact, the linebacker should keep inside leverage on the receiver and keep vision on him. His total concentration must be on the receiver. He should never look back for the ball unless the receiver looks for it, raises his hands to catch it, or teammates call "ball" to indicate that the thrower has released it.

An inside breaking route is usually doomed once a linebacker has made contact from an inside position.

Vertical Routes

Vertical routes scare linebackers, yet seldom have we had linebackers beaten deep. Much of this has to do with our style of coverage, that emphasizes zone help to man defenders.

Bill McCartney, former head coach at Colorado, used to say constantly, "Defense is knowing where your help is." How true that is in man-to-man. Our linebackers play vertical routes aggressively because of their help. Normally, they have deep-zone assistance on the outside (halves or thirds defensive backs) or the pressure of a blitz. With deep-outside-zone aid, they can be aggressive on the inside of the receiver. The same is true with blitz coverage, that should force an early throw. Linebackers should thus cover tight underneath and inside, forcing the long, outside throw.

On recognition of pass, the linebacker attacks the receiver just as he did in figure 7.3. He should attempt to jam the receiver and then "chew ear" when the receiver runs vertical. This is a descriptive term that reminds the defender to run on the receiver's inside ear hole, shadowing him from underneath. Remember, the shortest throw for the passer is still inside. Force the receiver wide to the deep help or at least away from the quarterback (see figure 7.4). Always maintain inside positioning.

Linebackers are often not knowledgeable about pass-interference rules on deep throws. Your staff should drill these situations and discuss them because frequently a defender will be in excellent location yet create an unnecessary penalty.

When chewing ear on a vertical route, the linebacker should run with his arms at his sides. In college it is legal to face guard, that is, run with arms waving in front of the receiver's face to distract him. The face guarding slows the linebacker. He cannot run fast flailing his arms in that fashion. Face guarding usually causes the linebacker to lose control, and he makes contact with the receiver coming back to an underthrown ball. We witness this repeatedly in college football.

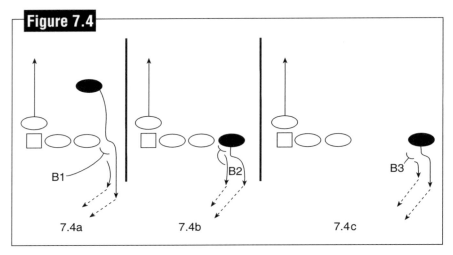

Figure 7.4

7.4a　　　　　　7.4b　　　　　　7.4c

Linebackers must jam the vertical release and chew ear from all these alignments.

Eliminate interference calls by training defenders to sprint with their eyes focused on the receiver's eyes and arms. When the arms go up to catch the ball or the eyes get large as the ball approaches, the defender can turn to the ball. If the linebacker is attempting to catch the ball, the officials should not call interference on contact.

If beaten deep, the linebacker should forget playing the ball and sprint to catch up to the receiver.

Outside Routes

These patterns are double-edged swords for the linebackers. The good news is that these are the most difficult routes to complete because they are farthest from the passer. The bad news is that they are the most challenging routes for the linebacker to defend. The closer the receiver is to the quarterback, the more difficult it is for a linebacker to defend the outside route.

We teach the linebacker the same consistent approach as he presses the receiver. We want the defender to jam the receiver. Strong, physical players are particularly adept at knocking running backs and tight ends to the ground as they come under control to make their outside breaks. As the receiver begins to chop his feet, the linebacker should attack under his pads with the outside hand.

As the receiver widens, the linebacker should accelerate his feet, putting his body between the quarterback and the receiver. Many teachers contest this point. Some believe that the defender should always stay behind the receiver on outside routes. Both beliefs have their selling points and these are ours:

- This is the passer's longest throw. When the quarterback sees the defender behind the outside pattern, he feels comfortable with a clear window to the receiver.
- This is the passer's longest throw. When the quarterback sees the linebacker underneath the outside route, he knows that a short throw can be intercepted for a touchdown. When he throws, he usually overthrows because of that fear.

Figure 7.5a gives the quarterback's perspective of the two positions a linebacker can take on a running back's flat route. When B1 plays underneath, the quarterback sees his helmet in the throwing lane even if the running back has some separation. When B1 plays

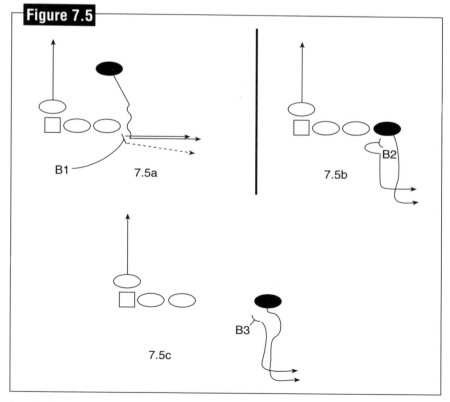

Figure 7.5

7.5a

B1

7.5b

B2

7.5c

B3

Linebackers must jam and accelerate, playing underneath the outside routes.

behind the receiver (dotted line), the thrower is less inhibited to make the toss.

Either method is sound. When the linebacker plays underneath, however, he must not look back to the passer until the ball is thrown. When a young linebacker peeks early he loses vision on the receiver. A veteran receiver will then turn upfield for a potential big play.

Rarely do linebackers look back to the quarterback early on inside or vertical routes. The inside routes grab their attention quickly. The vertical paths frighten them into focus. The outside routes, however, tempt even the veterans. They must stare at the outside breaking receiver until the passer throws the ball.

No Route

What does the linebacker do when the man he is assigned to blocks? There are two very sound reactions, and we employ both during the course of a season.

- The linebacker can free up and play as a short-zone defender like B2 in figure 7.2. He can now assist with crossing routes and be prepared to force a scrambling quarterback. The disadvantage of freeing the linebacker is that the screen is not well covered. A running back will fake a block and then slide away from an unsuspecting linebacker. Meanwhile, a blocker sets for him, and the other man defenders are chasing receivers with their backs turned to the quarterback.

  Our staff tries to choose this style when the offense is big on crossers but not on screens. In any case, the linebacker must always keep his assigned receiver in his vision.

- The second reaction by the linebacker when his receiver blocks is to continue to press him across the line of scrimmage.

When a running back is assigned to block the linebacker over him and the defender moves toward him, the back stays in the backfield to engage the linebacker. If the linebacker were to drop into zone coverage, the running back would usually check him for blitz and then release on a route. When a linebacker continues to press the back, he keeps the running back from becoming a potential receiver and adds pressure to the quarterback.

Against screens, the linebacker presses the receiver and has the opportunity to make a negative-yardage tackle.

Courtesy of Jim Ryan

■ One of four linebackers I coached at William & Mary who went on to the pros, Jim Ryan played 10 seasons for the Denver Broncos after not being drafted. Jim's pass coverage skills were outstanding. His academic drive and positive leadership made him a highlight in my coaching career.

Other Man Principles and Reminders

- Maintenance of an inside alignment on the snap and throughout the receiver's release is crucial. "If you're even, he's leaving." The linebacker who is head up gives the receiver two ways to beat him. Take away the inside.
- The linebacker should study a receiver's split. The wider a tight end flexes, the more obvious it is that the play will be a pass. Usually, a wide receiver who is running an outside pattern will reduce his split. A wide receiver who is running an inside route will generally open up his split.

- A receiver can make a sharp cut only when he raises his shoulders and gathers himself under control. When he is low and sprinting full speed with his head down, he will not make a sharp break.
- When a quarterback scrambles, the linebacker must stay focused on his receiver.
- When assigned a man in motion, the linebacker should maintain inside leverage and the same distance from the receiver that he had before the snap. When the ball is snapped, the linebacker should play the receiver for the three basic kinds of routes and deny, chew ear, or accelerate.

Man-to-Man Drills

We have used many man-to-man drills over the years. Here are some that we found particularly effective.

Identification Drill

This drill has a lot of flexibility and is excellent for training linebackers in man coverage identification, either when introducing a man coverage or when reviewing man coverage assignments on game week. Simply set up all the receivers that the linebackers would possibly have in coverage. It might only be two running backs, but more likely a coach would have to review all sets, including three-back (short yardage, power-I) and one-back formations, tight end obligations, shifts, and motion.

Review until everyone is completely comfortable with their assignments. Remember, an identification error means someone is free.

If a coach reviews man-to-man roles only on paper, he's asking for errors. A tip sheet is important, but actively reacting to the sets creates confidence in the players and the coach.

Base Route Drill

Introduce the base route reaction by initially working two linebackers at a time without a passer.

For inside linebackers put cones where the offensive tackles would align. Then position two running backs or two tight ends as shown in figure 7.6.

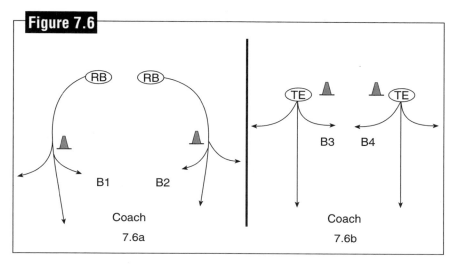

Inside linebacker's base route drills versus running backs and tight ends

The coach directs the routes on both sides. On "ready hit" the assigned receivers run the prescribed inside, vertical, or outside pattern. The coach evaluates the linebackers' responses. The coach should also have a receiver block to cover that reaction by the linebacker.

The coach can later add a quarterback and ball. It is particularly important that the passer throw to the vertical route to teach the linebacker to turn to the ball and avoid pass-interference calls.

The same drill can be set up for outside linebackers with a tight end and wide receiver or a tight end and running back, depending on the scheme employed.

Competitive One-on-One Drill

I have witnessed this potentially productive drill deteriorate into a one-sided offensive show at many practices that I have attended.

First, be sure the linebackers have been well grounded in the mechanics of man coverage. This should never be their introduction to man-to-man drills. If so, a coach will lose their confidence in a hurry. Run the basic route drill several times before conducting a competitive drill like this.

Put limits on the offense. The quarterback must be accountable to a stop watch. He has no pressure and ideal conditions. The receivers should run a limited number of realistic routes. I once saw a linebacker corps lose its confidence in 10 minutes because an offensive coach ran a high percentage of deep routes with no time constraints. I saw more deep running-back patterns in 10 minutes than I usually saw thrown against our defense in a season.

Teamwork means working for the good of both offensive and defensive groups. Script the snaps so the routes are realistic and both units learn in a positive environment.

If inside linebackers are included, set up a drill similar to that shown in figure 7.6. Add a quarterback and a timer to keep the throws gamelike. Use either tight ends or running backs.

Figure 7.7 shows the same drill with outside linebackers versus quality offensive personnel at wide receiver and tight end. If the scheme never puts outside linebackers on wide receivers, work them only against running backs or tight ends.

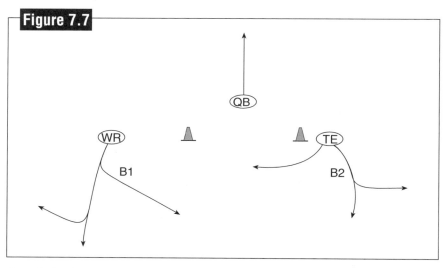

Figure 7.7

Outside linebackers work one-on-one competitive drill versus a WR and TE.

Again, agree to or script the routes ahead of time. This will be an emotional drill because of the competition. As a head coach, I never wanted either side to have an unfair advantage.

7-on-7 Drill

This old standby is just as critical for man-to-man coverage as zone. The drill is outlined at the end of chapter 6. Keep in mind that screens and bootlegs are not a challenge in 7-on-7. Use team periods during game week to test the reaction of the defense.

PART III

:25 SECONDS

Courtesy of University of Illinois

A significant part of football occurs before the snap. Coaches must communicate critical information to the players, and players must communicate among themselves. During this period a well-coached defensive unit can learn much that will help individual players and the whole unit be more effective. If even one player from the linebacking corps is not ready, the whole team effort can unravel.

Chapters 8 and 9 will present the volume of information that an observant and prepared linebacker can gain while the :25-second clock is ticking between plays.

Chapter 8

First :12 Seconds

For players and staff the first :12 seconds of the :25-second clock can be some of the most anxious and exciting moments in the game. Coaches and defensive leaders must exchange information quickly and precisely. Team leaders must then accurately pass on the vital calls to the entire unit.

The communication must be clear. One inaccurate word can change the whole concept of a defensive call. The communication must be quick. Our goal is to break our huddle within :12 seconds so that we will have time to study the opponent at the line of scrimmage.

Signals

Today, most offenses signal either the personnel grouping going into the game or the formation and play to be run. A few send in messengers with that information before every huddle. When-ever a defense can decode the personnel that the offense will use, it is a benefit. Although rarely will you be able to recognize plays by deciphering sign language, if you can do so it can be extremely valuable.

A defense has time with the :25-second clock to wait for the offense and respond. It is not as easy for the offense to respond to a defensive call. Defensive coaches routinely wait until the offense declares its personnel before submitting a call. Only :15 seconds may remain on the clock when the sideline signals a defense. For the offense to decode and alter a call is much more difficult.

Our staff introduced offensive and defensive signals the first day of practice. It is a language of its own that must become second nature. The time is precious on Saturday. The players and coaches must feel comfortable with the signal system. The team should use signals on every snap of 7-on-7 and team periods at every practice session throughout the year.

As the scheme unfolds, we will gesture the base calls frequently. We give those repeated calls multiple signals. For example, a common front or stunt might have three different hand motions. A blitz coverage, if decoded, could be attacked effectively by the opponent's offense. Even though we might blitz with man coverage only six times per game, we would use three different manners of signaling to hinder any stealing.

A staff that is in a league for an extended period should change its signal system every two or three years. Television often catches our sideline while transferring calls.

Back in the mid-1970s, it was legal to scout the spring game of an opening opponent in the fall. At William and Mary we began the season with powerful Virginia Tech, so I drove to Blacksburg to see the game in April. I had no idea I'd get so much information. I studied their offensive signal caller and wrote down the signals opposite the play I saw. By the time I got back to Williamsburg, I had matched many plays with their corresponding hand gestures. Thankfully, they didn't vary the signals in September.

As the game approached, we prepared a linebacker on the sideline to decode the offensive signals and transfer the play to our huddle. When the huddle knew the specific play that the offense would run, the linebacker could check a stronger call into the teeth of the play. We upset Virginia Tech that day and were aware of 70 percent of the offense before the snap.

It got so bad that when we picked up a reverse signal, our players couldn't contain their excitement and yelled "Reverse." The quarterback called timeout, looked at our sideline, and said, "That's ridiculous!"

I've never been part of stealing signals to that extent before or since. Offenses conceal their signals or mask them by using dummy callers. We still, occasionally, get formations or plays.

Courtesy of University of Colorado

■ Alfred Williams played as a true freshman as our rush linebacker. He was not a powerful run player early on, but he was an immediate-impact pass rusher. Alfred and Simeon Rice were similar. Alfred won the 1990 Butkus Award and became All-Pro after being drafted in the first round.

Huddle Procedure

The purpose of the huddle is to communicate information that is essential for every member of the unit. Communication is so vital that the coach should give each athlete a specific place in the huddle configuration so all can see the speaker's lips and hear his words. If all do not clearly understand the signal caller, the possibility of giving up a large gain increases dramatically. We instruct our players to call "Check, check" if they are unsure of the defensive command. At that alert, the leader immediately repeats the communication, without question.

We assign one player, usually an upperclassman lineman, to huddle discipline. On the field it is his responsibility to set the table for our vocal commands. He ensures that team members align properly and that no one talks when the leaders are addressing the huddle.

We teach our linebackers who transfer the call from the sideline to the team these basic concepts:

- Clarity: They must have eye contact with their teammates and mouth the words clearly so teammates can read their lips when the crowd noise is high.
- Confidence: No matter what the circumstances, we want our leaders to show boldness when they give the call and a faith that the result will be positive.

We use two linebackers in our huddle communications. The first addresses the huddle with down and distance information. He tells the squad, "Men, it's third and 15. Be sure to drift in the undercoverage," or "Guys, it's second and 6. They run inside 80 percent of the time." This linebacker's knowledge is basic to strategy, but many times younger players in the huddle are unaware of the down and distance, let alone the opponent's tendencies. This linebacker studies all week to be an expert at down and distance and to share the opponent's tendencies. Also, because this linebacker has learned communication skills, he can take over the signal responsibilities due to graduation or injury.

While one leader is conveying the down and distance information, the signal caller is outside the huddle receiving the defensive call from the sideline. We station him away from the huddle with his back to his teammates. Why? This is probably the time of greatest anxiety for the signal caller. The coach is waiting for the offense to declare its personnel. The defensive staff may be making suggestions, and meanwhile the :25-second clock is running. Panic can set in. We instruct the linebacker never to show anxiety before the team. When he turns around to give commands, he should demonstrate confidence, not apprehension.

If at some point the signal caller misses part of the signal, he should have a quick motion to the defensive coordinator to repeat the entire signal. Our linebackers grab their face masks for a repeat. Often young signal callers depart for the huddle without all the intended information. We have an over-and-out signal that reassures the linebacker that he has permission to leave eye contact with the sideline coach.

Active Sideline

We assign definite chores to linebackers not playing on the field. This keeps them mentally and emotionally into the game and can provide useful information for strategy.

Linebackers on the boundary can signal or fake signals. They can chart the play-by-play sheets, formation tendencies, or other items. Instruct them to watch their positions as if they were playing. On any snap, the active sideline should be able to tell the coach what happened to the linebacker's key and how the offense blocked him. An active sideline that takes its obligation seriously can provide useful information during the game.

Alignment

Once the huddle breaks, each defender uses his cue about where to align, usually based on the defense called and the positioning of the offense. For example, if a "50 defense" means that the outside linebacker aligns over the tight end's outside shoulder one yard off the ball, the linebacker first locates the tight end and then positions his body as taught over the tight end.

Defenses are often defeated because they simply align improperly. Put a premium on lining up correctly. This takes no ability. Coaches need to train it as a priority, and players must discipline themselves to align appropriately every time.

Players can attain proper depth from the line of scrimmage by always working individual drills on lined fields. A linebacker can sense a depth of four yards or a safety eight yards if he is daily watching depth by the field markings.

Stance

When I began coaching linebackers I was a real stickler on stances. There was a place and position for every part of the body. Now we teach concepts of stance within parameters that allow some freedom to each individual.

One concept has to do with the height of the stance. The farther from contact, the higher and less formal the stance may be. In chapter 3, we discussed the importance of being pad under pad when taking on a blocker. When a linebacker aligns five yards deep from the line of scrimmage, blockers rise significantly in their attempt to block. The deeper linebacker can then use a taller stance because he will contact a higher threat.

Twenty years ago inside linebackers were customarily two and a half yards deep. To get under an offensive lineman's pads, they had to hunker down in a very low two-point stance. Some nearly had their hands on the grass.

Another concept involves the base—the first thing a linebacker must learn about stances. Most linebackers play with a stance that is too wide. In their attempt to get down and dirty, they spread their feet wide to lower their center of gravity. Although this does sink the hips, it also restricts movement significantly (see figure 8.1).

Figure 8.1

This stance is too wide. The linebacker will false step inside to narrow his base from this hunkered down stance.

How can one tell if the stance is too wide? Easy. Watch the initial step. When a linebacker steps under himself to move, rather than gaining ground on the first step, he is operating with a base that is too wide. The initial step should take a linebacker toward the ball. If the defender steps under himself, have him narrow his stance. His first step should be clean and outside the base, never a move inside his base (see figure 8.2).

Figure 8.2

This is an excellent base. Now the linebacker can cleanly move toward the ball.

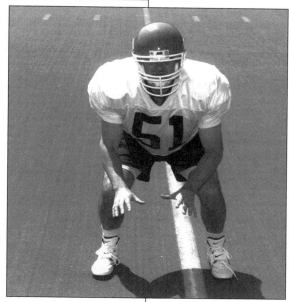

Chapter 9

Final :12 Seconds

Ideally, the defensive huddle will break with about :12 seconds on the clock. This should permit the linebacker to survey the offense for clues before the snap that will give his unit an edge by knowing the offense's intentions.

This :12 second pre-snap period differs from the first :12 second interval, described in chapter 8, because coaches have little input. Now the players are in charge. They, not the coaches, make the decisions and do the communicating.

This chapter will deal with types of keys players focus on before the snap, the line stances and splits that they can interpret, and ways to identify formations. The players must recognize, digest, and communicate all this information before the snap.

Keys

Two coaches can use the same scheme with identical techniques and yet differ radically with their keys. The keys of the up-front players must be coordinated if they are to respond in concert to a multitude of offensive threats.

Over the years linebacker keys have ebbed and flowed. I was trained in the era of the single wing and the wing-T. The misdirection of those offenses had coaches teaching lineman keys. When a linebacker watched a back for his primary movement, he was often led astray.

Today the running-game blocking schemes are simpler, and most linebackers key backs. We will investigate the benefits of the various keys. Obviously, both can be successful.

Back Keys

When linebackers key running backs their reactions are usually clear and unsophisticated. The beauty of running-back keys is their simplicity with double-gap responsible linebackers who fast flow. Back keys are really tempting (see figures 9.1 and 9.2).

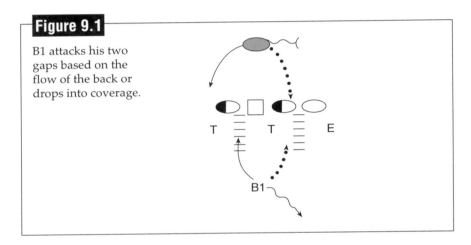

Figure 9.1

B1 attacks his two gaps based on the flow of the back or drops into coverage.

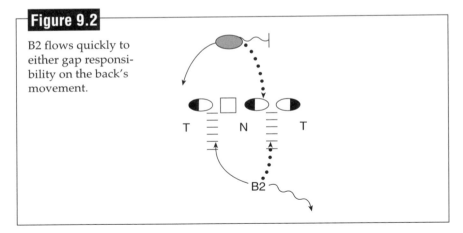

Figure 9.2

B2 flows quickly to either gap responsibility on the back's movement.

Back keys are confidence builders for inexperienced players and coaches. The rules that players usually learn are the following:

- When my key comes to me, I attack my frontside gap.
- When my key goes away, I attack my backside gap.

- When my key shows pass block or a pass route, I drop into my coverage rule.

Back keys lend themselves to aggressive, attacking, two-gap players.

Lineman Keys

Keying a lineman is more complex. Rather than having three basic running-back paths, a lineman may have to react to five to eight courses. So why consider it? Linemen rarely lie. They are the truest keys.

With play-action pass, a running back lies. He fakes a run and those who key him lose movement to the receivers. Usually linemen show pass protection.

When defending the winged-T offense, linebacker coaches often must compromise their back keys or decide to be unsound against the offense's weakest or least frequently used plays because of the misdirection in this offense. The counter play is popular in nearly all offensive attacks today (see figure 9.3).

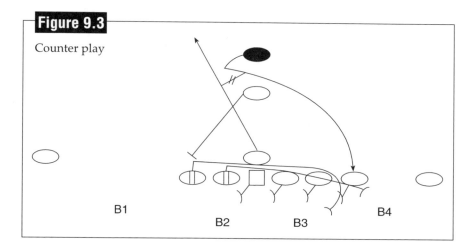

Figure 9.3

Counter play

B1   B2   B3   B4

Every back in figure 9.3 (QB, FB, and TB) starts toward the linebacker's left, yet the play will counter to the right side. With back keys, the linebackers will all false step to the initial backfield flow.

When the linebackers correctly read the players on the line of scrimmage, they will react immediately to the right without any false steps. Linemen are more difficult to read but more truthful.

Another advantage in focusing on linemen is that linebackers can more readily recognize tips from their stances that will alert them to particular plays. We will discuss this in more detail later in this chapter. Keying linemen makes linebackers more aware of their blocks. When focused on a back key, an unsuspecting linebacker will often contact a lineman. This can lead to a poor hit-and-shed base.

Triangle Keys

In an attempt to combine the two keys previously described, many coaches teach keying a triangle of backs, linemen, and the ball. It gives the player the potential fast flow of a back read with the caution of a pulling lineman who says "not so fast" on plays like that diagrammed in figure 9.3.

© Jessen Associates, Inc.

■ Simeon Rice was six feet, five inches tall with long arms and he ran faster than most wide receivers. Many felt it was all natural ability, but Simeon worked diligently at his conditioning. He and Bruce Smith were the most alarming pass rushers I've ever been associated with.

Personally, I believe having a prime key is critical. The linebacker needs a key he can depend on no matter what offense is being employed against him. The triangular system is sound but requires exceptional coaching ability. It also opens the door for a linebacker to guess because he is uncertain about the clarity of multiple keys.

Back reads are very clean although they can be deceiving with play-action passes and counters. Pure line reads are truest but take tremendous discipline and require time to learn. The triangle keys attempt to mesh the two, but at some point one key must take priority over the other or the linebacker cannot move with confidence.

Offensive Line Stances

Another advantage of reading offensive linemen is that, when a linebacker concentrates on them, they can tell a defense so much. The modern era of offense has brought excitement because of its multiplicity. Thirty years ago an offense might learn ten mirrored formations and three pass protections for the entire season. Today a team might install that much in two days of spring practice. It is not unusual to review a five-game scouting breakdown and find that you will be facing an offense that uses 60 formations and seven pass protections. While the assignments have skyrocketed, the teaching time is roughly the same. Something has to suffer.

What has happened is that we see poorer fundamentals. Pass protection in the modern era is a priority. Coaches teach it better than in the past. Run blocking varies with the teams, but squads have universally limited the number of running plays and simplified their blocking schemes. Coaches today do not stress run blocking and line stances as they did in past decades.

It is rare that we cannot find an opposing lineman who will tip us off as to run or pass by his stance. We assign certain coaches on our staff to study each lineman. Our players up-front routinely scrutinize opponent's tapes for an informer. Through our research, we define the *tipster* and the *messenger*.

The tipster is the lineman whom we identify as being an informant through his stance. On some teams we can identify only one, while on other teams we can find as many as three. Years ago it was difficult research, and a staff longed for just one guy who would spill the beans. Now almost every team has one.

Another factor has been the advent of videotape and the exchanging of "tight copies." This copy covers only from tight end to tight end and focuses on the linemen. We can now see stances much more clearly than before 1990 when only "wide copies" were exchanged.

The messenger is the defensive player who is in position to decode the tipster's stance. We make him accountable for giving accurate information. Frequently we choose two or three veterans for this prestigious detail. Players love it and long to give their teammates clues before the snap.

We communicate about three types of stances:

- Run stance: This body position is typified by having weight forward, head low, and the back heel off the ground.

- Pass stance: The lineman who is to pass protect has weight back on his heels, head level higher, and little weight on his front hand.

- Pull stance: This can be confused with a pass stance, but if the other linemen are in run stances this is probably a pull. When the other tipsters are in pass stances, it is probably pass. Another clue for a pull stance is the lineman's depth. Pulling 300 pounders usually must cheat back off the line of scrimmage to make the trip on a pull. Any penetration can derail them so they sit back off the line to avoid stunting defenses.

Our defense uses coded words to communicate to the entire team the information gained from stances. In 1990, we featured two mature linebackers in Dana Howard and John Holecek. As a pair, I've had none better at recognizing opponent's stances and accurately predicting the plays. In a Big Ten conference game that season, our opponent ran only four base runs from a multitude of formations. When both sides of the line tipped run, both linebackers would call "Reno," and the front dug in for an inside or outside zone play. When one side was "Reno" and the other showed pull, or "Cobra," the front knew it was a counter, as shown in diagram 9.3. When both sides informed us of pass stances by calling "Pinto," the defense prepared for pass or draw.

That day Dana and John not only gave us the advantage of knowing run or pass but also usually knew the type of run and its direction before the snap. That kind of display requires experience, trust, and a lot of training.

Two other examples jump out from my background. A Big Ten center put his free hand on the ground when a run was called and used only a three-point stance with pass. It was about 90 percent consistent, and so were we that day. At Colorado, we noticed an offensive guard who put his off-hand on the side of his leg when run blocking and on his thigh when in pass protection.

These obvious signs are not common, but most teams indicate the three categories in some way. During spring practice one of our offensive line coaches felt the defense knew the plays ahead of time and suspected that they were privy to a script. I had him stand behind the defense with me during an unscripted scrimmage. On nine consecutive plays, our defense correctly called run or pass.

Offensive line stances today can reveal a lot to linebackers who will study and be observant. It is, however, more natural for linebackers who key linemen. Those who key backs or a triangle do not invest the same energy into it.

Line Splits

Also helpful before the cadence are the offensive line splits—the distance between linemen. Three or four opponents each year will vary these splits considerably depending on the play. Typically, an offense will alter their splits in this manner:

▪ With a perimeter run, the linemen will often tighten their splits so that the corner is closer to the ball. It brings the defense closer and makes getting outside them easier (see figure 9.4).

A linebacker who observes this tendency could make an adjustment to get the defense more width.

Figure 9.4

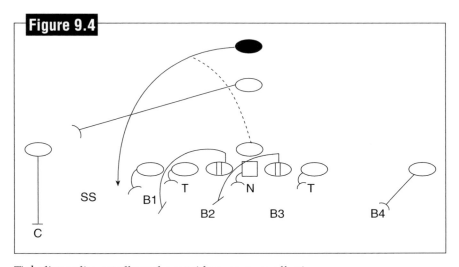

Tight line splits usually make outside runs more effective.

- With an inside run, it is common for the offensive line to widen their splits to spread the defenders farther apart. This creates natural holes before blocks are even attempted (see figure 9.5).

  A well-taught linebacker could check to another front or stunt to give added population to that big split area.

Figure 9.5

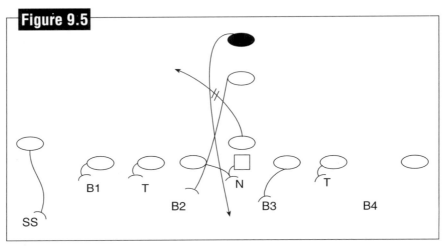

B2 is being exploited by large line splits on an isolation play. His help is spread farther from him.

Many teams keep constant line splits. They don't derive the benefits of splitting but neither do they give anything away to defenses that adjust well.

In 1980, we had a very competitive Peach Bowl squad at Virginia Tech. On October 25 we played an instate rival, the University of Richmond, well coached by Dal Shealy. Dal is currently the executive director at the Fellowship of Christian Athletes (FCA). It was always scary facing his offense, and that October day in Richmond it was frightful.

Virginia Tech finished that season leading the nation in rushing defense. We were overwhelming favorites to beat our smaller competitors that day.

Dal Shealy aligned with the largest line splits I have encountered in my career (see figure 9.6). The center-guard splits were four feet, and the guard-tackle splits were five to six feet. Barry Redden, an NFL first-round choice, ran through our vaunted defense for 233 yards. We never adjusted effectively. Our great outside linebacker Robert Brown (10 years in NFL with Green Bay) was so far from the ball that he was not a factor in stopping Redden. We learned a lot that day about preparing our defense for huge splits.

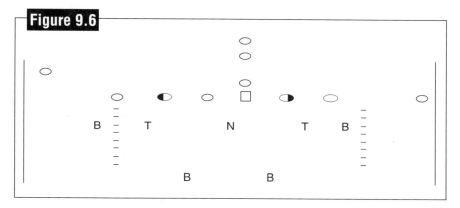

Full-field diagram of Richmond's offensive line splits.

■ Richmond's huge line splits widened defensive fronts then shredded them with an inside running attack. With the ball in the middle of the field the tight ends were often on the old college hash marks.

Formation Identification

Most defensive units have a player or players who identify the opponent's formations in some fashion. Often a linebacker calls out the backfield set by name (for example, I backs, split backs, and so forth). Each week defenders memorize tendencies based on the backfield looks. We choose one linebacker to be the backfield expert. Each week we also assign him any checks that accompany the various looks. Those checks can influence fronts, stunts, or coverages. From the first practice in fall camp, this linebacker has the job of identifying all backfields by name. It must become a habit if he is going to do it on Saturdays.

Few fans appreciate the enormous amount of information available to a defense :25 seconds before the offense snaps the ball. The simpler the defense, the more time it can spend gaining this knowledge. The more seasoned the linebackers, the more likely it is that the defense can use this information profitably.

PART IV

TECHNIQUES

We define techniques as the specific requirements of a position in a particular scheme. As disclosed in chapters 3 through 7, every system devised by coaches must accommodate the fundamentals. No linebacker can escape the essential nature of the fundamentals.

The techniques involve alignments, keys, reactions, responsibilities, and adjustments that are specific to a team's defensive design. In the following chapters, we will teach a variety of common linebacker techniques.

Chapter 10

Linebacker Technique Terminology

A linebacker or coach should be able to recognize styles of play similar to his own. To accomplish this task we need a common language to describe the techniques. We use *numbers* for techniques in which linebackers play unprotected over blockers at the line of scrimmage. We use *names* for techniques in which a linebacker is protected by a fellow defender from the potential blocker directly over him.

Numbered techniques have two digits when the linebacker plays off the line of scrimmage. The first digit refers to his frontside responsibility (see figure 10.1).

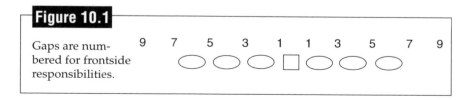

Figure 10.1

Gaps are numbered for frontside responsibilities.

9   7   5   3   1   1   3   5   7   9

Any linebacker off the line of scrimmage would have a double-digit technique beginning with a 3 if he is responsible for the frontside guard-tackle gap or a 5 if accountable for the tackle-end gap.

His second digit has to do with his backside movement. When the linebacker is required to "fast flow," or run, on action away from him, he is given the second digit of 1. Usually a fast-flow linebacker must fill an unattended backside gap as in figure 10.2.

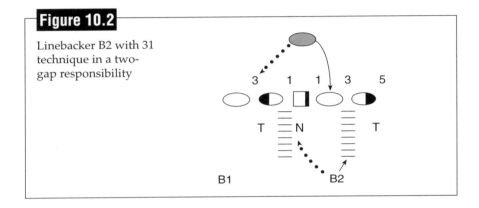

Figure 10.2

Linebacker B2 with 31 technique in a two-gap responsibility

The 31 technique linebacker has the 3 gap with flow to him and the away 1 gap with flow away.

When the linebacker's backside obligation is to shuffle with no particular gap responsibility away from him, he is a single-gap player. His backside digit, in our system, is a 2. Figure 10.3 shows a 32 technique player. Other defenders are responsible for all backside gaps.

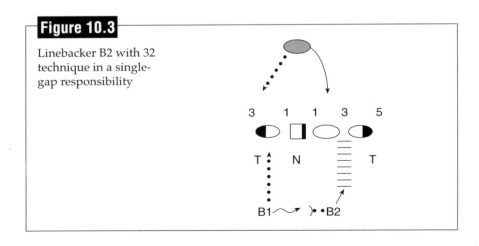

Figure 10.3

Linebacker B2 with 32 technique in a single-gap responsibility

Numbered techniques with single digits refer to outside line-backers on the line of scrimmage who are liable for that gap only, on flow to or flow away (see figure 10.4).

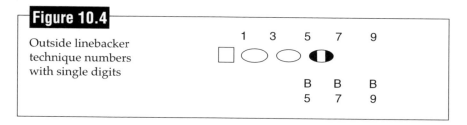

Figure 10.4

Outside linebacker
technique numbers
with single digits

An outside linebacker could be responsible on the line of scrim-mage for the 5 gap (tackle-tight end gap), the 7 gap (referred to as the alley), or contain (referred to as a 9 technique).

We use names for linebacker techniques that provide some pro-tection for the linebacker. Figure 10.5 shows a *nest* technique. We call it a nest because the linebacker sits in a protected cradle that can be designed for weaker or younger players.

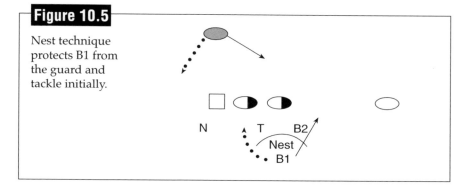

Figure 10.5

Nest technique
protects B1 from
the guard and
tackle initially.

One other consideration is whether the linebackers will play on one side (left or right) only or flip-flop and work both sides. Funda-mentally, it is an advantage to play on only one side because then a linebacker can usually take on blockers with just one side of his body. We did this at William and Mary, which put a real premium on find-ing left-handed players. Jeff Hosmer was particularly strong with his left-footed base. The William and Mary system had him taking on blockers with that side for four years.

For the past 17 years, I have flip-flopped our linebackers. This forces them to be equally effective with both sides of their body but limits the number of techniques that they must learn. Many schemes today feature linebackers who must master five or more techniques. We prefer teaching them just one or two techniques so that they can execute with confidence and be more aware of the pre-snap information reviewed in chapter 9.

Now that our terminology is familiar, the next chapters will describe in detail each technique.

Chapter 11

32 Technique

Today this is a standard technique employed by many reduction defenses for their "Oklahoma" side linebacker (that is, the linebacker playing unprotected over a guard). For me, its roots go back to the 50 defense that utilized a head-up nose guard playing both 1 gaps flanked by two mirror-imaged inside linebackers with 32 technique obligations.

This is a shuffle technique with flow to or away from the linebacker. It has a single-gap duty that requires the athlete to play slow on the backside to stop cutbacks.

Alignment

Because the 32 linebacker is assigned the frontside 3 gap and is in no rush with flow away, we align him wide over the offensive guard. The linebacker's inside foot covers the outside foot of the guard. We begin at a depth of four yards off the ball.

Keys

Linebackers in this technique can focus squarely on the guard or backs. We will analyze both in detail here. His initial steps are critical. The first step should ideally take him closer to the ball. Anything else we classify as a false step.

Guard Reads

The advantages of keying linemen were presented in chapter 9. In this technique keying on the guard helps the linebacker decipher play-action pass and counters. Rarely does the guard give false information.

Although a staff should drill eight different guard paths in fall camp, rarely does a single offense use them all. Each guard path could represent a variety of plays, but often they immediately indicate just one.

Let's review each. We will begin with the *clean* blocks. We describe them in this manner because they are simple to understand and respond to.

Base

We rarely see this block anymore except by some wishbone teams on their counter dive plays. It is still an excellent block to begin guard-recognition drills because it can isolate on the approach and the feet for the hit and shed, described in chapter 3.

With a base block, the linebacker should approach the guard with outside leverage. He should settle with the inside foot forward and planted. The linebacker should get pad under pad and explode off the base with the hips, keeping the outside arm free to make a play in the 3 gap (see figure 11.1).

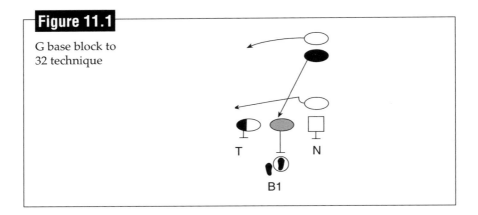

Figure 11.1

G base block to 32 technique

The defender should immediately recognize the play as an inside running play. We work this block only early in fall camp and never revisit it unless our opponent that week uses it.

Reach

This has become a very popular block in the past decade and one that we need to drill daily. With a guard reach block (an outside path by the guard to gain outside position on a defender), the linebacker shuffles for width first and then takes on the guard with his inside foot. Once he sets the base, he should squeeze the blocker with the ball inside. When the ball gains width, the linebacker simply pushes off the inside foot to pursue (see figure 11.2).

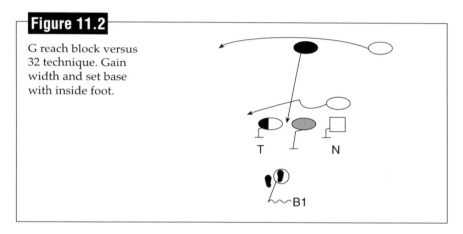

Figure 11.2

G reach block versus 32 technique. Gain width and set base with inside foot.

Initially linebackers are too aggressive with the reach block. They naturally want to attack upfield rather than gain width. When they run upfield, the linebackers are more likely to be reached and they often contact the guard with improper footwork.

There is no rush. The linebacker should take on this big threat on his terms. He should be under control, gain width to protect the assigned 3 gap, and settle on a firm base from which the hips can uncoil.

An experienced linebacker and coach can also make another adjustment. The wider the guard's path, the wider the play. After viewing tape, it will become obvious that the tighter the guard reach, the more likely it is an inside play. The linebacker should then lean heavily on his inside foot to constrict the hole. The wider track of the lineman will indicate a perimeter play and quicker pursuit by the linebacker.

Remember, when using this method the linebacker does not want to run upfield on a reach block. If he aligns at four-yard depth and takes on the guard at three-yard depth, that's ideal. He cannot, however, lose his outside arm. That is why we align him so wide over the guard. The linebacker should be unreachable both by alignment and key.

Pull Frontside

This is another clean block and a fun one for the linebacker. He may get a pre-snap indication of pull from the guard's stance. A pull toward the linebacker tells him that there is no 3 gap threat and he can immediately overlap to the 5 gap and beyond.

In chapter 4 we studied pursuit and pressing open seams. Here the pull alerts the linebacker of an opening. He can begin pressing before seeing the running lane. What a deal! Figures 11.3 and 11.4 show typical plays with guard-pulling schemes frontside.

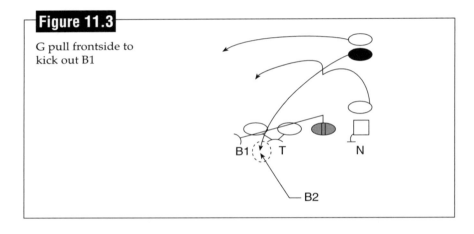

Figure 11.3

G pull frontside to kick out B1

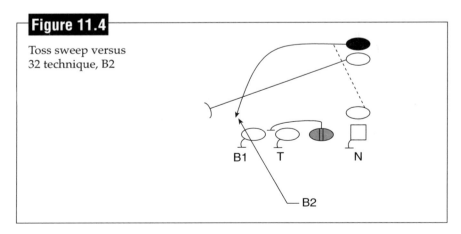

Figure 11.4

Toss sweep versus 32 technique, B2

With the play in figure 11.3, the linebacker can make a negative-yardage tackle based on a read. Most fans will think that he blitzed.

In figure 11.4, the guard will likely be taught to cut the linebacker in the 5 gap. Most coaches teach the defender to use the machine-gun drill described in the hit-and-shed drill section in chapter 3 (figure 3.13). Because this is a confined area, we teach our linebackers to cut the guard! Many coaches are shocked at this, but it is truly a better method. Cutting the guard allows the linebacker to penetrate and be aggressive. He forces the ball carrier to bounce outside and regularly gets a two-for-one trade by knocking off the fullback or backside guard.

Pull Backside

This is another block that the guard's stance may tip. With guard pull away, the ball will usually follow. Remember that in 32 technique the 2 means shuffle on the backside. Also recall from chapter 4 that we give shuffling linebackers the freedom to press any opening.

When the guard's helmet pulls away, the linebacker should shadow him with a shuffle, looking for an opening to press. It could be a quick-hitting influence trap as in figure 11.5. In this case the linebacker should easily beat the tackle's block and press the ball carrier.

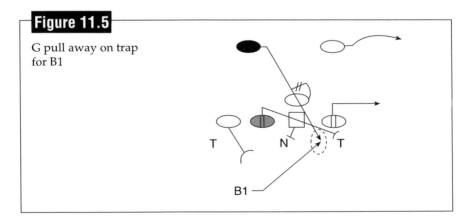

Figure 11.5

G pull away on trap
for B1

T   N   T

B1

Figure 11.6 shows the popular counter play. Even though the entire backfield is moving toward B1, he should step laterally with his right foot. There should be no false steps. Now, rather than pressing the far 1 gap as he did versus the trap in figure 11.5, he will continue to shuffle to the opening outside his tackle in the 5 gap, and then press it as shown in figure 11.6.

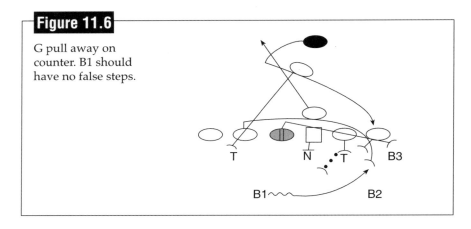

Figure 11.6

G pull away on counter. B1 should have no false steps.

In figure 11.7, we see a guard pull away on a pass play. This common bootleg look has the whole backfield move initially toward the linebacker, but his key goes away. The well-trained linebacker (B1) will step with his left foot inside following the guard. Once he recognizes pass, the linebacker moves with the quarterback to the opposite seam, described in "Action Passes" in chapter 6. Most often he will cover a drag route by a backside receiver.

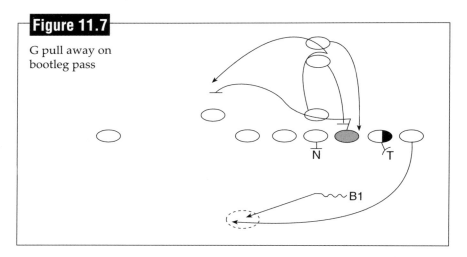

Figure 11.7

G pull away on bootleg pass

Pass or Draw

The fifth guard picture is also easily recognizable. Frequently our messengers will call out "pass" based on a tipster's stance as related in chapter 9.

When the guard shows pass, the linebacker must yell "Pass, pass" as he retreats in zone coverage or presses a receiver in man.

Draw is also a strong possibility with this guard look. We teach our linebackers to <u>keep vision on the guard</u> as they retreat in coverage. Most opponents set their guards briefly to show pass and then release them to block the draw. We train daily the linebacker's reaction to pass and quick-set draw. They will learn to differentiate the two similar reads.

Once he recognizes draw, the linebacker yells it out to alert defensive linemen to retrace their steps to the line of scrimmage. At the same time the linebacker accelerates to the blocker's outside shoulder and forces the ball carrier back inside (see figure 11.8) to B1.

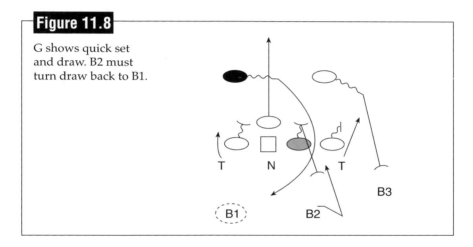

Figure 11.8

G shows quick set and draw. B2 must turn draw back to B1.

In 1985, we had a turnaround season at Colorado, going to our first bowl game under Bill McCartney and demonstrating our first dominant defense in Boulder. We consistently failed, however, to defend the draw. We sought the advice of other college and NFL experts, but the best advice came by studying our cut-up tapes of all the draws from that season. We discovered

- that the pass rushers had to retrace their steps directly to the line of scrimmage when they heard "draw,"
- that the backside linebacker was unblocked far more frequently than any other defender, and
- that the frontside linebacker had to turn the ball back to the free defender.

Many opponents will attempt to make play-action pass blocks look like run blocks. This is an arduous task, especially for a 300-pound lineman. Even guards engaging other linemen on pass must be softer and higher to be effective pass protectors.

Down

The down block begins a series of three *gray* blocks, so termed because they initially look similar to the linebacker. They are not clean like the five previously described. How a coach teaches these three determines the confidence of the guard-read linebacker.

When the guard blocks down on the nose guard, attack the open 3 gap with outside leverage on the blocker. Usually this is a lead blocker, such as a fullback, on the isolation play. A linebacker must dominate fullbacks. Many players feel satisfied to trade one for one when engaging a burly fullback. Our linebackers grade positively only when they tackle the running back or force him wide to another defender. A collision with the lead block derailing the runner is our goal. We seek penetration and desire to run through fullbacks (see figure 11.9).

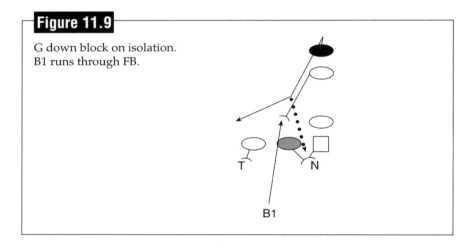

Figure 11.9

G down block on isolation.
B1 runs through FB.

B1

A down block occasionally will be accompanied by a lineman trapping the inside linebacker. We do *not* run through linemen but instead settle on our base as shown in figure 11.10.

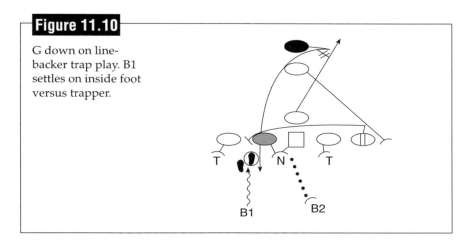

Figure 11.10

G down on line-
backer trap play. B1
settles on inside foot
versus trapper.

Veer

The veer is a gray block because, within it, is a down block. Initially
the two blocks look identical. They are frontside schemes and most
opponents use both. Defenders must practice these two each week.

The veer block is, perhaps, the prime reason that coaches deep-
ened their linebackers in the 1960s. Before that, linebackers played
tighter to the line of scrimmage. Obviously, it was an advantage for
the linebacker to be closer to the fullback when defending the isolation play (figure 11.9). When the offensive tackle also blocked down,
the linebacker now got blindsided.

In reaction, coaches set linebackers four yards deep and emphasized to the defensive tackles that they needed to jam the offensive
tackle when he veered inside. Now the linebacker could react forward to the guard key, but when he saw the 3 gap closing with those
two big bodies veering inside, he would slide outside.

Our linebackers find this reaction very natural. The depth allows
them vision and they wouldn't penetrate the 3 gap anyway when
they see it closing. The defensive tackles now take control of the 3
gap. The linebacker is responsible for the 5 gap, including the quarterback versus veer-block option teams (see figure 11.11).

The veer scheme is a versatile frontside block. Teams use it for
trapping wider-playing tackles and as the frontside design for pow-
ers, counters, and many forms of option.

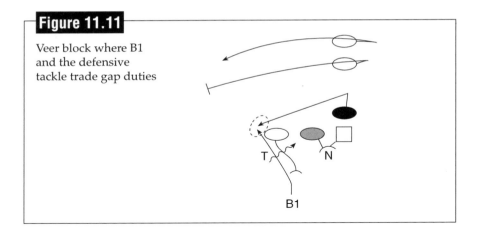

Figure 11.11

Veer block where B1
and the defensive
tackle trade gap duties

Scoop

The final gray block also has the guard engaging the nose guard,
but rather than being a frontside block, this is a favorite backside
pattern. The guard and center attempt to work together to pin the
nose and linebacker away from the play (see figure 11.12).

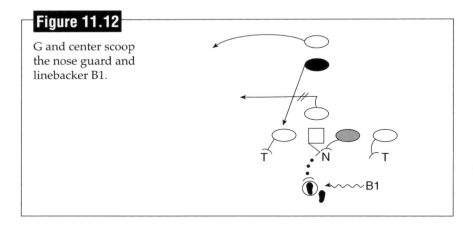

Figure 11.12

G and center scoop
the nose guard and
linebacker B1.

Quite often the guard will narrow his split so he can get closer to
the nose guard and get his helmet between the ball and the nose.
Ideally, the linebacker will see that the guard's helmet is flat and
partially hidden from his view. If it were a down or veer block, the
linebacker could plainly see the guard's helmet as shown in figure
11.13. The guard would normally split wider with a down or veer
scheme, too.

Figure 11.13

Solid line shows path of
G's down or veer block.
Dotted line indicates G's
scoop block.

Unfortunately, with today's larger and sometimes sloppier line-men, it is not always easy to detect a scoop from its frontside rela-tives, the down and veer. What do we do? Make it simple. Tell line-backers that when in doubt always play all gray blocks as an open 3 gap and attack. If wrong, as the defender moves forward and senses the ball away, he can shuffle backside. That's the beauty of 32 tech-nique. There is no rush with flow away.

The reverse is not true. The athlete cannot shuffle backside on a down or veer block. He will be out of position to play the isolation (figure 11.9) or a veer scheme (figure 11.11) with false steps inside. Again, when in doubt the linebacker should play all gray blocks as frontside plays.

When the center gets through to the linebacker on a scoop scheme as in figure 11.12 (dotted line), how does the shuffling backside line-backer react? He establishes his hit-and-shed base with his near foot, jams the center, and stays behind the ball for cutback. Nearly a quarter of a 32 technique linebacker's tackles will come playing off a center's scoop. He will be severely tempted to cross the center's face. A line-backer can do that only when there is no threat of cutback.

Remember back to chapter 4 when we stated that the longest run-ning plays break behind the backside linebackers. No place is our strategy to prevent that more evident than having the 32 technique linebacker shuffle behind a scoop block. He must stay behind the ball.

Back Reads

Thirty-two technique can be used successfully with the linebacker reading the backfield. The coach must choose a consistent back or backs to key in each backfield set. For simplicity we will use only the I-formation in this presentation.

Back reads are used because they are simple. A linebacker in 32 technique needs to know quickly if the play is a frontside run, back-side run, or pass. When coaching a defensive scheme with many techniques to master, a coach usually finds back keys attractive.

Below are examples using 32 technique while keying backs. The linebacker will focus on the tailback in the I.

Tailback Inside

When the tailback takes an inside path at the linebacker, the linebacker will attack the 3 gap while reading the blocking scheme on the run. Usually, this is an isolation play as shown in figure 11.14.

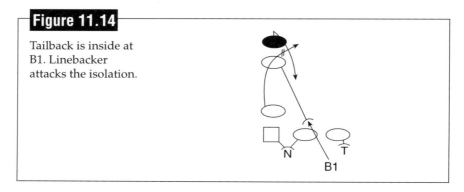

Figure 11.14

Tailback is inside at B1. Linebacker attacks the isolation.

The linebacker's reaction should be exactly like that on the guard down block in figure 11.9.

Tailback Outside

When the tailback's path is wide, the linebacker shuffles frontside, checking the open 3 gap for another back's threat. He should keep the outside arm free by maintaining outside leverage on all blockers (see figure 11.15).

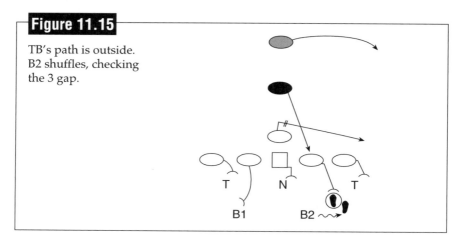

Figure 11.15

TB's path is outside. B2 shuffles, checking the 3 gap.

When the same backfield action occurs and the 3 gap is closed due to a veer block, the linebacker should slide outside to the 5 gap. He now has quarterback option responsibility (see figure 11.16).

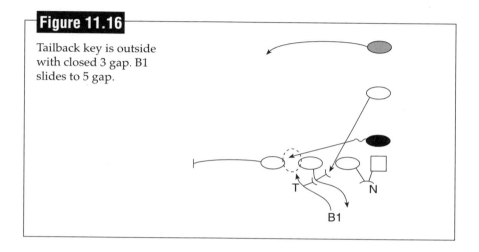

Figure 11.16

Tailback key is outside with closed 3 gap. B1 slides to 5 gap.

Tailback Away

With flow away, the linebacker should shuffle toward the flow, staying behind the ball for the cutback. In 32 technique, teammates defend both 1 gaps (see figure 11.17).

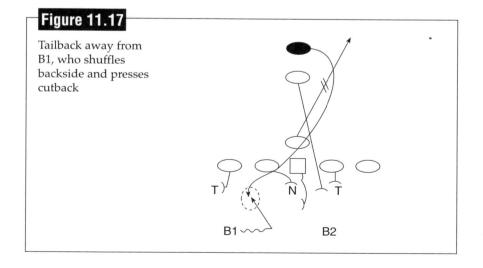

Figure 11.17

Tailback away from B1, who shuffles backside and presses cutback

Tailback Pass

When the tailback shows pass blocking or runs a pass route, the linebacker responds with his man or zone coverage duties.

32 Responsibilities

Whether keying a guard or a back, the responsibilities in this technique are identical. The linebacker is responsible for the immediate 3 gap and then playing inside-out on the ball with flow to him. With option to the linebacker, he must check the dive when the 3 gap is open. When the gap is closed, he should slide outside and play the quarterback-to-pitch phases. With flow away, he should shuffle inside-out on the ball checking for cutbacks.

Adjustments

- The key can vary from team to team. The truest key is the guard, but back reads have their place.
- Against big line splits to the linebacker, the linebacker should walk up tighter on the guard, anticipating an inside play, or check to a penetrating charge by a defender in the 3 gap.
- When faced with small splits, anticipate an outside play and deepen the linebacker and widen him to the gap.
- Anytime the nose guard widens his alignment or stunts to a wider alignment, play the linebacker in a wide 32 technique with the same guard or back reads as he had in 32 technique (see figure 11.18)

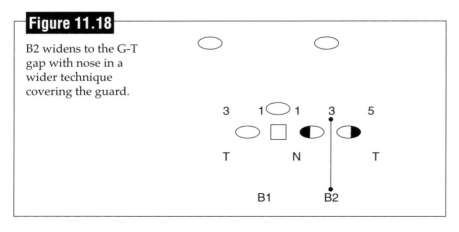

Figure 11.18

B2 widens to the G-T gap with nose in a wider technique covering the guard.

32 Technique Types

This technique requires experience (when the defender uses guard keys) and discipline with flow away. It does not demand speed because of the backside duties. Rarely do rookies play here because of the time it takes to learn how to respond soundly to the eight guard paths. It is a thinking man's position. Players perform it best when it is mixed with few other techniques. My best linebackers at this technique have ranged from six-one to six-four in height, from 206 pounds to 235 in weight, from 4.7 to 5.1 in speed, and from 4.3 to 4.55 in the jingle-jangle. All were bright, dynamic leaders with an internal drive to be great performers.

Chapter 12

31 Technique

Even many in the profession would not notice the difference between 31 technique and 32 technique before the snap. It would take film study to determine the subtle variation between the two.

The frontside responsibilities are identical, but the backside obligation involves a free gap. The 31 technique linebacker cannot favor his frontside 3 gap and react slowly to his backside duty. He is on a teeter-totter balancing himself between two equal gap responsibilities. Refer to figure 10.2.

This is a shuffle technique with flow toward the linebacker just like 32 technique but with a scrape to the away 1 gap on a play backside. This two-gap technique requires a quick read of flow and clean footwork.

Alignment

Because of the balancing act between the two gaps, we align the 31 linebacker with just a slight outside position over the offensive guard. His inside foot splits the stance of this lineman, so the defender can maintain outside leverage on frontside blocks yet cross the guard's face on run action away. We ask the 31 technique to align four yards deep off the football.

Keys

This is strictly a back-read technique because it employs a fast-flow linebacker. Backfield keys permit flow without much hesitation. The gray guard blocks (refer to chapter 11 make guard keys less suitable for this style.

Reads

The frontside back reads for 31 technique are identical to those presented for back keys for 32 linebackers in figures 11.14, 11.15, and 11.16. There is absolutely no difference except that the 32 technique aligns with decidedly more width before the snap.

With flow away, however, the 31 technique changes radically. Instead of using a controlled shuffle, staying behind the ball at all costs, the 31 linebacker moves quickly, as though his hair were on fire. His backside footwork is measured and must be clean and consistent.

With flow away, the 31 linebacker steps laterally with his inside foot and then crosses over with his outside foot, pointing it at the far 1 gap, for which he is responsible. This is the first time we have advocated a crossover in the heavy-contact zone. The crossover is necessary to cross the face of the near guard as a cut-off block (see figure 12.1) or the center versus a scoop. The 31 linebacker rips his outside shoulder through the guard or center using the same-side foot as his strong base.

As the linebacker scrapes toward the far 1 gap, he must read whether the gap is open or closed. When the gap is attacked by the offense and open, the linebacker must square up and press the open seam to make the play (see figure 12.1).

Figure 12.1

B1 scrapes to the open 1 gap and presses the fullback.

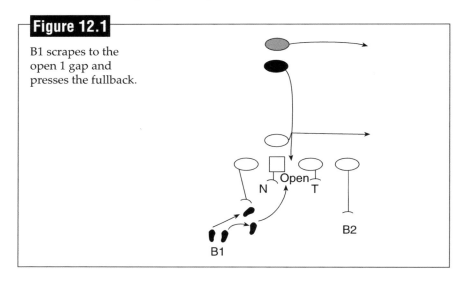

With flow away and the far 1 gap closed, the linebacker should square up and play inside-out on the ball. He should be prepared to shuffle and press to either side of the closed gap (see figure 12.2).

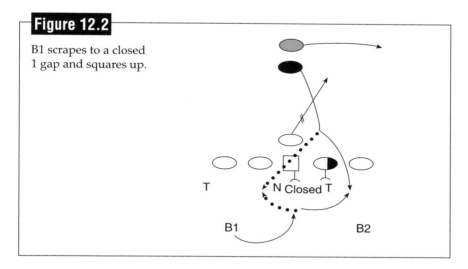

Figure 12.2

B1 scrapes to a closed 1 gap and squares up.

When the flow away is an outside threat, teach the linebacker to pursue, staying inside the ball without pressing into the away 1 gap. This happens with toss-sweep teams. The backside linebacker now can alley pursue (discussed in chapter 4) to maintain proper leverage on the ball carrier (see figure 12.3).

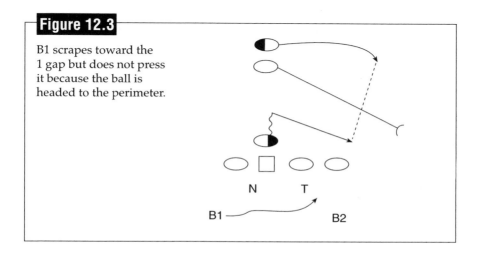

Figure 12.3

B1 scrapes toward the 1 gap but does not press it because the ball is headed to the perimeter.

When the backfield action shows pass, the 31 linebacker responds to his zone or man duties within the scheme. Finding a suitable pass key on run down and distances is difficult in fast-flow execution. The 31 defender is less likely to be as active in coverage as the 32 linebacker. The fast-flow linebacker is obviously more vulnerable to misdirection because he must move so quickly to reach his far gap and the ball may be countering back to his frontside responsibility.

31 Responsibilities

The linebacker is responsible for the immediate 3 gap and then playing inside-out on the ball with run action toward him. With option toward the linebacker, he must check the dive when the 3 gap is open. When the gap is closed, he should slide outside and defend the quarterback-to-pitch phase. With flow away, he should check the far 1 gap, then pursue inside-out on the ball carrier.

Adjustments

- Keys are difficult to vary because line reads are so ill-suited for the fast-flow nature of this technique.
- Against small splits, the 31 linebacker can deepen just like his 32 counterpart. With huge offensive line splits, however, the 31 technique has limited ability to crowd the line of scrimmage because on flow away he must be able to scrape to his backside 1 gap. The added width and his moving toward the line present him with a poor scrape angle that is too horizontal.

31 Technique Types

This technique requires less experience because it uses a more simplified key than a 32 linebacker does. It does need a quicker, more athletic player to respond to rapidly changing backside conditions.

My most effective linebackers at this technique have been in the six-foot-one range and between 210 and 225 pounds. Generally, they have been faster and more agile than my great 32 technicians.

Drills for 32 Technique

Although the two techniques, 31 and 32, are closely related, we drill them very differently. Young players are like fans—they love to watch the ball. That becomes a handicap when teaching the guard read to 32 technique linebackers.

We execute all individual drills with guard keys without a backfield. We align an inside linebacker with a stand-in nose guard and defensive tackle flanking him, as shown in figure 12.4.

1. We execute each of the eight base guard paths, and the linebacker must react correctly. Any scoop or pull away must force a shuffle backside, but we never consider it perfect unless the athlete presses the first opening past the nose guard. We do this drill daily in camp and use it to begin each hard work practice during game week. It is the most essential technique drill we do for a linebacker's confidence. We train all movement without the benefit or distraction of a backfield. When in doubt, the linebacker *always* believes his guard key.

2. The next progression is 9-on-7 or the inside drill in which a scout unit or the varsity offense includes a backfield. Counter plays and play-action passes quickly tell the coach of the linebacker's trust in his key.

Figure 12.4

Drilling the guard keys for the 32 technique, B1

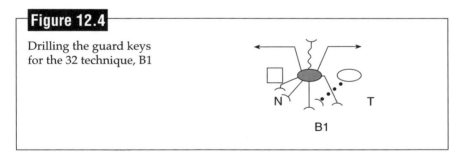

B1

Drills for 31 Technique

The 31 technique drill varies significantly. Now the emphasis shifts to initial steps based on a chosen backfield key. The keys will change slightly with each backfield type, and the drill must work all back actions. Line spacing is vital to permitting 31 linebackers to visualize their twin gap responsibilities.

1. Define the gaps with a stationary seven-man sled, seven padded posts cemented in the ground, or just seven cones if finances do not permit more lavish equipment. Figure 12.5 shows a seven-man sled drilling area with a ball over the center so the linebackers can have proper depth. Cones mark the positions of defensive linemen so the 31 technique can recognize his gap duties.

   The coach simulates the backfield sets and paths. He can see the linebacker's eyes and initial steps. A pair of fast-flow players can work this drill together, like B1 and B2 in figure 12.5. They immediately reset and do a repetition in quick order. The coach can rearrange the cones easily for new fronts and different assignments. Add scout linemen to simulate particular blocks the linebackers must respond to with fast-flow assignments.

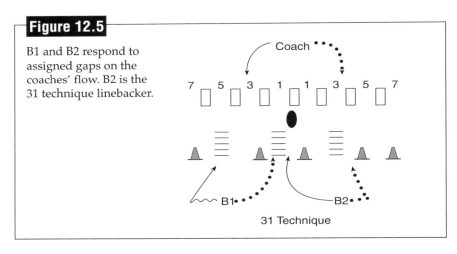

Figure 12.5

B1 and B2 respond to assigned gaps on the coaches' flow. B2 is the 31 technique linebacker.

31 Technique

2. Just as in 32 technique, the next progression for the 31 linebacker is the 9-on-7 drill. Now an offense from tight end to tight end runs plays. This progression combines keys and blocking schemes in a critical test of the linebackers' understanding of the concepts.

Chapter 13

51 and 52 Techniques

The similarities between the techniques described in this chapter and the 31 and 32 techniques discussed previously are striking. It is rare that inside and outside linebackers share the same methods, but both inside and outside linebackers frequently use the 51 and 52 techniques.

In 1978, Bill Dooley, the head coach at Virginia Tech, introduced me to the eagle defense when I joined his staff. His scheme required an inside linebacker to play over a tackle to the reduced side (see figure 13.1). This was very customary in an eagle package.

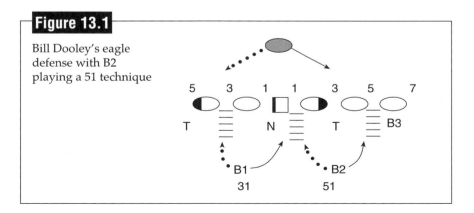

Figure 13.1

Bill Dooley's eagle defense with B2 playing a 51 technique

In the 1990s, the 4-3 defense soared in popularity. Its outside line-backers, particularly to the tight end side, played a technique like Bill Dooley's eagle linebacker (see figure 13.2).

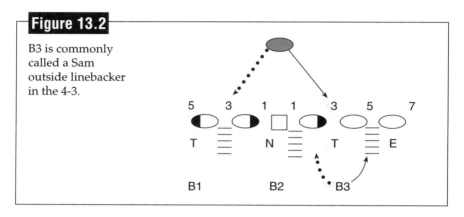

Figure 13.2

B3 is commonly called a Sam outside linebacker in the 4-3.

Quite often reduction fronts will kick both tackles down over the offensive guards, making an inside linebacker liable for the 5 gap (see figure 13.3).

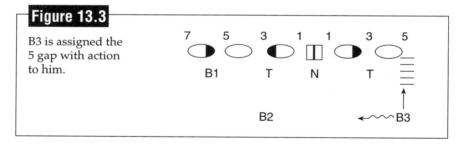

Figure 13.3

B3 is assigned the 5 gap with action to him.

The above illustrations are a few examples of both inside and outside linebackers having 5 gap obligations. For the inside line-backer who has already mastered 31 or 32 technique, the transition can be comfortable. The backside responsibilities can vary just as they do with a defender playing over a guard. The second technique digit may indicate a fast-flow style to another gap *(1)* or a cautious shuffling movement with no gap obligation on action away *(2)*.

52 Technique

This double-digit description is used when a linebacker has the 5 gap when flow is toward him and is slow with action away. Figure 13.3 is a fine example of this style of play. The linebacker has a single-gap duty, and with flow away he moves without a specific gap assignment.

Alignment

The 52 linebacker aligns with his inside foot covering the outside foot of the offensive tackle at depth of four yards off the ball.

Keys

Linebackers in this technique can read the tackle they align over or a running back. Both keys are sound, but just as we found in 32 technique, the line key is generally more dependable on counters and play-action passes. Versus tackle trap teams, this can be a particularly effective read.

Tackle Reads

The linebacker can use the guard reads detailed in chapter 11 to key the offensive tackle. Generally, the tackle is not quite as athletic as the guards on run blocks. He fears the linebacker's speed and maneuverability. This can be an excellent matchup for linebackers.

The tackle's possible blocking paths are shown in figure 13.4. The linebacker's reactions are the same as they were in 32 technique. These two techniques are interchangeable. Only the alignment differs, so using these two techniques in the same scheme is efficient teaching.

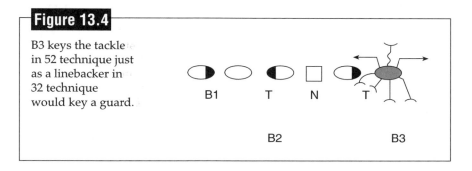

Figure 13.4

B3 keys the tackle in 52 technique just as a linebacker in 32 technique would key a guard.

By reviewing the guard-read section of chapter 11, the coach or linebacker will clearly understand the 52 technique responses to a tackle. Those new to the 52 concept ask most frequently about the veer block. A tight end is now required, and he blocks down with the tackle (see figure 13.5). In this situation, linebacker B2 starts forward toward his 5 gap responsibility. When he feels the tight end coming down and sees his fellow defensive end close with him, he slides outside to the alley.

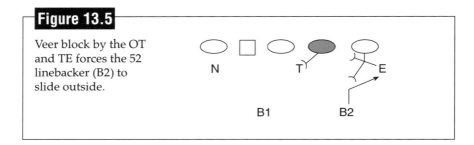

Figure 13.5

Veer block by the OT and TE forces the 52 linebacker (B2) to slide outside.

Versus the option, the 52 technique takes what shows in his gap. When the tackle blocks down, the linebacker must be ready to squeeze the dive. With a tackle reach or veer, the 52 linebacker widens for quarterback.

Back Reads

Fifty-two technique is easily adaptable to a backfield key. Again, review this section in chapter 11 with 32 technique. They are identical.

52 Responsibilities

The linebacker is responsible for the immediate 5 gap when it is open. He then plays inside-out on the ball. Versus option, he must play the dive with an open 5 gap. When the gap is closed, he should slide outside to the alley and play the quarterback-to-pitch phases. With flow away, he should shuffle inside-out on the ball, checking for cutbacks.

Adjustments

- The key can vary from series to series if necessary. The tackle is truer, but the backfield key is simpler to learn.
- Adjustments to line splits do vary from a 32 technique. With large splits, the 52 linebacker should align tighter to the ball, but we do not have him make a check to a penetrating charge as suggested for the 32 defender. This is because the defense

has already been knocked down or concentrated for strong interior play.

- With small line splits, the linebacker should deepen and widen, anticipating a perimeter play.

- In pass situations or when pre-snap information indicates pass, we often instruct the 52 linebacker to walk up on the line of scrimmage and engage the tackle before dropping into his coverage. This can slow the offensive tackle from freeing up to help his adjacent guard (see figure 13.6). Linebacker B3 in figure 13.6 also needs to walk up and blitz occasionally to make the tackle honor his presence.

Figure 13.6

With a heavy pass tendency, B3 walks up on OT. He engages the OT to force the OG to pass protect without OT help.

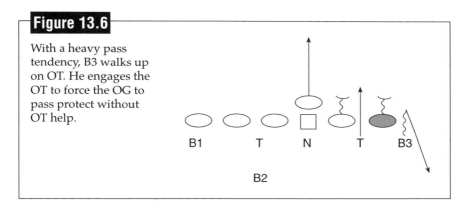

52 Technique Types

This technique is unique because both inside and outside linebackers use it frequently. Usually, it is a variation for the inside linebacker and, because the reads are so similar to 32 technique, the transition is easy. Some inside linebackers feel uncomfortable, however, if the blocking schemes force them routinely into the alley or 7 gap.

For the outside linebacker, this is often a base technique. Generally, outside linebackers are faster than their inside counterparts and operate with more ease in the open spaces of the alley.

51 Technique

This double-digit technique is used when a linebacker has the 5 gap frontside and runs because of a second hole responsibility on the backside. The eagle defense, so popular in the 1970s, assigned two linebackers to three gaps utilizing the 51 technique and its cousin the 31 technique. Review now figure 13.1 earlier in this chapter. When flow moves toward the 51 linebacker, it is away from the 31 player, so he runs backside and the gap farthest from the ball is left vacant. This is a concept common to many defensive packages.

The 31-51 relationship is just as close as the 32-52 correlation. In the eagle defense (figure 13.1), those techniques can be used together, and linebacker coach can drill them efficiently. In the 4-3 scheme, a 51 technique can also be used as shown in figure 13.2. Now the 51 linebacker works in conjunction with a middle linebacker, but he has the same duties.

Alignment

The 51 linebacker aligns with his inside foot splitting the stance of the offensive tackle. He is tighter than the 52 technique because he must cross the tackle's face on action away. We ask the 51 linebacker to be at least four yards deep.

Keys

The linebacker initially keys backfield action for flow.

Reads

With flow to the linebacker, he should approach the 5 gap, reading the blocking scheme in front of him. He should stay square to the line of scrimmage and take on all inside blockers with his inside foot. He should not penetrate the 5 gap but instead settle on his base.

The 51 technique needs to stay in the 5 hole even when the backfield action is all inside him. He cannot cross the offensive tackle's face with flow to the 3 gap. He has quarterback to pitch on all options off those inside fakes (see figure 13.7).

The 51 linebacker is unique because with action to him, he reads the tackle's frontside blocks. With flow away, he runs just like the 31 technique defender.

Let's look at the frontside block reactions in 51 technique:

Base

Figure 13.7 illustrates a base block reaction. The linebacker approaches with outside leverage and sets his base on his inside foot with his outside arm free in the 5 gap.

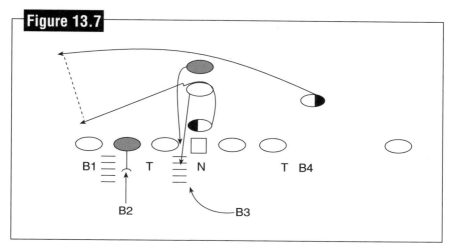

With flow to him, B2 must keep outside leverage on the OT for option or bounce-out.

Reach

The 51 defender shuffles for width to maintain outside leverage on the tackle. Just before contact, he sets his base with his inside foot and squeezes the tackle versus an inside play or pushes off the inside foot in pursuit on a perimeter run (see figure 13.8).

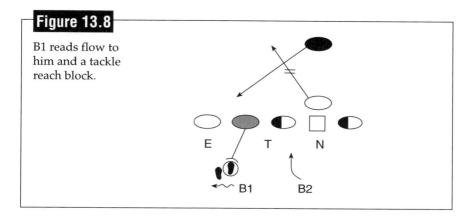

B1 reads flow to him and a tackle reach block.

Down

With action to the linebacker and the tackle down block, the defender should approach the 5 gap and then squeeze the double team with his inside foot up and hips square. He must be prepared to take on any inside blocks with his near foot or tackle the first threat to the double team (see figure 13.9).

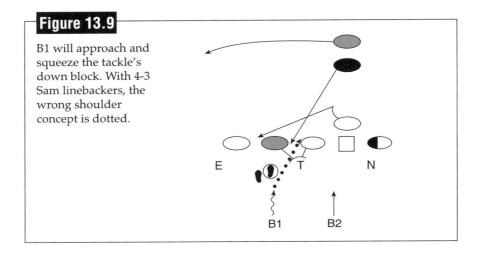

Figure 13.9

B1 will approach and squeeze the tackle's down block. With 4-3 Sam linebackers, the wrong shoulder concept is dotted.

The 4-3 defenses have developed the *wrong shoulder* concept with the 51 technique linebacker and have achieved outstanding results. We will look at this concept again when discussing 7 and 9 technique outside linebackers in chapter 17. Refer to figure 17.8 in that chapter.

Now the 51 linebacker, upon recognition of a down block, fills the hole with penetration and attacks the lead blocker with his *outside* shoulder, or wrong arm. The intent is to close the inside passage for the ball carrier immediately and to spill him outside to defenders who can run him down. In figure 13.9, B1 would go inside the full-back (dotted line) and bounce the runner to the end and safety defending the perimeter. B2 will often overlap inside-out pursuing on the same play.

Fold

This was once a very popular method of blocking to the reduced defensive tackle. In 51 technique the linebacker approaches and squeezes just as he did versus the down block. As the guard folds around, the defender must set his base and explode his hips to constrict the hole (see figure 13.10).

At Virginia Tech, Ashley Lee, our 182-pound freshman 51 linebacker, saw the fold block often. It led our staff to develop the hawk technique that we will discuss in chapter 14.

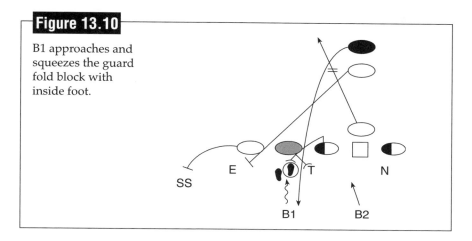

Figure 13.10

B1 approaches and squeezes the guard fold block with inside foot.

Veer

This scheme was a favorite of Nebraska's Tom Osborne when we faced him at Colorado. He loved to give the ball to his fullback off the belly play with this block. The linebacker must follow his read progression.

Flow to him starts the defender forward. Reading the tackle down confirms action to him. As he approaches, he feels the end closing the 5 gap with the tight end so he slides to the 7 gap or alley (see figure 13.11).

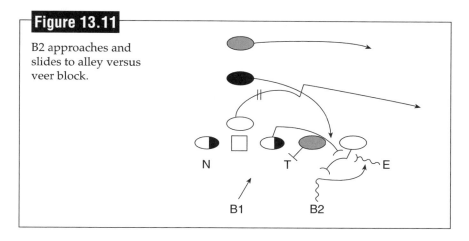

Figure 13.11

B2 approaches and slides to alley versus veer block.

With flow away the linebacker fills the near 1 gap when open and attacked. If there is no threat to that gap he continues to pursue inside the football (see figure 13.12).

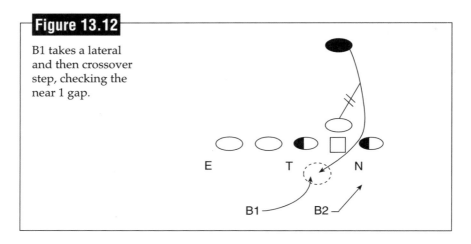

Figure 13.12

B1 takes a lateral and then crossover step, checking the near 1 gap.

51 Responsibilities

This is perhaps the most challenging technique that I ever had to coach. It is a 2 gap obligation with a backfield read for flow. On the frontside, however, the linebacker had to recognize at least five frontside blocking patterns. With action away the 51 linebacker focused on open and closed gaps. All these things happen very quickly, and it takes an outstanding athlete to make it work. The linebacker is responsible for the immediate 5 gap with action to him. With ball direction away, the defender is responsible for the near 1 gap and then inside-out on the football.

Adjustments

- When playing against a quick tackle, the linebacker should deepen his alignment and play more head up.
- When an offensive tackle runs the linebacker past the 1 gap, it is probably because he is breaking down rather than pressing through the open 1 gap.
- When an offensive tackle takes a big split and then runs a flat course to cut off the linebacker, have him play back door and squash the tackle's body parallel to the line of scrimmage. The lineman has little power with his shoulders turned to the sideline (see figure 13.13).

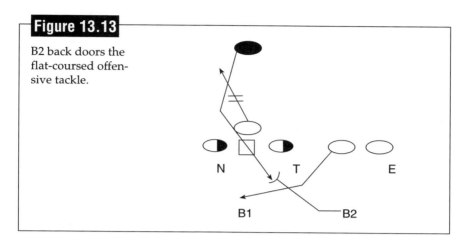

Figure 13.13

B2 back doors the flat-coursed offensive tackle.

- In 1980, the undersized Ashley Lee started for Virginia Tech as a 51 technique. Ashley was quick as a hiccup and made many plays, but he had difficulty with the frontside blocking schemes in the 5 gap due to his inexperience.

We adjusted with a "Falcon" call. The *F* in falcon was to remind Ashley that on all frontside action, the end had the 5 gap. Now he ran to the alley on flow to him and ran to the near 1 gap on flow away. It eliminated the line reading and taking on all the powerful 5 gap blocks (see figure 13.14).

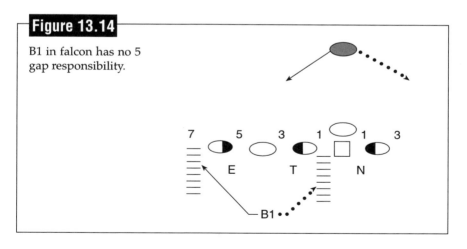

Figure 13.14

B1 in falcon has no 5 gap responsibility.

- When the reduction was set to the split end side, we enjoyed compressing the outside linebacker over the tackle and giving him 5 gap responsibility. This protected the reduced linebacker. He was now off the line without a free gap in front of him. This became our first named, rather than numbered, technique. We called it *nest* technique because the linebacker was protected, as if in a nest (see figure 13.15).

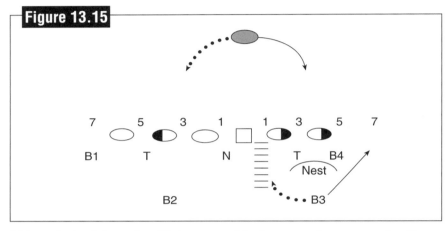

Figure 13.15

B3 keys the back for action. He is protected in the nest and can run to the alley or near 1 gap.

51 Technique Types

Because these linebackers can be sheltered somewhat, they do not have to be the best at taking on blockers. They do need wonderful movement skills, particularly when put in the alley. They need the quickness to cross the face of linemen based on backfield flow. Speed and agility are required because they often play in the alley, running down perimeter plays and avoiding cut blocks by backs and pulling linemen. When protected, size is not a strong prerequisite.

Chapter 14

Hawk Technique

This is a classic technique that the defensive staff at Virginia Tech created after the 1979 season. This technique formed the cornerstone of three consecutive top-10 defenses in Blacksburg and then laid the foundation for the outstanding defensive units at Colorado and Illinois in the '80s and '90s, respectively.

The first mention I have of *hawk* in my records is from the winter following the 1979 season. We introduced it on the field on April 9, 1980. It may have originated elsewhere before that, but we fashioned it independently that winter.

Bill Dooley had brought the eagle package with him from North Carolina in 1978. It formed our base until we conceived hawk. Since the 1980 season, the hawk front has dominated our game plans and has become synonymous with the defensive philosophy of those on our defensive staffs for nearly two decades.

What is the difference between the hawk and eagle fronts? The front four were nearly identical, but the linebacker concepts were dissimilar. The eagle featured two inside linebackers who were assigned to three gaps. They always voided the space farthest from the ball. Each linebacker had two holes to defend. The hawk linebackers were 1 gap players. We permitted them to pay more attention to that particular gap and didn't force them to make hasty decisions based only on backfield action.

The eagle seven-man front had to defend the potential of eight gaps as shown in figure 14.1. The alleys (7 gaps) to both sides were the duty of someone in the forcing unit.

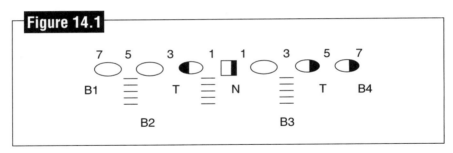

The alleys are defended by B1 and B4. The six interior gaps are defended by only five players in eagle.

The hawk defense was aided by an overshifted coverage that brought a safety six to eight yards deep inside a tight end. When the tight end blocked, the safety defended one alley. This permitted the front to slide the reduced linebacker (B2) inside as well as the outside linebacker (B1). Now the seven-man front defended only seven gaps as shown in figure 14.2.

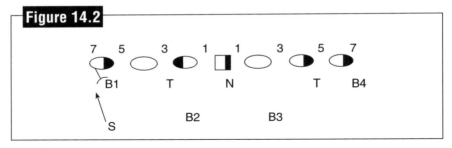

The alleys are defended by the safety and B4. The six interior gaps are defended by six players in hawk.

B2, in figure 14.2, became Mr. Inside. He not only had an interior gap to him but also became a real thorn in the side of the offense with flow away. B2 aligns so far inside that it becomes difficult to stop his pursuit backside. This was all possible due to coverage adjustments made by our superb secondary coach, Steve Bernstein, who spent 12 years with me perfecting the support from our secondary.

A coach uses hawk when he wants to take away the inside running attack. It is an aggressive, attacking style of play.

Alignment

The hawk linebacker aligns three to four yards deep. The wider the guard-center split, the tighter the hawk linebacker should position himself. The defender should advance closer to the ball on any tendencies or pre-snap information that indicates inside run.

The hawk can vary the width of his alignment quite a bit. We align him anywhere from stacked behind his defensive tackle to the middle of his 1 gap (see figure 14.3).

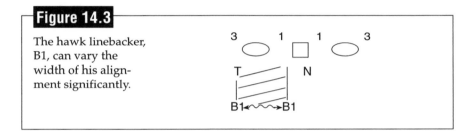

Figure 14.3

The hawk linebacker, B1, can vary the width of his alignment significantly.

Most coaches in this scheme do not often enough use this alignment flexibility. A well-trained hawk linebacker knows formation tendencies. For example, when the tight end is frontside 75 percent of the time in the running game, the hawk should use that flexibility to slide toward the tight end. When run is away, he benefits considerably by aligning closer to the center.

Keys

This key varies with the offense more than any other technique discussed thus far. In 1980, we read only backfield action. I had mistakenly believed that linebackers could not effectively key linemen when they were covered by a defensive lineman. In the early 1980s, counter plays caused our hawk linebacker many false steps. One spring we experimented with guard reads and have used them extensively ever since.

Hawk is a named technique because the linebacker is initially protected by the defensive tackle, who always plays over the guard to the hawk linebacker's side.

Guard Reads

Mr. Inside responds by pressing the immediate 3 gap unless on his path he recognizes that all threats are in the 1 gap. With flow away, he shuffles and presses the first open seam. It is therefore a frontside press and backside shuffle style of play.

Hawk requires the linebacker to master only five basic guard paths, as opposed to eight when keying guard in the complementary 32 technique (see chapter 11). Hawk also has few gray, or confusing, reads. There are two frontside run patterns, two backside, and pass. Sounds simple. Let's take a look at them.

Hat On

When the guard puts his helmet within the cylinder of the defensive tackle's body, the linebacker should start toward the 3 gap and read the near back's path. He should take the fullback away. If there is any doubt he should press the 3 gap aggressively (see figure 14.4).

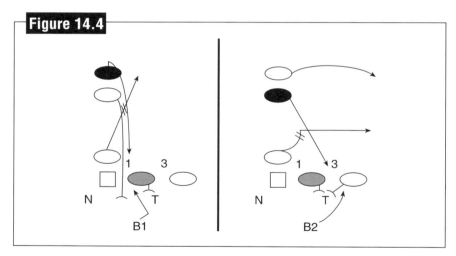

Figure 14.4

B1 and B2 face hat-on blocks.

Linebacker B1 begins to press the 3 gap and recognizes a threat to the 1 gap. He naturally reacts back to the isolation. B2 presses the 3 and hugs the double team to tackle the fullback when he is given the ball.

Fold

With the guard pull to him, the linebacker attacks the 3 gap, hugging again the tackle's down block, that will put the linebacker on an inside-out path to the ball.

We portrayed the fold block versus the eagle defense in chapter 13 and described it as a popular scheme in the early 1980s, when our Virginia Tech staff was experimenting with hawk. We found the evolution from eagle to hawk was a real benefit to smaller linebackers defending the fold block (see figure 14.5).

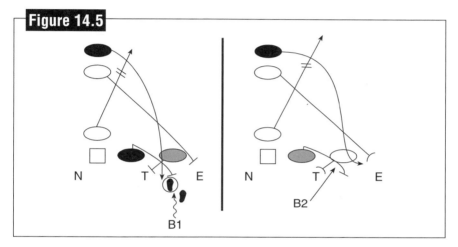

Figure 14.5

N   T   E   N   T   E

B1   B2

Eagle linebacker B1 faces fold from the outside. Hawk B2 attacks inside the fold.

Eagle linebacker B1 faced a guard running on his track and kicking out B1. Hawk linebacker B2 pressed inside the guard, who had to adjust and get his shoulders turned to block on B2. We found this to be a much more awkward path for the guard. Hawk reaction also forced the ball outside to an overshifted coverage rather that giving it a chance to run inside the linebacker.

With guard pull to the linebacker and no inside threat, the linebacker begins to press the 3 gap and then alleys, finding the first cavity to fill (see figure 14.6).

Scoop

When the guard shows scoop, the linebacker should shuffle backside looking for a place to press (see figure 14.7). This is a huge advantage for the hawk system. A scoop scheme should never cut off a linebacker aligned inside him, especially when protected by the hawk defensive tackle. This player must consistently make plays versus scoop offenses.

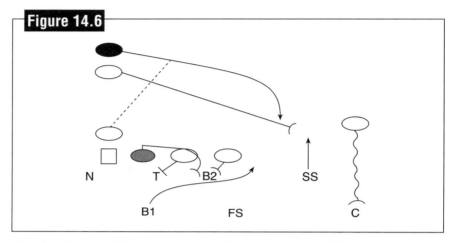

Guard pull sweep. B1 presses the 3 gap, then adjusts with width.

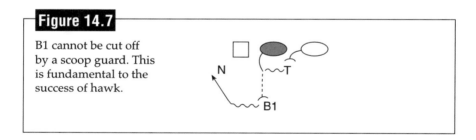

Guard Pull Away

With guard pull away, we teach the linebacker simply to shuffle and press the first open gap. Now the line must block back, and usually the frontside tackle is responsible for the hawk defender. We make him aware of this on every pull away. The linebacker must now be prepared to read the offensive tackle's block and fill the open seam (figure 14.8) or go topside the offensive tackle (figure 14.9).

Guard pull away often indicates bootleg pass. The linebacker begins shadowing the guard. When he recognizes pass he reacts to

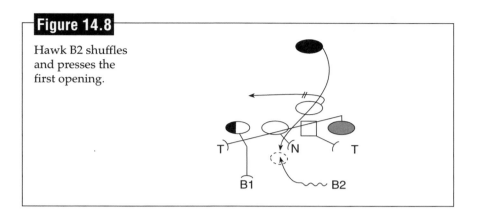

Figure 14.8

Hawk B2 shuffles and presses the first opening.

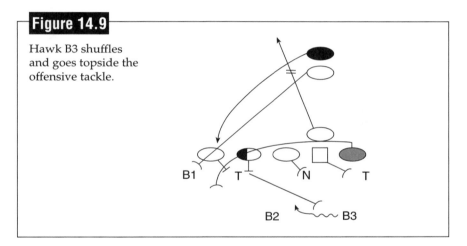

Figure 14.9

Hawk B3 shuffles and goes topside the offensive tackle.

the route. Against bootleg he should open to the opposite hook, and he should run with any drag, just as the 32 technique did in figure 11.7.

Pass or Draw

With guard pass protection, the linebacker yells "pass" and opens his hips to his key receiver or moves forward in man coverage. Draw is also a strong possibility. Most offenses choose to run the draw away from the protected hawk linebacker. When the offense runs toward the hawk linebacker, a lead back usually engages him, not a lineman (see figure 14.10).

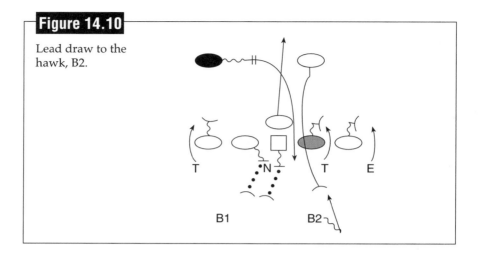

Figure 14.10

Lead draw to the hawk, B2.

T

N

T

E

B1

B2

Now the linebacker screams "draw" and retraces his steps while sprinting to the outside edge of the blocker. He should always force the draw inside.

Back Reads

The back keys are even less sophisticated than the guard reads. We simply have the hawk linebacker mirror his key. When in a back read, an adolescent should be able to perform without mental errors.

One Gap

When the 1 gap is attacked, the linebacker should attack it. He must keep his outside arm free (see figure 14.11).

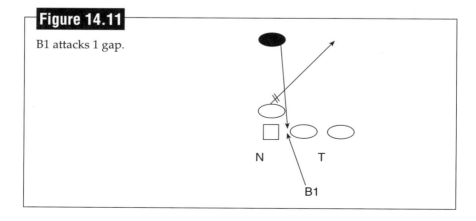

Figure 14.11

B1 attacks 1 gap.

N

T

B1

Three Gap

When the 3 gap or wider is attacked, the linebacker must press the 3 gap as shown in figures 14.4, 14.5, and 14.6 earlier in this chapter.

Action Away

When flow is away, the linebacker should shuffle backside to stop cutbacks first, then pursue staying inside-out on the ball. Review figures 14.7, 14.8, and 14.9.

Pass

This is difficult to recognize versus strong play-action clubs. The coach must find a suitable key or a coverage that takes pressure off the hawk linebacker. Guard reads have an obvious advantage here.

Hawk Responsibilities

The linebacker is challenged with taking away the inside running threats. With no inside resistance, the linebacker should pursue inside-out to the ball.

Adjustments

- With big splits the linebacker aligns in the middle of the center-guard gap three yards deep. We permit veteran linebackers to blitz through a large gap once they have proven themselves trustworthy.
- With small splits across the line the linebacker should deepen to five yards, anticipating a perimeter play. He should shade to the side of the offense's perimeter tendencies when possible.
- When the center-guard split is cut down to the reduction, it generally denotes a scoop block. The linebacker should slide toward the center.

Hawk Types

This technique does not require as much experience as many others. The keys are simple, and the duties are not complex. It is an ideal position for less mature players.

Interestingly enough, two of the best I have tutored at hawk have been vastly different physically. Small Ashley Lee was extremely effective because of his movement. Linemen could not cut him off. Dana Howard, the 1994 Butkus Award winner, was 48 pounds heavier than Lee as a true frosh. Dana was a thug versus the inside run. Big Ten opponents quit trying to run the isolation at him. He chewed up fullbacks.

Chapter 15

Middle Linebacker Technique

This particular technique was popularized in the National Football League. Many NFL Hall-of-Fame linebackers were middle line-backers that kids grew up wanting to impersonate. Each era had their featured guys in the middle, and many old-timers are still revered for their exploits of decades ago.

At Illinois, a real treasure was the opportunity to bring back NFL Hall-of-Fame legends like Ray Nitschke and Dick Butkus to speak to our squad. Their legacy was an intense style of play that influenced the demeanor of the Illini 30 years after they graduated.

Ray Nitschke, the Green Bay Hall of Famer, spoke to our 1990 Big Ten cochampions in Champaign Friday evening before a game at Memorial Stadium. It was one of the most stirring messages I have witnessed on the field.

Until the 1990s, college defensive packages used two inside line-backers more often than a middle linebacker as the NFL did. As the decade progressed, the 4-3 scheme became more popular in college circles, and even reduction fronts began to stack linebackers to give a 4-3 middle linebacker appearance occasionally.

For the 4-3 teams this technique was the principal method of play for their man in the middle. For the packages with two inside line-backers, this technique was a change-up. In both, the responsibilities were relatively simple.

Almost all of the middle linebackers have a 1 gap open in front of them and a 3 gap open to the opposite side (see figure 15.1). We term this a 13 technique because they are unprotected to the near 1 gap and backside must fill the 3 hole.

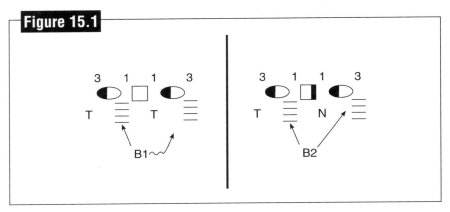

Figure 15.1

Middle linebackers B1 and B2 both have typical assignments of a near 1 gap and far 3 gap.

Alignment

We ask our 13 technique linebacker to align directly over the ball three yards deep. If his primary key is the backfield he may need to offset slightly to see past a quarterback and get good vision on his key.

Keys

The majority of middle linebackers key backfield action, yet two other keys need to be considered strongly when assigning 13 technique duties.

Backfield flow is attractive to coaches and players because of its simplicity. It is not cumbersome for the innate or naive player in the middle. For schemes that use this technique as a change-up, it is very tempting to have the linebacker use an unsophisticated key for direction. If action goes to this side, he fills the near 1 gap. When it goes away, the middle linebacker presses the 3 gap. It's neat and easy but too neat and easy for some.

A few, like Steve Wilt, head coach at Taylor University in Upland, Indiana, still teach the time-honored center read to their middle linebackers. The advantage is that the center often blocks the 13 technique and the linebacker is, of course, watching him. The center is also a truer key than backfield action. As we have noted before, linemen will tell of play-action pass and misdirection, while running backs try to deceive on those plays.

A third consideration for those mixing the eagle or 50 defenses with a stack look is to key the guard, particularly if the linebacker is already trained in that key, as is a hawk linebacker (chapter 14) or 32 technique (chapter 11).

We will now study this technique and how it varies with each key.

Backfield Reads

The coach's film study usually identifies a player or combination of players that the linebacker will key for flow as a middle linebacker. As mentioned before, if the quarterback obstructs that view, the linebacker may have to offset slightly. This can occur particularly with the I-formation.

Frontside Flow

When aligned in a 13 technique and action coming toward the near 1 gap that is open, the linebacker fills it aggressively with his near foot and hands or near foot and shoulder.

When the frontside 1 gap is closed, he continues to pursue, looking to press the first open gap available as he feels the path of the runner (see figure 15.2).

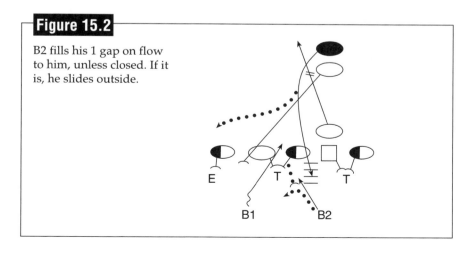

Figure 15.2

B2 fills his 1 gap on flow to him, unless closed. If it is, he slides outside.

With an immediate perimeter threat as shown in figure 15.3, the middle linebacker need not check the initial 1 gap but instead pursues topside the center's block in rapid pursuit of the next opening to the ball.

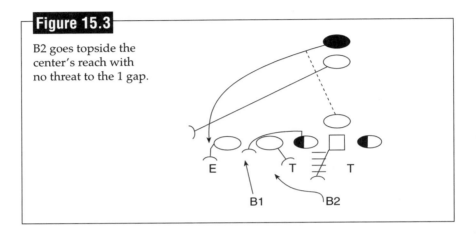

Figure 15.3

B2 goes topside the center's reach with no threat to the 1 gap.

Backside Flow

When action is away from the immediate 1 gap, the 13 linebacker has the 3 gap obligation. Now he simply presses the guard-tackle gap. When it is open he fills it. When it is closed he goes topside all blockers, staying behind the ball (see figure 15.4).

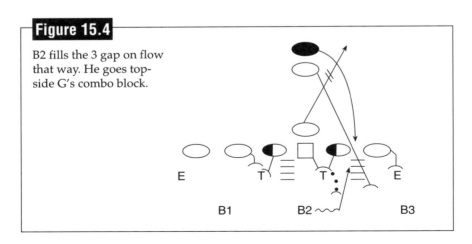

Figure 15.4

B2 fills the 3 gap on flow that way. He goes topside G's combo block.

Pass

When the backfield indicates pass, the middle linebacker reacts to his zone or man-to-man rules. Play-action pass and bootlegs can be particularly effective versus a back-read middle linebacker.

Shuffle and Press

When employing other defenses as a base, such as the 50, eagle, or wide tackle 6 schemes, the coach can simplify middle linebacker technique even further. Coaches can tell the linebacker to use a backfield key for flow and to shuffle to the indicated direction, looking to press the first open seam.

Now the linebacker can work uninhibited by front or most stunts. Our staff chose to use this method when we would check our linebackers to a stacked alignment as in figure 15.5.

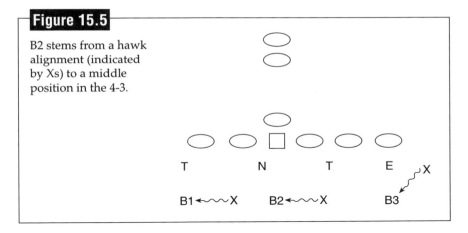

Figure 15.5

B2 stems from a hawk alignment (indicated by Xs) to a middle position in the 4-3.

Here, B2 aligns in hawk technique (chapter 14), and on the check all three linebackers stem to a 4-3 look. Now B2 doesn't have to consider the gap responsibilities of those aligned in front of him. He does not need to be aware of line twists or games. He is free to fit almost anything by simply shuffling and pressing the first open seam.

Center Reads

Steve Wilt, the head coach at Taylor University, shared with me recently that at a clinic of nearly forty 4-3 defensive coaches, only two staffs had their middle linebackers key the center. While coaches rarely use line reads for this position, they should consider them if they use a limited number of techniques in their defensive package.

Base Block

As the center's helmet attacks him, the linebacker should approach and set his base with his foot down the middle of the center's body and his free arm in his assigned gap. The contact surface can be hands or shoulder. The defender should then separate and find the football (see figure 15.6).

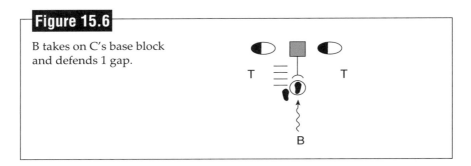

Figure 15.6

B takes on C's base block and defends 1 gap.

Reach or Zone Block

As the center's head attempts to reach him, the linebacker knows that flow is in that direction. When the center reaches toward his 1 gap duty, the defender must play in that gap with his near foot. When the center reaches the other direction, he will combo block with the guard. The middle linebacker immediately presses the 3 gap to that side (see figure 15.7).

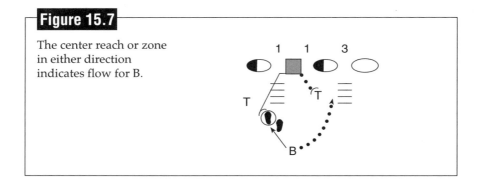

Figure 15.7

The center reach or zone in either direction indicates flow for B.

Block Back

Many believe the toughest reads for the linebacker with a center key are when the center blocks back. The hat placement is, indeed, at a different angle than when the center reaches or zone blocks. On the block back, the center's eyes are fixed on that near lineman.

Steve Wilt trains his Taylor middle linebackers to step toward the center's initial hat placement and see the nearest guard. When he feels the guard pulling across his face, the linebacker redirects and fills from inside-out on the influence trap, veer trap, and power or counter blocking patterns (see figure 15.8).

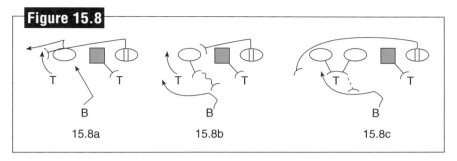

Figure 15.8

15.8a   15.8b   15.8c

B steps toward center's hat and then redirects on the G pulls.

Center Pull

While we do not regularly see this block during the season, we expose the linebackers to it in fall camp so they can recall it during a given week or recognize it when they do not expect it. Some toss sweep and counter teams use it (see figure 15.9).

The middle linebacker can mirror the pulling center with no false steps. He should be aware that the frontside tackle will probably be assigned to seal him inside.

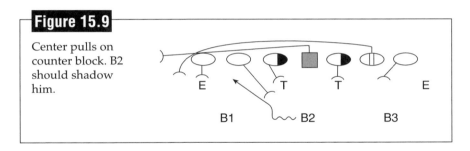

Figure 15.9

Center pulls on counter block. B2 should shadow him.

E   T   T   E

B1   B2   B3

Pass

A real benefit of center read is on pass plays. Now the middle line-backer recognizes pass instantly, and play-action pass loses its hold on him. Once he recognizes pass, the defender must yell "pass" and keep the center in his vision briefly for draw (see figure 15.10).

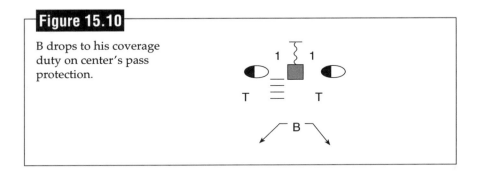

Figure 15.10

B drops to his coverage duty on center's pass protection.

Guard Reads

The third possible key is probably the least used by middle line-backers and their coaches, but it is a viable option. In fact, if the hawk technique described in the previous chapter is used, the play-ers already know keys and reactions to flow. Only the gap assign-ments change.

Review chapter 14. If the guard to the 3 technique tackle places his hat on the tackle or pulls toward him, the middle linebacker re-acts to his frontside gap (see figure 15.11).

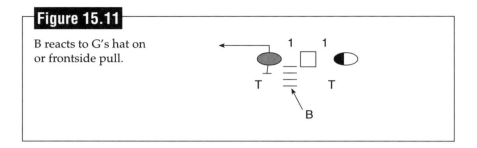

Figure 15.11

B reacts to G's hat on or frontside pull.

When the guard key scoops or pulls away from the 3 technique tackle, the middle linebacker would read it as flow away or play to his right in figure 15.12.

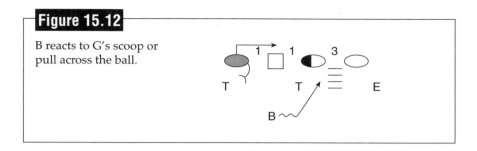

Figure 15.12

B reacts to G's scoop or pull across the ball.

With the key in pass pro, the 13 technique yells "pass" and retreats to coverage or responds to draw (see figure 15.13).

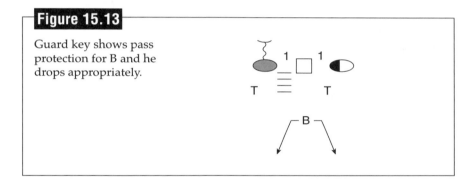

Figure 15.13

Guard key shows pass protection for B and he drops appropriately.

Personally, I find the guard read an easy transition to teach to linebackers trained in hawk technique. It also avoids the false steps that the center block back reads can produce.

Determining the perfect key for the middle linebacker can be arduous. It has as much to do with fitting the entire scheme as it does with just this technique.

Middle Linebacker Responsibilities

The middle linebacker is usually responsible for two inside gaps when threatened. These can change depending on the defense dialed up by the signal caller. Normally he has a 1 gap and a 3 gap on either side of the ball. Once the frontside gap is defended, the middle linebacker roams from there to the sideline, always inside-out on the ball. Versus option, this linebacker is responsible for the dive first. He can then overlap to the outside phases of the option.

Adjustments

- The larger the offensive line splits, the tighter the 13 technique can play to the line of scrimmage. We normally align at depth of three to four yards and would never get tighter than two and a half yards. If the split to the 3 technique side was huge, the linebacker could blitz the near 1 gap.
- With tight line splits, the middle linebacker can deepen to four yards, anticipating an outside run or pass.
- Some 4-3 teams often assign the tackles both 1 gaps. They can do this by stunting or playing both tackles in head-up alignments on the offensive guards, but with inside gap duties (see figure 15.14).

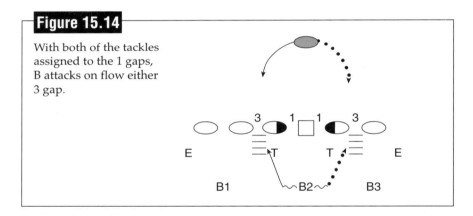

Figure 15.14

With both of the tackles assigned to the 1 gaps, B attacks on flow either 3 gap.

Middle Linebacker Types

The term *middle linebacker* conjures an image unlike others. The player chosen for this role must have some special qualities.

This guy must be the wild-eyed competitor. His intensity can never be doubted. He must portray the fire of his defensive unit. His enthusiasm must pour out to his teammates in visible fashion. Who can forget the bulging, frenzied eyes of Mike Singletary of the Chicago Bears or the toothless, scowling face of Jack Lambert leading Pittsburgh's vaunted Steel Curtain.

Physically, the middle linebacker must be a heavy-contact player. He must be able to hit and shed from tight end to tight end along the line of scrimmage. He must prowl that area as though it were his domain. He must always be prepared to press upfield to the ball carrier.

Speed is always a plus, but it is not a defining quality at this position. Here we want the competitor who loves to hit and hates to lose. We expect a middle linebacker to be near every running play. He needs to be special!

Chapter 16

5 Techniques

The previous chapters have discussed the most common inside line-backer techniques. The inside linebacker roams exclusively over the center and guards, usually with depth off the line of scrimmage. Outside linebackers operate exclusively from the tight end to the sideline, on or off the line of scrimmage. The area where they frequently share various schemes is the tackle-tight end gap (see the shaded areas in figure 16.1).

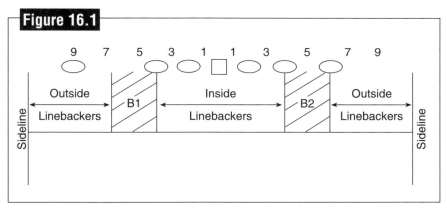

Figure 16.1

B1 and B2 in shaded areas could be identified as inside or outside linebackers depending on the coaches' scheme.

Chapter 13 discussed 51 and 52 techniques. These styles defend from depth the shaded gaps in figure 16.1. Some systems consider 51 and 52 linebackers inside defenders, while in other defensive packages outside linebacker coaches teach the 51 and 52 linebackers.

In contrast, this chapter presents 5 gap responsibilities almost always associated with outside linebackers. Although they, too, defend the shaded area in figure 16.1, they do it from the line of scrimmage. This is a rare assignment for an inside linebacker.

Coaches and defenders must understand the principles of perimeter run defense. Every sound defensive scheme has a 5, 7, and 9 gap player to the frontside of an outside run. We liken this principle to the mechanics of a swinging gate (see figure 16.2).

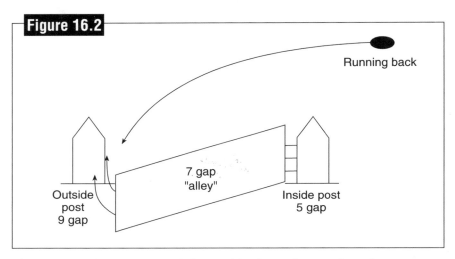

Figure 16.2

Running back

7 gap
"alley"

Outside
post
9 gap

Inside post
5 gap

The principle of perimeter run defense is like the mechanics of an effective swinging gate.

A defense must close the passageway for a running back by establishing a frame made of the 5 gap defender and a contain player or the sideline.

These two posts must maintain the line of scrimmage or work across the line for negative yardage. If the offense displaces either post, the gate will not function properly and an opening will likely exist for the runner.

The alley player closes the seam inside the frame made by the 5 and 9 techniques. The alley, or 7 gap, defender must be an active tackler. He becomes the swinging door that is the moving barrier to the running back's progress. Against a strong outside team, the defense features the performance of the alley player.

In a 1983 Colorado game, we made a wise scheme decision, but a terrible personnel choice. We designed a perimeter defense that always had an unblocked 7 gap player. The posts set the frame on the line of scrimmage, and a free-swinging door went one-on-one in a narrow passageway with the ball carrier. Time after time our alley player missed the tackle for minus yardage. We learned a hard lesson that personnel dictate the perimeter scheme, not vice versa.

A variety of perimeter run schemes can utilize various personnel at 5, 7, and 9 gap duties. Each is sound as long as the frame players can maintain the line and the alley defender works inside-out and is a productive tackler.

The gate principle leads to another defensive concept important to outside linebackers: Defense is knowing where your help is. When an outside linebacker plays 5 technique, he knows that he is the inside post on perimeter plays and has much outside help. He must usher the ball to the sideline and not permit the runner to cut inside him. He must not be soft in the 5 gap.

Another element that is different for outside linebackers and their inside companions is time. Things happen more slowly for linebackers involved with the 5, 7, or 9 gaps as opposed to those who align over a center or guard. Inside linebackers frequently don't recover from a mistake because the ball is so close to them. An outside linebacker does not have to rush to anything, and he can more than likely recover from an initial poor read or step. It takes much longer for the ball to challenge the outside defender. The outside linebacker, however, must have discipline and patience.

This chapter will deal largely with two single-digit outside linebacker techniques that defend the 5 gap. Remember, a single digit in our terminology means the linebacker is on the line of scrimmage and involved in defending only one gap, whether action is to or away from him.

Wide 5 Technique

In our scheme we call this position the rush linebacker. It is a relatively simple position that permits a player to feel comfortable with his duties. When opposite a tight end, he must dominate the end in the run game. When pass develops, he rushes the quarterback often and should strike fear in the heart of an offensive tackle because of his acceleration. If a rush can do those two things well, he will have extraordinary success at this technique. With no tight end, we adjust to a loose 5 technique that we will discuss later in this chapter.

In 1980 at Virginia Tech, we had our first dominant rush in Robert Brown. Robert was six-foot-three, 235, and had brute strength and tremendous competitiveness. He was the finest run player I've had at this position. He played 10 years with the Green Bay Packers after being drafted in the third round. Robert was quiet and unassuming, but he treated tight ends as second-class citizens.

By 1984 at Colorado, we started our first lanky rush in Dan McMillen, a six-foot-five, 225-pound model. Dan was an impressive pass rusher and a relentless pursuer. Until that season, our wide 5 techniques played in a two-point stance like all the other linebackers. Then Oklahoma State unveiled the outside zone play featuring Thurman Thomas. The tight end and tackle would come off and double team McMillen, getting initial movement, while Thurman would accelerate to that spot. By the second half, Dan was in a three-point stance, and our rush linebackers have been employing it ever since.

The next premier rush linebackers in our defense were Alfred Williams and Simeon Rice. Both were first-round draft choices. They had similar body types. At six-foot-five, 230 as freshmen, they were elusive pass rushers and strong enough versus the run. In 1996, Alfred was an All-Pro after winning the 1990 Butkus Award. Simeon Rice was the NFL Rookie of the Year in 1996 and registered an NFL record 12-1/2 sacks in his first season.

Alignment

Our wide 5 linebackers use a three-point stance with the near foot back in a heel-to-toe relationship. The feet are normally shoulder-width apart, with the tail slightly raised and the back flat. Most of the player's body weight should be over his feet. He must focus on his key once the center addresses the ball.

The linebacker should align with his outside foot down the middle of the tight end's body. This puts the linebacker firmly inside the tight end and entrenched in his 5 gap. His depth will vary based on his experience and the quickness of his initial step. Begin the young rushes deeper so they can feel the planted base on contact as described in chapter 3. Once they have success setting their base, move rush linebackers closer to the blockers at the line. Whenever the base is sloppy, move rush linebackers back. Too many coaches emphasize hands over feet at this technique. Without a proper base, the wide 5 linebacker will not prevail.

Key

Overwhelmingly, coaches and players prefer initially to key the tight end in this technique. The tight end blocks them often, and players enjoy a visual key on the prominent blocker. Have them focus intensely on the end's helmet.

A minority of wide 5 linebackers key the offensive tackle while stepping toward the tight end. Now the tackle becomes their visual key and the tight end a pressure key. They see the tackle and feel the tight end. The advantage with a tackle key is against the pass. As soon as the tackle shows pass protection, the linebacker can rush or drop into coverage. He knows immediately that pass or draw is likely. With the tight end key, he may not recognize pass as early.

Tight End Reads

The following descriptions outline the wide 5's reaction to the common movements by his tight end key. Each game week requires trimming the number of blocks down to a manageable number so that proper repetition can be given.

Base Block

When the tight end's helmet moves, the linebacker should attack with a short power step, setting the base with the near foot to the tight end. He should launch the contact surface with the hip explosion off that base. We use hands as our primary way to take on blockers at the line of scrimmage. The linebacker seeks to put both hands with thumbs up into the chest plate of the blocker and immediately "bench presses" to get separation from him.

The wide 5 technique is only one step from contact, but it is the crucial step. Without a firm base, the chance for success diminishes rapidly. Spend much time working this step that sets the base, and then use quick hands to ensure proper contact.

Now the linebacker must find the ball while controlling his 5 gap. When the ball comes into the linebacker's gap, he should make the play with his inside pad (see figure 16.3).

When the ball carrier bounces outside B2 (dotted line in figure 16.3), the linebacker works across the tight end's face to the ball, but not until then. The alley player is responsible for the bounce-out—remember the swinging-gate concept.

Figure 16.3

B2 controls his 5 gap versus a base block.

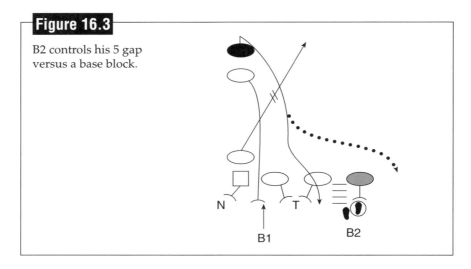

Versus option, the wide 5 linebacker has the quarterback *inside* the tight end's block. The linebacker should force the quarterback outside to the alley help, then shed the blocker and pursue.

Reach Block

The wide 5 player reacts to the tight end's outside hat placement by stepping with his outside foot and attacking the inside edge of the blocker with correct hand placement. With toss sweep he must locate the ball and defend the 5 gap for cutback. He is the inside post shown in figure 16.2. This linebacker must maintain the line and push the ball to the alley (see figure 16.4).

Once the ball crosses the linebacker's face, he should quickly shed the tight end and pursue inside-out in the alley (see figure 16.5). Often the tight end will reach too wide and allow the rush defender to come underneath his block. Now the linebacker can get to the alley quickly and be disruptive as part of the swinging gate.

Zone Block

At Colorado we feared Oklahoma State's Thurman Thomas and Barry Sanders running behind this scheme. It put tremendous pressure on a wide 5 technique and forced us to play our rush in a three-point stance.

The tight end reaches and the outside linebacker responds just as he did initially versus the sweep in figure 16.5. The linebacker will then feel the inside pressure of the offensive tackle as the tight end tries to combo off to any alley threat (see figure 16.6).

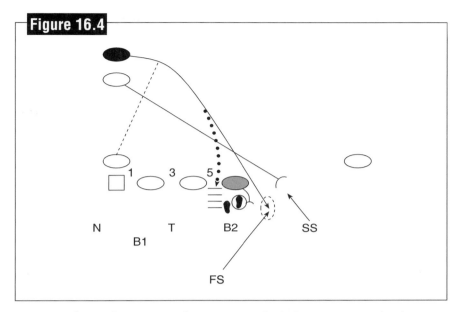

B2 attacks the reach, staying in the 5 gap until the ball carrier crosses his face.

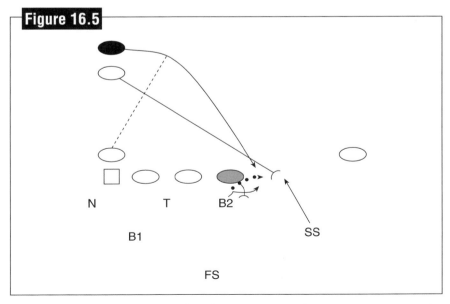

B2 can cross the TE's face only when the ball is outside him. B2 can run under the overreach by the TE (dotted).

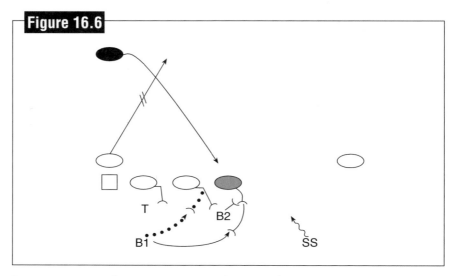

Figure 16.6

B2 must maintain the line by defeating the TE on the zone block.

We teach the rush linebacker to defeat the tight end and maintain contact with him. When the tackle takes over the block, the defender needs to lean back over his inside foot if the ball has not gotten width. When the ball carrier has width, the outside linebacker should be able to run under the separating tight end and away from the tackle.

In figure 16.6, B2 must realize where his defensive help is. Linebacker B1 should press the 3 gap, forcing the tackle to come off his combo block on B2. Now B2 can work alone against the end.

Outside Blocks

A multitude of schemes are presented when the tight end releases outside. After the initial step with his outside foot, the rush will recognize that the end's helmet is gaining width and not attacking the frame of his body.

At once the defender must counter by staying square and stepping inside to constrict his 5 gap from the next inside threat (that is, the tackle, fullback, guard, or ball).

Tackle Fan. This is a common block and alarms outside linebackers because it occurs so quickly. This block puts a premium on quick footwork. The rush steps toward the end and then must redirect instantly with weight over his inside foot to thwart the tackle (see figure 16.7).

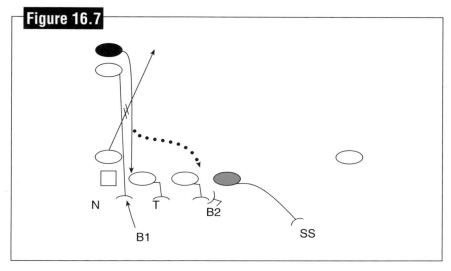

Figure 16.7

Tackle turns out on B2. He must constrict the 5 gap after stepping toward the TE key.

Linebacker B2 needs to constrict the 5 gap and tackle the runner on the bounce-out (dotted line in figure 16.7) with his outside arm. This is a scheme that is much easier to read and recognize with a tackle key.

Power. This is another frequently used blocking pattern at all levels of competition. It is less challenging for the wide 5 because it grants him a lot of time to react. Now as he steps back inside, he sees the fullback charging and sets his inside foot while launching his near shoulder off his coiled hips. The linebacker does not want to get upfield—he wants to stay near the line. He should squeeze inside and always keep his outside arm free for the expected bounce-out by the runner. Usually a wide 5 linebacker has inside help as demonstrated by B1 in figure 16.8.

G Block. This is a frontside guard kick-out on the wide 5 linebacker. The reaction should be identical to fan and power. The alignment of the rush forces an outside release by the tight end, that permits B1 to press inside B2 as shown in figure 16.9. Now, linebacker B2 must just stay square and not get upfield to open a vertical seam.

Counter. This popular blocking pattern gives the outside linebacker a lot of time to decipher the scheme. He needs patience as he squeezes back to the blocker with his shoulders square and his inside foot up.

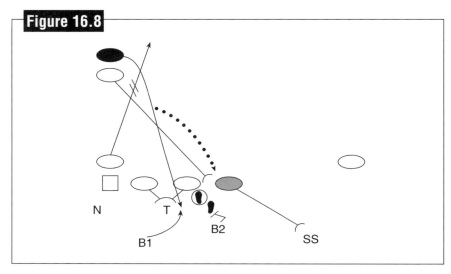

Figure 16.8

B2 reacts back inside to threat from FB. B2 is square to the line of scrimmage with his inside foot up.

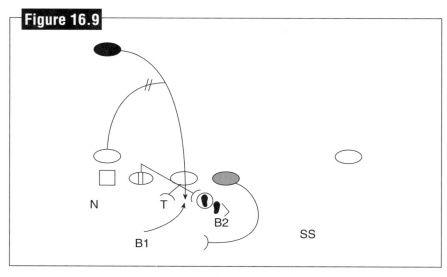

Figure 16.9

B2 protects B1 from the TE by forcing the TE around B2. B2 then engages the pulling guard with his inside foot.

The wide 5 technique wants to force the ball back to B1 and be prepared to push off his inside foot in pursuit of the potential bounce-out (see figure 16.10).

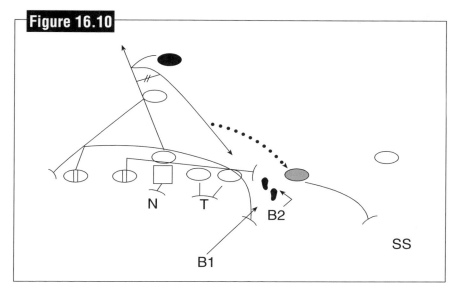

Figure 16.10

B2 reacts inside to backside pulling G.

Options.　A variety of option plays begin with the tight end block-ing outside. We have our rush step back inside as the tight end arcs. Upon reading option, we instruct him to feather the quarterback from the line of scrimmage. He should never get upfield or turn toward the quarterback. He wants to be able to push off his inside foot and overlap to the pitch versus a quarterback who is an impos-tor as a runner. He should force the quarterback to hold the ball as long as he can to give the other defenders more time to pursue (see figure 16.11).

The wide 5 look can present an option dilemma for wishbone teams. At Colorado our offense ran the three-back option every spring. The base triple-option play left unblocked all three defend-ers of the dive, quarterback, and pitch (see figure 16.12).

Passes.　With his key releasing outside, the wide 5 linebacker can experience numerous pass actions. Unless on a stunt or in cover-age, he must get upfield and contain the quarterback.

This is a relatively simple recognition on long-yardage downs versus pocket passes. With play-action throws on run downs it gets stickier for the outside linebacker (see figures 16.13 and 16.14).

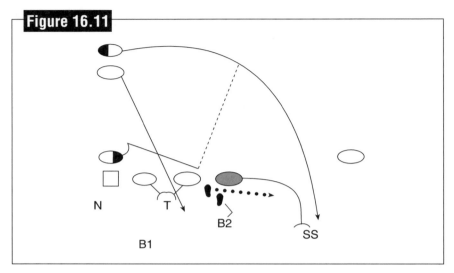

B2 feathers QB and then pursues with depth behind the line to pitch (dotted lines).

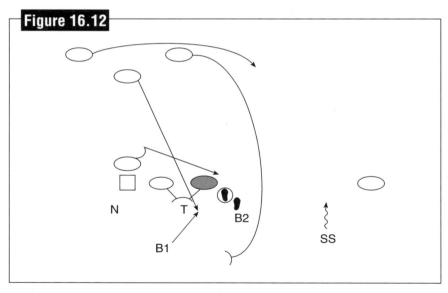

B1 presses FB. B2 feathers QB. The SS has pitch on our base triple-option defense.

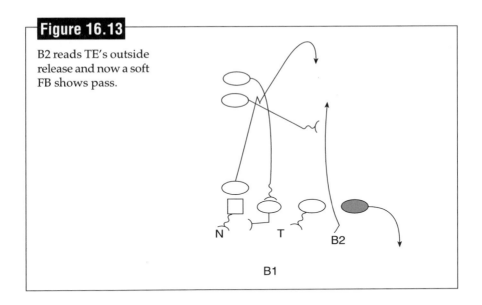

Figure 16.13

B2 reads TE's outside release and now a soft FB shows pass.

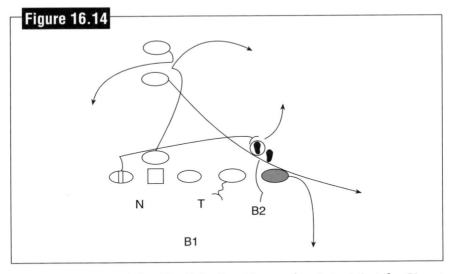

Figure 16.14

B2 reads G's pull and the QB off the line. He uses hands to defeat the G's cut block.

Inside Block

The wide 5 linebacker aligns inside the tight end and should *never* permit the end to block inside him. This is a cardinal error. When a tight end tries to block inside, the linebacker must squeeze him down inside to protect the inside linebacker, B1 (see figure 16.15).

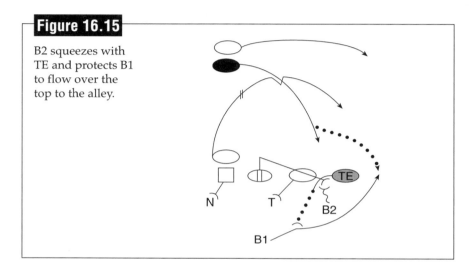

Figure 16.15

B2 squeezes with TE and protects B1 to flow over the top to the alley.

When the next blocker attacks, the wide 5 linebacker should play him inside-out and bubble the ball carrier to the inside linebacker, B1, who is working free in figure 16.15.

If a tight end is assigned to block B1, we force him to release outside and around the wide 5 linebacker, never inside him.

Cut-Off

When the tight end's headgear comes inside the frame of the linebacker's body quickly, it is a run play away. Often the end will attempt to cut the rush's outside leg with a low chop block to get him off his feet.

The linebacker steps toward his key and then reacts to the low helmet by putting his inside hand on the opponent's helmet and outside hand on the tight end's shoulder pads. The wide 5 technique should maintain inside leverage on the end to defend his 5 gap. The athlete must defend cutbacks curling back to him (see figure 16.16).

Anytime flow goes away from a 5 gap player, he should squeeze square, looking for inside blocking threats as he does with the counter, reviewed in figure 16.10. Then the linebacker must close

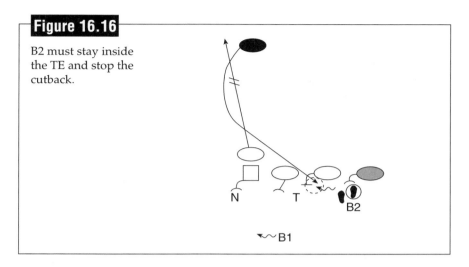

Figure 16.16

B2 must stay inside
the TE and stop the
cutback.

N   T

B2

B1

the area between himself and the nearest inside defender while
checking for cutbacks, reverses, and naked bootlegs.

With reverse, the wide 5 technique should see it coming or hear
"reverse." When he recognizes reverse, the linebacker needs to get
vertical quickly and aggressively attack the outside edge of the runner. He should force the runner inside (see figure 16.17). A looping
tight end or quarterback will usually have the assignment of blocking the rush near the line of scrimmage.

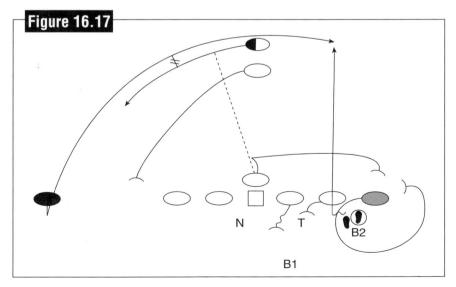

Figure 16.17

N   T

B2

B1

B2 is challenged with a reverse. He must get upfield and disrupt it.

Responsibilities

The wide 5 linebacker is responsible for any runs to his tackle-end gap. With option frontside, the linebacker has the quarterback regardless of the blocking scheme. When the tight end engages him, he should get help in the alley outside the end. Versus run away, the 5 gap linebacker must squeeze inside and check for cutbacks, reverses, and naked bootlegs. When pass shows, the outside linebacker either drops in coverage or rushes with contain responsibility. With a pass key the rush needs to be aware of draw. When he hears "draw" or feels it, he should sprint back to the line of scrimmage, retracing the path that got him there. Rushers too often run around the pass protector and open up a huge hole for draws (see figure 16.18).

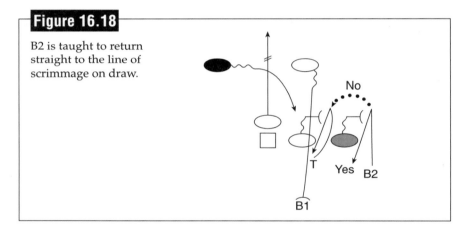

Figure 16.18

B2 is taught to return straight to the line of scrimmage on draw.

Adjustments

- The key can vary from tight end to offensive tackle by opponent or by down and distance. On long-yardage downs, we usually have the rush key the football, not anyone at the line, to get a jump on his pass rush.
- In pass situations or when the defense has spotted pass stances on the offensive line, the wide 5 technique should get into his best pass-rush stance and key the ball.
- Versus a split end, the linebacker can stay in a wide 5 alignment over the ghost of the tight end or move down to the tackle in a loose 5 technique, that we will discuss later in this chapter. In either case he would key the near tackle.

- When the tight end flexes up to three yards, the linebacker should stay in a wide 5 alignment and key the end. When the end widens more than three yards, the linebacker should close down and play a loose 5 technique.

Wide 5 Types

A younger performer can play this technique if he has the physical tools. It requires few mental adjustments, but a standout rush must be a natural pass rusher and also be able to punish tight ends one-on-one versus the run.

Our most productive rushes have been in the Alfred Williams and Simeon Rice mold. Their height, long arms, and acceleration made them imposing figures. Surprisingly, some shorter nose guards have made the transition to wide 5 technique rather well. Traditionally, the wide 5 linebacker has led our defenses in sacks and often in minus-yardage plays.

Loose 5 Technique

We have discussed this technique previously in this chapter because it is the prime method of play the rush linebacker uses when aligned to a split end. He still has the same inside support from his team-mates but has no outside threat from a tight end. Now almost all blockers come from the inside, and the tackle becomes his focus before the snap.

Most rush linebackers prefer loose 5 over wide 5 because the key is truer, the tight end does not disrupt the pass rush, and all threats are in the vision of the linebacker's key.

Alignment

Our loose 5 linebacker aligns in a three-point stance with his inside foot slightly back at a toe-to-instep relationship with the outside foot. His feet are about shoulder-width apart, just as described for the wide 5 stance.

Now the rush puts his inside foot on the inside edge of the offensive tackle's outside foot. His depth will vary depending on the quickness of his first step and his experience. As with the wide 5, begin inexperienced players deeper until they can set their base confidently versus those big tackles.

Key

The linebacker keys the tackle's helmet unless faced with a heavy pass tendency. If pass is indicated he will key the ball while choosing his pass-rush strategy.

Tackle Reads

The tackle reads are simple and true compared to reading the tight end. Today's tackles are huge, but a linebacker's movement is a real advantage for him in the alley.

Base Block

When the tackle's headgear moves, the linebacker attacks him with a short power step with the near foot setting the base. He should launch the hand punch with hip thrust off that base. He should place both hands in the chest plate with thumbs up. The linebacker should control the line of scrimmage, keeping his outside arm free.

A base block will generally indicate an inside play such as an isolation. The loose 5 must squeeze the tackle's block and anticipate the ball bouncing out to his free arm. He must stay square by keeping his inside foot up. That foot position is fundamental for his alley pursuit. He must be able to push off the inside foot and open his hips to the alley.

Reach Block

The linebacker should step with his inside foot. As he reads the helmet of the tackle reaching toward him, he should widen with him and drive upfield, keeping his shoulders square to the line. The loose 5's width and speed advantages over the tackle should serve him well. Now the defender must lock out his arms to get separation from the tackle's body and keep his feet moving.

As the linebacker controls the tackle's reach block, he should try to force the ball outside. He then accelerates to the ball carrier, leaving the tackle behind (see figure 16.19).

Other Blocks

All the other blocks described in the wide 5 section of this chapter pertain to the loose 5 technique. Review the figures 16.7 to 16.17. Only those in which the tight end engages the linebacker are inappropriate because no tight end exists for the loose 5 linebacker.

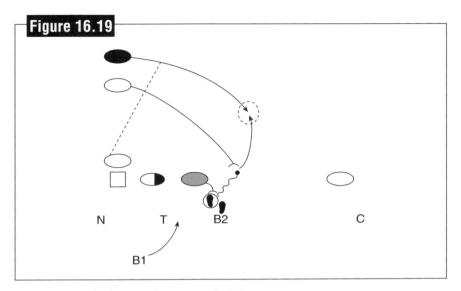

Figure 16.19

B2 defeats reach, then machine guns the FB.

These two techniques are naturally compatible. The near foot is inside for the loose 5 and outside for the wide 5, but both have identical gap duties and react to the non-tight end blocks alike.

Responsibilities

Resposibilities are identical to those of the wide 5 technique (see page 231).

Adjustments

- The loose 5 keys the tackle unless it is an obvious pass situation. The linebacker then keys the ball and rushes the passer first while reacting to run schemes.
- The loose 5 can also widen his alignment extensively on definite pass downs to add horizontal pressure on the tackle.

Chapter 17

7 and 9 Techniques

The final two techniques that we will explore involve outside line-backers. These two are more closely related than any others we have examined. Most packages that employ one use the second as a varia-tion. Against a tight end, the two can be indistinguishable. Against a split end, the differences are more readily apparent.

We describe both techniques by single digits in our terminology. That means these players are generally responsible for one gap and often play at or close to the line of scrimmage. Specifically, the 7 technique is an alley player who must have someone with contain duties to his outside, while the 9 technique is the "outside post" in the swinging gate (see figure 16.2). All his help is to the inside (see figure 17.1).

In figure 17.1, B1 and B2 can look identical to the untrained eye. To a tight end, however, the perimeter play of the two will be

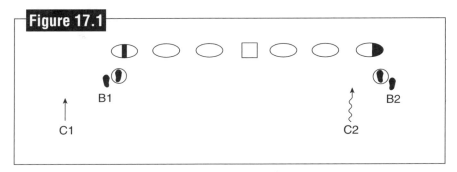

B1 is a 7 technique while B2 is a 9 technique. Notice how the corner support differs for the two techniques.

distinctly different. The 7 technique relies on C1 being the outside post, while the 9 technique (B2) funnels everything inside to C2.

Although the alignments of the 7 and 9 techniques can seem similar, the physical characteristics can vary decidedly. It is rare to find an athlete who can perform the techniques equally well. In my more than 30 seasons, I have only had two: Kanavis McGhee of Colorado, an NFL second-round draft choice, and Kevin Hardy of Illinois. These two could not only muscle with large tight ends but also be finesse players as wider-playing 9 techniques.

Usually a coach recruits to a 7 or 9 technique based on his scheme. Often he changes his defensive structure because of the outside linebacker personnel available. I began my career coaching 7 techniques as a base. In 1980 at Virginia Tech, we took a 191-pound backup strong safety and moved him to drop linebacker. Rick Miley became the prototype 9 technique in our scheme.

The cunning Miley couldn't muscle with the physical tight ends but he sure could finesse them. We sold him on the fact that quickness was his ally and that ends feared his athletic ability. Rick and many drop linebackers that followed him were productive despite their lack of size because they understood their roles.

Because these techniques are so closely bonded and similar in many reactions, we will work through them together for their alignment over a tight end. We will separate their play to a split end in the adjustment section.

Alignment

The 7 technique places his inside foot to split the body of the tight end. He is in a two-point stance with feet shoulder-width apart. He bends his body at the ankles, knees, and hips to produce maximum force in just one step. His eyes must focus on the end's helmet, and the linebacker's hands are waist high ready to punch as the front foot hits the ground.

Coaches set their 7 technique's feet in numerous positions. Most settings can be effective. It is imperative only that on contact the inside foot is in advance (that is, closer to the line of scrimmage), as described in chapter 3. We prefer that the feet be nearly even because the initial step can be with either foot.

The 9 technique aligns wider. We have him place his inside foot opposite the outside foot of the tight end. Review figure 17.1. We teach the same stances to both techniques.

Key

When aligned to a tight end, the outside linebacker keys the end's headgear first and then keys through the nearest blocker to the ball. When pass rushing on obvious pass down, the linebacker can look at the ball first.

Tight End Reads

The following descriptions outline the reactions of the 7 and 9 techniques to the various movements by the tight end key. The challenge for the coach is to present all these blocking patterns in early training sessions, but then curtail those used during game weeks so the outside linebackers gain confidence defending a limited number of schemes.

Base Block

This block usually indicates that the offense is running inside. The only threat to the outside linebacker is the ball bouncing outside. It is essential that the linebacker keep his inside foot up and his shoulders square so he can neutralize the block, and more important, so he can push off the inside foot to run down the bounces. Figure 17.2 illustrates the base block.

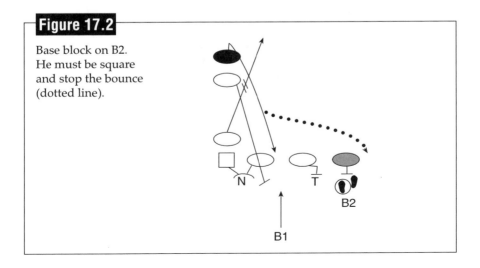

Figure 17.2

Base block on B2. He must be square and stop the bounce (dotted line).

Neither technique can afford to peek inside until the ball crosses the line of scrimmage. Nor can the 7 technique run around the tight end's block. This would open a large 5 gap seam inside.

Most 9 techniques are overcoached on the base block. Coaches often browbeat this finesse player to hunker down and get gritty against a block he doesn't have to master. What if the 9 technique is driven for width on an inside play? The 5 gap defender and the alley player should make the play for a negligible gain anyway (see figure 17.3).

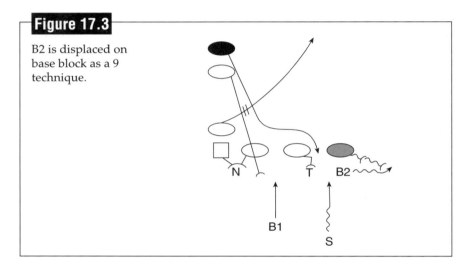

Figure 17.3

B2 is displaced on base block as a 9 technique.

N   T   B2

B1

S

Yes, I want the 9 technique to be physical, and we work him one-on-one against burly tight ends in camp. But I'm not going to become bent out of shape or make him feel inadequate over a low-priority block. For the 7 technique it's a point to emphasize, but not for the 9 technique.

Kanavis McGhee entered Colorado at six-foot-three, 210. We recruited him to be a crafty drop linebacker. By the time he was a senior, he was a substantial 240 pounds. As a freshman, Kanavis did not have success in our one-on-one drills versus the base block. He understood, however, that it was not critical to his position. His ego was not damaged in the process.

When the tight end blocks and option develops, both linebackers take the quarterback. The 7 technique does so because he always has a teammate outside him assigned for pitch. The 9 technique plays the quarterback when engaged by the end because he knows that the alley player (S in figure 17.4) will overlap to the pitch on the end's block (see figure 17.4).

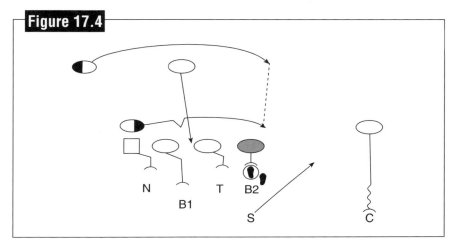

Figure 17.4

B2 takes QB as a 9 technique. The safety is free to take the pitch on the TE's block.

Reach Block

This single block defines the differences between the 7 and 9 technique linebackers better than any other. The reach block usually warns of a perimeter run, and that is where these two styles of play differ most dramatically.

As the 7 technique sees the tight end's head move outside, he steps toward it and attacks the end, much as he did versus the base block. He wants to control the end at the line, keeping his outside arm free. He drives the tight end backward and forces the ball to bounce outside to his help, the contain defensive back (see figure 17.5).

The 9 technique, on the other hand, *is* the contain player. Of all the blocks he faces, this is the one he must really anticipate and enjoy. When the tight end's helmet gains width, this linebacker steps with his outside foot laterally to maintain his outside leverage. Then he forcefully crosses over with his inside foot and works upfield to an ideal point that is two yards wider and two yards deeper than the end's original stance (see figure 17.6).

A savvy 9 technique knows that his help is all on the inside. In figure 17.6, four teammates can make a play when the 9 technique turns the ball carrier inside. None can make it for a negligible gain

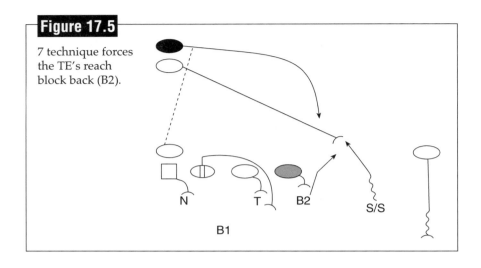

Figure 17.5

7 technique forces the TE's reach block back (B2).

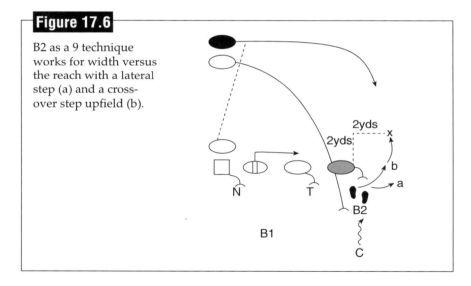

Figure 17.6

B2 as a 9 technique works for width versus the reach with a lateral step (a) and a cross-over step upfield (b).

when the ball goes outside the linebacker. A smaller, active linebacker can thrive against big ends with this technique. Jesse Penn was 215 pounds yet mastered this method against much larger opponents at end. He was tremendous in space to a split end, and this finesse technique allowed him success over tight ends, too. The Virginia Tech product followed in the Rick Miley mold, and the Dallas Cowboys drafted him in the second round.

Inside Block

There are a host of plays and second blocking threats ⟨when⟩ the tight end blocks inside. Fortunately, a single offen⟨se⟩ portion of the pictures we will discuss.

Generally, when the end blocks inside, the linebacker⟨s⟩ squeeze him. The 7 technique should protect the inside line⟨backer⟩ from the end's direct path. The 9 technique aligns wider and wi⟨ll be⟩ less able to disrupt the tight end. A defensive back, however, shoul⟨d⟩ fill off the end's tail when the end blocks inside versus a 9 technique.

Both linebackers should step inside with their inside foot, jamming the end with their hands. As they close inside they should shuffle to get their inside foot up and shoulders square to the line. They should point their feet upfield and search inside for the next blocking threat.

Outside linebackers must learn to tell the difference between an inside block and an inside pass release by the end. On pass, the tight end's head will be higher and his path more vertical as he runs his routes.

Let's investigate some of the standard inside blocking patterns we see.

Power

We train both techniques to play the power in the same fashion. The 7 technique, because of his alignment, can squeeze the hole more effectively and get a better jam on the tight end.

The linebacker must slide inside off his jam of the tight end. "One step is not enough, three is usually too many, two is just right," is a saying John Gutekunst used at Virginia Tech while coaching our drop linebackers. The key is to stay on the line of scrimmage and not get upfield, which creates a vertical seam for the runner. The defender should take on the fullback with his inside foot and shoulder. Should the ball bounce outside, he is in position to push off the inside foot in pursuit (see figure 17.7).

Several times in the past nine years we have had our outside linebackers wrong shoulder the power. Some defenses do it regularly. We have made that decision based on our personnel. The theory we have is that the wrong-shoulder method is effective if the outside linebacker can eliminate two blockers himself. Then, when the ball bounces to the alley a teammate can make the tackle.

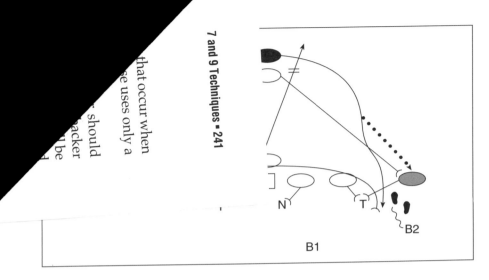

Wrong shoulder means that the 7 or 9 technique would hit the fullback with his outside shoulder and take the pulling guard with him (see figure 17.8). Now B1 realizes that the ball should bounce and that he must replace the 7 technique in the alley or the 9 technique with contain. Often we felt that our inside linebacker did not have the speed to make that tackle consistently in space.

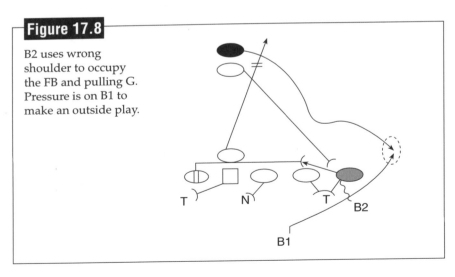

Figure 17.8

B2 uses wrong shoulder to occupy the FB and pulling G. Pressure is on B1 to make an outside play.

Option

Offenses use many blocking schemes for the option, but whenever the tight end blocks on the outside linebacker or inside, our 7 or 9 is responsible for quarterback. Both will have defenders outside them on the pitch when the end blocks inside.

Again, the linebacker should stay square and position his inside foot up so he can break to the pitch when the ball is dealt outside. The coaches must inform the linebacker of the quarterback's option ability. With an average quarterback, the 7 or 9 technique should play beneath the line of scrimmage and anticipate a pitch. He should never turn toward an option quarterback, even a great one. The linebacker must always slow play the option runner to give his teammates time to pursue (see figure 17.9).

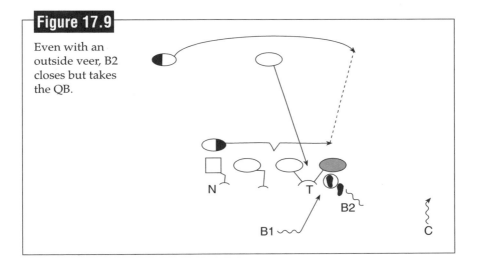

Figure 17.9

Even with an outside veer, B2 closes but takes the QB.

G Block

We used to see this block a lot, but it still needs work in camp. If the linebacker just follows his inside block progression, he will be fine.

The linebacker should squeeze the tight end's block and set his base with his inside foot to take on the guard pull. That will compress the hole and put the 7 or 9 technique in position to push off the inside foot for the bounce or quarterback (see figure 17.10).

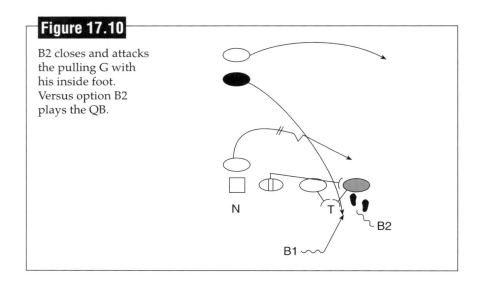

Figure 17.10

B2 closes and attacks the pulling G with his inside foot. Versus option B2 plays the QB.

T Block

In 1978 at Virginia Tech we began calling this blocking pattern the Virginia block because our bitter rival used it. It is still in vogue but not something we see weekly during the season. The purpose is to get the outside linebacker to squeeze with the tight end and then hook him with the pulling tackle. Versus a 9 technique some offenses have tried to kick the linebacker out and run inside him.

The real solution is to get into the tackle's mustache quickly before he gets moving very far. The 7 technique can attack more tightly. The 9 technique must gain width to turn it back to his inside help (see figure 17.11).

Counter

Once again this play begins with the end blocking inside. The 7 or 9 technique squeezes and will see all backs going away while the backside guard and tackle pull toward him. He should continue to slide inside with hips square to the line and his inside foot set just before contact with the pulling guard (see figure 17.12). We want to squeeze inside, and B2 is always ready for the bounce-out.

When the pulling tackle stays directly behind the guard, we have used the "bowling ball" adjustment. B2 dives at the feet of the guard, tripping both pullers and forcing the ball carrier to bubble.

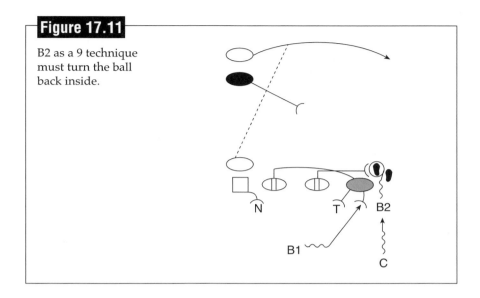

Figure 17.11

B2 as a 9 technique must turn the ball back inside.

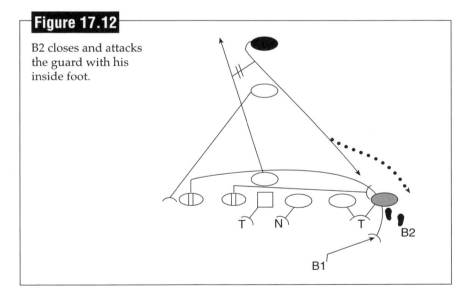

Figure 17.12

B2 closes and attacks the guard with his inside foot.

Pass

The maturity of an outside linebacker is often affirmed by his reaction to play-action pass. Through film study and experience, he can distinguish between an inside block and an inside pass release. It is difficult to fool a savvy 7 or 9 technique, even with play-action passes, because he discerns the end's intentions by his release. Often an end will flex wider, ever so slightly, and a veteran outside linebacker will perceive pass before the snap.

Figure 17.13 demonstrates such a release. The end's head will be high and going downfield. As the linebacker reads release, his vision should go inside to his next key. He will usually see the tackle in a pass set.

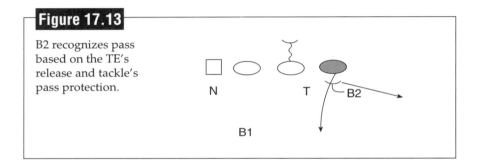

Figure 17.13

B2 recognizes pass based on the TE's release and tackle's pass protection.

The linebacker should jam the end with his hands and then react to his pass responsibility. As a 9 technique, he will usually be flat in zone coverage. A 7 technique normally would have a more restricted zone drop. Either could be in man or asked to contain rush on this key read.

Against action pass to the outside linebacker in zone, it must be very clear about when he contains a scrambling quarterback. In our system, a zone linebacker stays in coverage no matter how tempting it is to charge the passer on the run (see figure 17.14).

In this particular coverage B2 is the only defender who can take away the tight end's route. B1 is forced to help the defensive tackle contain, while B2 can come up only after the quarterback crosses the line of scrimmage.

Backside Blocks

When the tight end's headgear goes inside and the backfield action starts away, the linebacker must first check for a lineman pulling toward him, such as the counter in figure 17.12 or the reverse in figure 17.15. We call this a *mental trail*.

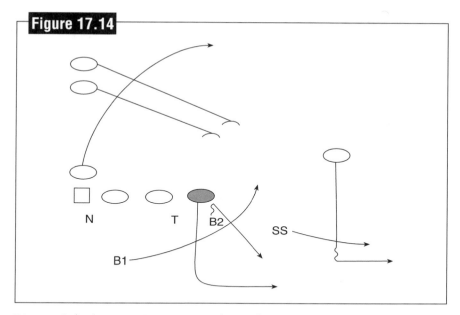

B2 must fight the natural tendency to charge the QB and stay in coverage.

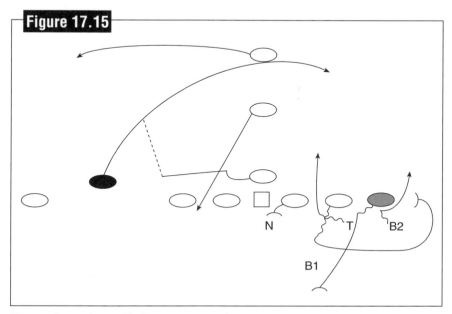

B2 must be patient with flow away to stop a reverse.

When run is away, the linebacker must shuffle down the line of scrimmage with hips square, compressing the area between himself and the 5 gap defender. He cannot take a deeper pursuit angle until he is positive the ball carrier has crossed the line. This attention to detail stops many huge runs (see figure 17.16).

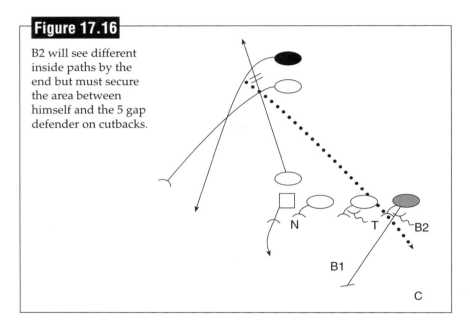

Figure 17.16

B2 will see different inside paths by the end but must secure the area between himself and the 5 gap defender on cutbacks.

If the defensive package has the 5 gap player upfield chasing the ball on flow away, the 7 or 9 technique must fold under him. Those two backside defenders must coordinate their movements (see figure 17.17).

When the tight end simply drives his helmet to the linebacker's inside jersey number, he is attempting to position himself between the defender and the ball carrier. The linebacker must attack the end with his inside foot and deliver a closing hip roll. He must drive the end inside and backward while he anticipates cutback (see figure 17.18).

Arc Releases

These tight end blocks are distinguishable from the reach blocks because the end's helmet is higher and pointed away from the line-

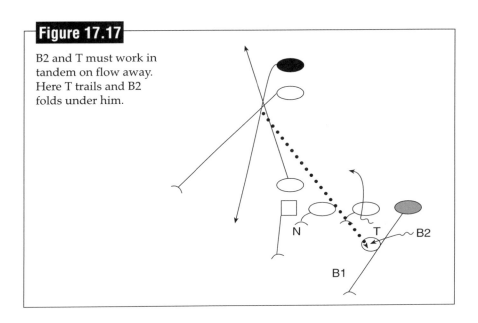

Figure 17.17

B2 and T must work in tandem on flow away. Here T trails and B2 folds under him.

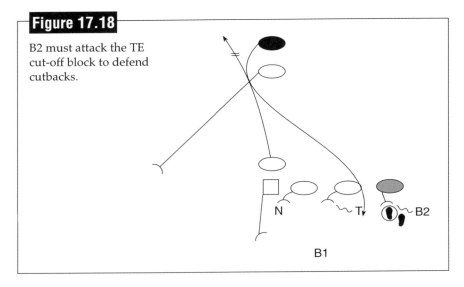

Figure 17.18

B2 must attack the TE cut-off block to defend cutbacks.

backer. Similarly, however, the arc release can point out the variation between 7 and 9 technique responsibilities.

With each of the plays, the linebacker should engage the tight end and ride him as he reads run or pass.

Option

The 7 technique knows that the secondary is rolled up outside him and has pitch. He is also aware that someone inside him should overlap to the quarterback. Therefore, the 7 technique can ride the tight end arc and defend the dump pass to him. Once option shows, he can come off the end and help as the alley player. When a teammate takes the quarterback, he can stretch to the pitch. If the option quarterback is running free, the 7 technique can constrict and feather him as described previously (see figure 17.19).

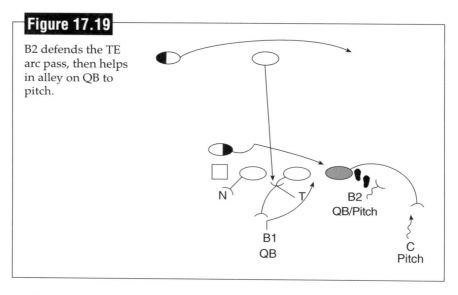

Figure 17.19

B2 defends the TE arc pass, then helps in alley on QB to pitch.

The 9 technique reacts with a completely different set of circumstances. With an arc by the tight end, this linebacker has pitch alone. He rides the end for width and then disengages to get upfield to the back. His inside help, a defensive back, defends the dump pass (see figure 17.20).

Sprint Draw

As the tight end arcs, the linebacker must ride him as he did versus the option. Quickly, he will recognize that all backs are inside and the near back is on a kick-out path toward him.

Now the sprint draw becomes just like the power described earlier. The 7 and 9 techniques must constrict and take on the near back with outside leverage (see figure 17.21).

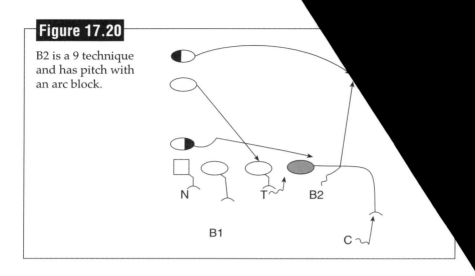

Figure 17.20

B2 is a 9 technique and has pitch with an arc block.

N T B2 B1 C

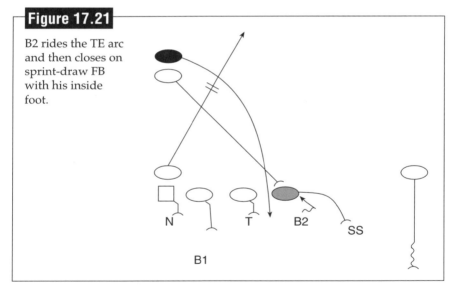

Figure 17.21

B2 rides the TE arc and then closes on sprint-draw FB with his inside foot.

N T B2 SS B1

We are now seeing little of this play to 7 and 9 linebackers. The tight end does influence the linebacker for width, but without the end blocking inside, the 5 gap defensive tackle is a thorn to this scheme.

Sprint-Draw Pass

Proportionately, we see much more sprint-draw pass to the 7 and 9 techniques than we do sprint draw. Now the linebacker rides the

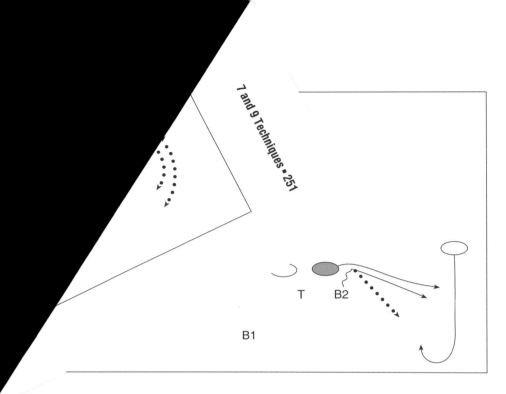

tight end. When he recognizes pass by the quarterback's action or the fullback's soft path, he must drop to his coverage responsibility (see figure 17.22) or rush the quarterback as his scheme dictates.

Pass Block

When a tight end shows pass protection immediately, the linebacker should drop to his zone, recognizing that draw is also possible. This block occurs regularly with some opponents when the end is on the backside of twins or trips as the widest receiver. The staff may consider rushing the outside linebacker and voiding the zone when the tendencies warrant it.

7 Technique Responsibilities

This linebacker is responsible for the 7 gap at the inside edge of the alley. With an inside block by the tight end, the linebacker is expected to protect the inside linebacker by jamming the end and compressing the gap. Versus option, the 7 technique always has quarterback first and then overlaps to pitch. With run away the linebacker squeezes, checking for counters, reverses, and cutbacks. Against pass the 7 technique drops or rushes as the coverage demands.

9 Technique Responsibilities

- This linebacker has contain duties versus the run when the tight end blocks outside.
- With an inside block by the tight end, the linebacker reacts just as the 7 technique does, but he cannot be expected to protect the inside linebacker from the end.
- Versus option, the 9 technique uses the block read. When the tight end blocks the outside linebacker or blocks inside, the 9 technique plays the quarterback. When the end arc blocks, the 9 technique works to the pitch immediately.
- The 9 technique's backside run duties are the same as the 7's.
- Versus pass, both linebackers drop or rush as the coverage demands.

7 Technique Adjustments

Most defensive packages place the 7 technique linebacker to the strength of a formation. We will review his adjustments within that framework.

- When he aligns to a wing, a 7 technique could maintain his normal alignment. A corner would outflank the wing so that the deployment would look sound on paper as shown in figure 17.23.

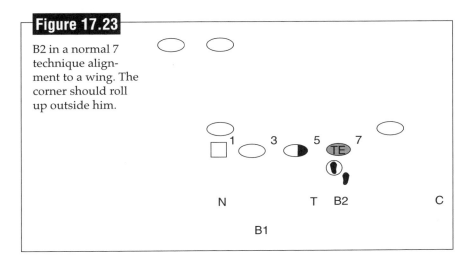

Figure 17.23

B2 in a normal 7 technique alignment to a wing. The corner should roll up outside him.

Unfortunately, if the wing is another big body (that is, a second tight end) a strong run threat toward B2 exists. We would normally put B2 in a three-point stance and penetrate the 7 gap with him when faced with this strong run potential.

If the wing were a wide receiver and deemed no blocking threat, our normal alignment in figure 17.23 would be satisfactory. We would train the outside linebacker to recognize the type of opposition he had and to adjust accordingly. We have even permitted him to check to a line slant in that direction when warranted.

▪ With twins or trips to his side there is no longer a tight end. Now the 7 technique must move out into space (see figure 17.24).

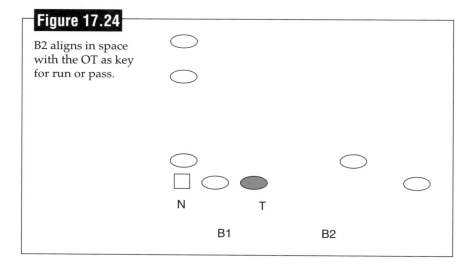

Figure 17.24

B2 aligns in space with the OT as key for run or pass.

N   T

B1   B2

Linebacker B2 keys the near tackle for run or pass. With run, he attacks the line of scrimmage, ready to jam the nearest wide receiver with his outside foot or a backfield blocker with his inside foot. Versus pass, B2 opens to the Z receiver and follows his coverage rules.

9 Technique Adjustments

A 9 technique in our defensive package can play to the strong or weak side. When on the strong side, we attempt to adjust as we did with the 7 technique. When on the weak side, more adjustments are usually required.

▪ Any coach caught unprepared for an unbalanced line never wants to be in that situation again. Most offenses have some form of it, but we defend it only twice per season on average. We work it every week, however, so our players are certain to recognize it and adjust.

Early in fall camp we teach our outside linebackers to identify and communicate unbalanced looks. We drill it in individual periods the first week in spring practice and in team shortly thereafter.

When an outside linebacker has no tight end and no wide receiver to his side, he has an unbalanced line. He must feel confident that he can identify it and make the appropriate checks to the defense.

Early in my Big Ten career, Wisconsin played nearly the whole first quarter in a variety of unbalanced looks. It surprised the staff, but our drop linebacker recognized it immediately and thwarted the Badger's extensive plans in those sets. By the same token Gary Moeller had Michigan go for an important two-point play, and it was the only unbalanced formation of the day. Our drop linebacker did not make a quick, forceful adjustment, and Michigan scored. The lesson was that we must train our defenders so well that they make those adaptations the first time.

Most unbalanced looks we defend have about three basic plays. Five plays designed specifically for an unbalanced set would be highly unusual. Be sound, but be able to adjust quickly and confidently.

▪ When the 9 technique aligns to a split end with a three-deep zone shell behind him, he can soundly adjust to a *walk* or *hip* location.

The *walk 9* puts the linebacker three to four yards deep, midway between the 5 gap defender and the split end (see figure 17.25).

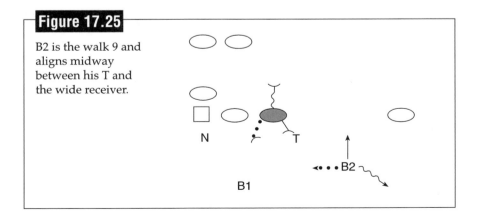

Figure 17.25

B2 is the walk 9 and aligns midway between his T and the wide receiver.

As a walk linebacker, B2 keys the tackle for run or pass. With run action to him, he has contain and always the pitch on option. With run away, B2 works with backside leverage, anticipating cutbacks. When the tackle shows pass, B2 assumes his coverage duties.

We use the *hip 9* alignment with some specialized coverages to get the outside linebacker closer to the forcing unit. It is also a favorite with the three-deep zone, particularly when the 9 technique is into the high school or college boundary. It is an excellent blitz position (see figure 17.26).

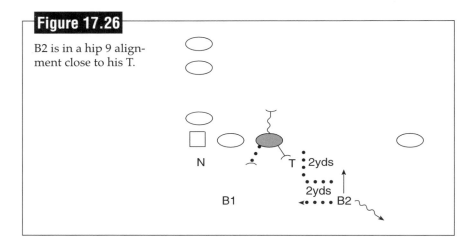

Figure 17.26

B2 is in a hip 9 alignment close to his T.

As a hip linebacker, B2 has the same keys and responsibilities that he had as a walk linebacker in figure 17.25. With the ball on the hash, however, B2 can still be a factor on throws to the split end while being a strong run force from the hip.

▪ When the 9 technique aligns to a split end with a two-deep shell behind him, we adjust with a *far* alignment. The far 9 linebacker begins with his outside foot covering the inside foot of the split end receiver, three to four yards deep (see figure 17.27).

The far 9 aligns inside the split end so he can be a forceful frontside run player. The split end has poor leverage to put his body between the linebacker and a perimeter run. On run away, B2 pursues with backside leverage for cutbacks and reverses. He is also critical on deep pursuit away.

Versus pass, the far 9 linebacker sinks straight back to take away the vertical route of the split end until the halves corner can break to it.

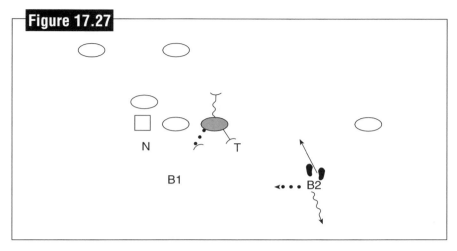

Figure 17.27

B2 is in a far 9 adjustment over the wide receiver.

Early in the scheme we actually cocked the far 9 toward the split end receiver, keying him. When the split end blocked the linebacker, we attacked him and then played inside him at the line. When the split end released for pass, the linebacker rotated his hips inside for vision on the ball as he retreated.

7 and 9 Technique Types

The player who can excel at these techniques is an excellent athlete and usually an experienced performer. Strength is a real priority for a 7 technique. A finesse defender can play the 9 technique. In fact, when he is in space, a strong safety is ideally suited to play hip 9, walk 9, or far 9. In pass situations we often substitute a second-team defensive back for our drop linebacker.

Normally our 9 techniques have been six-foot-two to six-foot-four and in the 215 to 225 range. They are usually excellent basketball players who have real ball sense.

Because of the coverages this is a more demanding position mentally than the wide or loose 5 techniques. Although it is not uncommon for a freshman to play our rush linebacker, rarely does a rookie play the 7 or 9 technique in our scheme.

Part V

TEACHING AND LEARNING

This section is directed primarily to coaches, but serious students of the game will also benefit from the information. Each chapter deals with a different aspect of teaching and learning. Coaching is teaching. Learning is critical to the success of playing linebacker.

Chapter 18 discusses the player-coach relationship and teaching style, along with tips for increased learning in the classroom and on the field. Chapter 19 speaks specifically to the organization of linebacker training sessions on the field. Chapter 20 looks at how a grading system can have special benefits for both coach and player.

Chapter 18

Teaching Style

A coach's teaching style arises from values he learns through the course of his life. The home usually provides the strongest influence on what he believes is important. That was certainly true in my case, and those values greatly influenced my philosophy on teaching.

I was born in September 1945 in Latrobe, Pennsylvania, known then and now for producing the legendary golfer Arnold Palmer. I was raised in Keystone, a village with a population of slightly over 60, located on a lake about 40 miles southeast of Pittsburgh.

Keystone had a convenience store that was open only during the summer for the fishermen who used the lake. There was no gas station, not even a zip code.

The men of Keystone were laborers and the women, housewives. No one in our town's history had ever gone to college until my oldest sister, Nancy, attended Indiana State Teacher's College, about 30 miles away. My father, Lou Senior, had an eighth-grade education. That was not atypical in towns like Keystone. My mother, Frances, had a high school diploma and always stressed education as the key to our futures. Mom would prove to be an inspiration to all of us by going to college late in her 40s to earn a degree. By the time Pat, my youngest sister, came along, we expected her to have a college experience. Nancy had set a standard. What a positive influence our parents had been for education.

I was the second in Keystone to attend college, thanks to football. Football was my passion. My parents used it to motivate me academically, as thousands of parents and coaches do each year. If my grades were not acceptable, I couldn't play. No other lines needed to be drawn for me. I worked academically to please my family and to play college football.

By 1963, four colleges—Rutgers, Penn, Cornell, and Rochester Polytechnical Institute—courted me seriously. I tell my players today that only those four institutions could even find Keystone, but that is stretching the truth just a bit.

I remember distinctly two events surrounding my decision to attend Rutgers College. First was the official visit to New Brunswick. I had never been on an airplane before. My parents bought me an expensive coat because they did not want me to be embarrassed while at Rutgers. On Friday evening, I arrived at the fraternity house where I was to spend the night. I casually hung my new jacket inside the door. The next morning I awoke and—you guessed it—my coat had been stolen. In 17 years of living in Keystone, I had experienced theft only once. That burglar stole a saddle, a piggy bank, and a pistol. To this day I cannot understand the mentality that prompts people to take something they have not earned.

The second defining event was the school visit by Dr. John Bateman, the Rutgers head coach. Coach Bateman met me at Derry Area High School to finalize my commitment. I was in awe. But what he did next put Rutgers in the lead permanently and influenced my recruiting as a coach for an entire career.

Coach Bateman took me out of school with him to visit my father. Dad was pumping gas at a one-bay garage on Ligonier Street in Latrobe. He had no help. Dr. Bateman, in shirt and tie, rolled up his sleeves and helped pump gas so he could talk to my father about Rutgers. Dad could not believe that a man of his status would spend hours helping a common laborer and his son.

That evening after the visit, Dad asked me what I thought of Rutgers. I told him that Rutgers was my first choice, and Dad responded, "Good, because that's where you are going!" Dad didn't know if Rutgers was better for me academically. He rarely saw me play in high school or college, but he knew John Bateman to be an honorable man, without a hint of arrogance. He would entrust his only son to John Bateman.

Keystone of the 1960s seems like a foreign town amidst today's values. I do not remember a divorce or even a separation in my 17 years there. A man's word was his bond. If you weren't going to do it, you had better not say it. Men kept their promises to their wives and children.

On the Rutgers campus, I met Bill Regan, one of 22 freshmen quarterbacks on our squad. Bill's father was a legendary high school coach in New Jersey. We both wanted to teach. We had similar values and forged a lifelong friendship. Bill has been a highly regarded and successful coach at Morris Knolls High School for over 25 years. Together we composed a common philosophy that I have used ever since. The words may not be verbatim, but this was my version for our staff policy book some 30 years later. Our shared feelings produced this teaching philosophy:

> Our football program should be an integral part of the education system. Football itself is neither good nor bad, it is a tool. Like any other tool, what it creates depends upon the design of the craftsman. Because of the immense popularity of football, it is perhaps the most unique tool in education today. It can be used to greatly influence the values of young men who partake in it. It also influences behavior of thousands of fans who see our student-athletes and imitate them. As much as we work toward winning, let's remember our role as teachers and our responsibility to use football to improve the lives of our young men.

Staff Qualities

What qualities make a linebacker coach special? Certainly he needs a base of knowledge and experience, but there is much more.

Three criteria are critical for success as a coach: hard work, loyalty, and a care for kids. A person must work diligently in any profession to have success. A coach does not punch a time clock, but he must be sure to turn over all stones to prepare a team for victory. When a coach has studied all situations and forged a detailed game plan, then it's time to go home. Until the coach has studied and determined the two-point play, for example, he cannot call the game plan finished. To do so would not be fair to anyone in the program.

Loyalty is a strong key on any staff. By signing a contract the coach commits himself to the team's effort. He should make only positive statements in public. Once the staff makes a decision, arguments cease and they go full-speed ahead to accomplish it together.

Many coaches *say* they love their players. That statement requires a lot of effort. A coach must be willing to get to know his men. He must be willing to devote time to their personal and academic lives.

Courtesy of Dewey King

When I entered Rutgers in the fall of 1963, I did not know **Dewey King.** Dewey was the Scarlet Knight's defensive coordinator. He was a proven strategist and had led the Rutgers defense to national recognition. Dewey wrote a celebrated book on pass defense entitled *Jericho.* He later became a Division I head coach at San Jose State. He influenced numerous lives and careers, including mine.

As a freshman, I played our six-game schedule as a running back. After the season Coach King approached me about playing defense for him that spring.

Rutgers College, nestled along the Raritan River in New Jersey, had only about 4,000 students on the campus in 1963. The King family lived in a dormitory on the Quad. The dorm next to theirs was Hegeman Hall, and I lived at 414 Hegeman. On warm days, students could hear and see Dewey's young children, Doug and Tiger, frolic in the courtyard. Players met weekly in his home for Fellowship of Christian Athletes meetings. All were welcome. Coach King's wife, Peg, was a mother substitute for many. We got to know Coach King personally. I liked what I saw. I wanted to play for him, and later I'd want to teach like him.

What made Dewey King so special? He did, absolutely, know his defensive scheme. There was a legitimacy about him. When I heard he was a Christian, my first impression was that he had to be soft. We all learned soon enough that was not true.

Dewey King had an infectious enthusiasm about his scheme and his players. He believed in both. He bred confidence in those around him. He demanded effort, and we gave it because of our trust in him. I thrived under his teaching style.

When my career ended, I really felt I'd sign an NFL contract. My fraternity brothers faked a call to me from the New York Giants before the draft, and I bought it hook, line, and sinker. Later, I realized what a limited corner and linebacker I had been, but Coach King made me believe that I could perform as well as anyone I played against.

Coach King and I spoke recently and revisited our upset of highly rated Yale in October 1966. In that game I twice hit Calvin Hill, the Dallas Cowboy's first-round choice, and created fumbles. Even then, I realized that the stunt called based upon Yale's backfield motion is what put me in such an advantageous position. Today, I value Coach's defensive wisdom even more than I did then.

Later, I considered playing professionally for a team in Richmond, Virginia. I asked Coach King for advice then, starting a practice that I have now followed for 30 years. Before every major professional decision I seek the advice of the man who earned my trust with his love. By the way, he told me to forget playing with Richmond in the minor leagues and come help him coach in the spring. He then advised me to get into college football and called head coaches until he got me an opportunity as a graduate assistant at the University of Pittsburgh.

Dewey King also taught a course on coaching football. I still have the textbook and some of my notes. He made a statement that I use a lot with my staff about handling young men. Coach said, "If you call a kid a dog long enough, he'll become one." There are times to be hard on players, but men live for encouragement. I was never a great player, but I always thought I was, because Dewey King told me so.

Coach persuaded me in July of 1965 to accept an all-expense-paid visit to Black Mountain, North Carolina, to work out with some NFL greats including Raymond Berry, Don Shinnick, Fran Tarkenton, and Jerry Stovall.

Garth Weber and Doug Clark, fellow athletes at Rutgers, drove me down. NFL Hall-of-Fame receiver Raymond Berry spent time running routes against me and then shared his faith while challenging me to commit my life to Christ. Five days later I became a "new creation" (2 Corinthians 5:17).

Raymond Berry continued to stay in contact and in July 1992 sent me a series of scriptures to help me during my coaching. Raymond was the featured speaker at the 1997 Illinois High School Coaches Association Clinic in Champaign, and we reflected on the relationship started by Coach King in 1965. Dewey King influenced my life dramatically as a player, coach, and Christian because of his work ethic, loyalty to Rutgers, and a deep love for his young men.

Remember, "a kid doesn't care how much you know until he knows how much you care."

If a coach has these qualities he can make a substantial difference in the lives of his players. Organizational skills will ensure that his work is efficient and not wasted. He will be dependable in accomplishing the little things for his players and staff.

At Colorado, Bill McCartney brought to our campus an engaging speaker, Steve Musso, to talk about goal setting. Musso made a lasting impression in several areas. I resolved, after he spoke, to design a mission statement for my squad.

In December 1991, Karen and I fashioned the mission statement after I became head coach at the University of Illinois. It hung in the most prominent area in the Irwin Football Complex. Every day our staff, secretaries, janitors, and players walked by it and were reminded of their purpose.

Each coach and player should have an individual statement of purpose. For both long and short range, goals can be designed and

▪ Chris "Crash" Cosh led Virginia Tech in tackles as a junior but missed his senior season due to a neck injury. He became a student coach for me, and turned his negative into a positive in his coaching career. He may be the best inside linebacker coach I have witnessed, and he's like a second son to me.

targeted. Without a clear purpose and plan, much less is accomplished.

Prepare for Meetings

For over 30 years I have observed coaches teach in the classroom before they take their players on the field. They use concepts much like those that chemistry professors use in a lecture hall before sending their students to the laboratory. Classroom time is precious if the labs and practices are going to be effective. My experience has shown that the best meeting-room teachers are usually the finest on-field coaches as well.

With the present NCAA time restrictions on meetings and practices, coaches must prepare diligently for their limited time in the classroom. They should thoroughly plan each meeting, giving thought to reviewing material from the previous practice to teaching the new concepts for the day.

Daily tip sheets were mandatory for our staff before every spring practice and before hard work days during the season. Each position coach gave me a copy so I could become familiar with their new material. This forced them to organize their teaching.

Each tip sheet had to be three-hole punched, labeled with the player's name, and placed in a binder. The binder had to include an attached plastic zip-lock pouch with pencils and a highlighter.

Tip sheets were typed or hand-written. They outlined what the meeting would accomplish and reviewed the information necessary for the player to perform well in practice. The binders allowed the student to organize the material and write notes or highlight what they are learning. Coaches encouraged the players to use more than just a visual sense in learning. Players could refer to the binder when they returned to their dorms.

I wrote out the linebacker tip sheets by hand. Chris Cosh, who coached our inside linebackers from 1992 until 1996, typed his. Tuesday's sheet, usually the longest, included formation tendencies plus calls for first and 10 and second downs. Wednesday's tips included three-down calls, blitzes, short yardage, and goal-line explanations. Thursdays sheets reviewed tendencies inside the 20, two-minute plans, and two-point defenses. Following are examples of tip sheets from Chris and me.

This is my 1990 tip sheet from Tuesday before a game against Wisconsin.

LINEBACKER TIP SHEET ▬▬▬▬▬▬

WISCONSIN

Tuesday, 1990

Pro Formations

A. Pro (25Run-26Pass)

   1. Runs favor TE side 19 to 6

   2. Passes favor X receiver

   3. Pro with "weak" backs have been 4 screens. ILB check to a "clamp" coverage with this backfield set

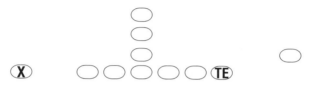

B. Twin Flip I (24Run-5Pass)

   1. Runs favor TE 17 to 7 with emphasis on sweep and power

   2. Last year Wisconsin ran iso and bounce to split side

   3. ILB check to hawk with a fin call to the TE side

C. Unbalanced (3Run-3Pass)

   1. ΔLB will check cover O, ELB will check hawk

   2. Like to boot screen to stub side of formation

   3. Run power, bounce, and iso to twins; ELB is H/C versus the unbalanced check.

D. Twin Open I (4Run-2Pass)
  1. Used at NW and versus us two years ago
  2. Coverage will be 0 or 2
  3. Like to run draw and waggle to the 5 technique tackle

1-10 Calls (69Run-55Pass) 56% Run

1. Fd Hawk, 2
2. Fd Hk Nose, 2
3. St-Fd Hk Loop, 0-2
4. Sht Hk (Star), 1
5. Sp Tilt Check, 2/5—ILB call Rip or Liz to TE and play 32 technique
6. Sp Tilt Nato Swap, 2/1—ELB play like Gopher

3 WRs (37Run-78Pass) #1 formation.

We will hold our emphasis on it until Wednesday but experiment with TITE Hawk, 4 today. ELB call Rip/Liz to TE.

1. ELB: play over OT at LB depth. TE has been thrown the ball on 3 delays (short dropper) and 2 drags. Key OT for reach, pass, pull, etc.
2. ILB: with TITE play 32 Tech and still short drop versus 3 WRs. Favor the counter (5x) and Zone (5x). You must stop X under when Y drags.

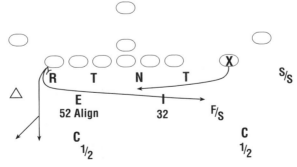

FB cuts on draw and iso in two back formations.

On pages 271-273 is a 1995 typed tip sheet that Chris Cosh wrote before our Wednesday practice for Iowa.

Those tip sheets are of tremendous value the following season. A coordinator or coach can quickly get the facts behind all his teaching from the previous year. I still have a tip sheet on mimeographed paper from a spring practice on April 18, 1967.

Other points we stress on meeting preparation are to put additional diagrams or notes on white boards or chalkboards *before* the meeting begins. Have tapes marked and in the VCR ready to play. Inefficient coaches waste time by searching for tapes during meeting time or fast forwarding to find a particular play. An organized teacher has those things rehearsed and can cover more material.

Spoken communication and demonstrations also make teaching more effective. Have the players verbalize concepts to their peers. The coach will hear of their knowledge if he forces them to speak. Demonstrations use movement to visualize and walk them through the learning process. Some of our finest meetings were held prepractice on the field in walk-through sessions.

Most of all, the coach must take time to prepare for his meetings. They are critical to the learning curve. Research suggests that meeting time and visualization may be as important as practice time for certain performance skills.

Prepare for Practice

Plan each practice detail. A coach should mentally review how to improve each proposed drill to increase learning and the quality of repetitions.

A linebacker coach must concentrate on the field. If he does not focus during practice, neither will his players. The coach should require all of his players to hear his instructions and be aware of every call. Too often a coach prepares only one player at a time in a specific drill. The finest teachers have everyone in their group aware of the calls. One linebacker may be doing a key drill, but the others at his position are behind him stepping physically at the correct angle. They are active mentally on the snap while they are viewing the drill itself. When a player is asked for the defense or coverage that is about to be executed and doesn't have a clue, he should be sent off running. A serious linebacker learns a lot when he is watching.

On the field, train the linebackers to move rapidly from one drill to another. It helps if a coach is in good physical condition so his

LINEBACKER TIP SHEET █████████████████

IOWA

Wednesday, November 1, 1995

Today's Installation:

- 3rd 6+
- Short yardage
- Goal line
- Funnel
- Pressure

Effort: Experience—It's not what happens to a man, it's what a man does with what happens to him.

3rd 6+ (7Run-32Pass) 17% Run

1. Personnel groups
   - Pro = 7Run-23Pass, I-backfield is 100% run!
   - Double flanker = 0Run-5Pass, stop 3-step passing game.
   - 3 WRs = 0Run-1Pass
   - Flanker = 0Run-1Pass
2. Calls
   - St-Fd 40 Fin, 4-2
   - St-Fd Double Rat, 4 or Dog O
   - St-Fd 40 Double Pick, 4
   - Wk-Sht 40, Funnel Hot
   - St-Fd Nickel Fin, 8 Hot-8 Clamp

Short Yardage (7Run-1Pass) 87% Run

1. Heavy
   - Strong placement will be made
   - Rush LB align head-up the heavy tackle
   - Split back = pass
   - I-back = run

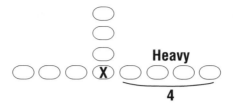

2. Strong backs on 4 snaps

3. Strong Heavy Dart I—This call will be made when I-backs are anticipated. Dart will be executed only versus the I.

Goal line (3Run-4Pass) 42% Run

1. Heavy calls
   - St. Heavy, 4
   - St. Heavy Dart I, 4
   - Pinch Run Check toward the strength

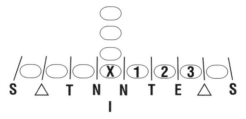

2. Pinch Run versus Heavy One Back
   - ELB count to #3
   - Align inside #3
   - 4 pt. Stance, key ball, and penetrate gap

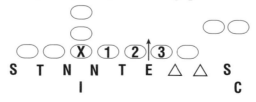

Funnel Coverage

1. ELB—Flat

2. ILB—Hook to TE, with no hook threat then short drop

Pressure – Split G Blitz, Key

1. Pro I

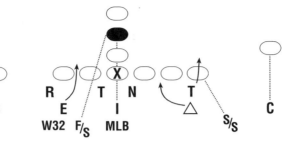

2. Pro Split

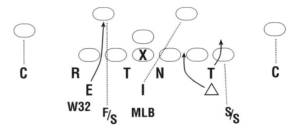

energy stays high throughout practice. When the horn blows for the end of a period, stop the drill at once if the linebackers are expected to join another group in the next period. Do not make another coach wait for you by running over the time allotment.

Do not condone mistakes on the field. Many coaches yell and curse, but the important issue is to make players repeat mistakes until they correct the errors. All motivated players want to execute properly. They appreciate repeating poor snaps, even though they may not show it. Rather than saying, "You moron, can't you get this right?" I usually prefer saying, "John, that's not like you" or "That's almost perfect, do it again like this and you'll have it!" It's the Dewey King principle. Express confidence in his ability and affirm that he will do it well.

Do not condone penalties. When a player hurts the team with a violation, let the linebacker know that it is not acceptable. The entire team pays a price for his lack of discipline. Usually, we penalize the entire unit with instant grass drills for individual penalties. Bill McCartney once made a statement to our Colorado staff that haunted me as an assistant coach, but I believe there is much truth to it: "An undisciplined player is coached by an undisciplined coach." That presents a challenge to us as teachers.

An exceptional defense is usually a superb fundamental team. A coach should take pride in spending enough time on the building blocks of linebacker play. Players who are fundamentally sound are confident and know that they are improving each day.

That reminded me of a story told by Bo Schembechler in Boulder at one of our Colorado High School Clinics. Bo said that he was looking to hire a young, enthusiastic position coach on defense and happened to attend a clinic in California. He was intrigued by a young Division II college coordinator who was a polished speaker and quite handsome. The young coach used all the modern buzz words and seemed to have an answer for everything in his defensive philosophy. Suddenly a local high school coach said, "But tell us, Coach, why you gave up over 400 yards per game." The youngster responded, "It wasn't because of scheme, it was *only* tackling." Bo was no longer impressed.

Players must master fundamentals and techniques to be successful. If asked to learn too many techniques, a player cannot gain the boldness to be great. This quotation hung for years in our defensive staff room: "If we don't have time to teach it well, let's not put it in." Every assistant coach could use that idea to get rid of any new scheme. Be known as a confident, fundamental defense.

Linebacker coaches should not forget that coaching is teaching. A remarkable academic instructor could be a tremendous coach if he had the knowledge to impart. An effective athletic coach could be a successful chemistry teacher if he had the background and desire to teach it.

One major difference exists between athletic education and the teaching of most other academic disciplines. That is motivation. I was a strong student, yet when I sat in my calculus or physics classes in college, I would frequently watch the clock as we neared the end of the period. During football meetings, I always sat on the edge of my seat. Football, for most players, is a *want to*, not a *have to*. As teachers of this activity we have the potential to sway the lives of young men. Let's make it a positive experience.

Chapter 19

Practice Organization

In this chapter, we will discuss ways to organize practice to teach and train linebackers progressively. The practice format may change during the year to meet specific objectives and make adjustments as circumstances dictate.

Most teams begin practice with some form of stretching and total body movement. The purpose is usually to warm up the muscles and increase flexibility. After speaking to a number of speed development experts, including Willie Williams, the University of Illinois associate head track coach, we made speed improvement a daily part of our prepractice format. We devoted the initial minutes of team practice to total body warm-up, flexibility, and speed.

Because the warm-up and speed movements often included the shuffle and backpedal, the linebacker coaches didn't need to repeat those actions as often in their individual work.

After stretching, our squad spent 20 to 25 minutes daily on special-teams work. This period often included some excellent tackling drills. When we ran tackling drills the linebacker coaches could skip that form of tackling in their weekly progression during individual practice periods.

I have witnessed other staffs where the practice structure was quite different. In some, the linebacker individual periods began directly after 10 minutes of stretching. Now all warm-up and speed improvement activity fell into the hands of the position coaches.

276 - Complete Linebacking

For this chapter's purpose we will assume that the players have warmed up thoroughly and addressed speed improvement before the individual segment of practice.

Individual Periods

Linebacker coaches are seldom pleased with the amount of individual time they get. Linebacker coaches must do all the drill work for the fundamentals in chapters 3 through 7 and the training of the techniques they use from chapters 11 through 17 in their individual teaching. By the time their players reach the first group period, the rest of the staff expects the linebackers to be performing the necessary techniques properly.

Later we will review practice schedules for various times of the year. It will be noteworthy how the amount of time dedicated to fundamentals and techniques fluctuates throughout the year. One thing should remain constant, however. Never should a hard work day go by without attention to fundamentals and techniques.

Fundamentals

We discussed the fundamentals in detail in the opening chapters of this book. Work on hit and shed, pursuit, and tackling skills daily in full-length practice sessions. Time constraints do not always permit daily work on zone and man coverage fundamentals.

During early spring practices and fall camp, spend approximately 40 minutes on the fundamentals. When the season begins, the coach can drill the ABCs with quality in 15 minutes. Remember that an excellent scheme built on faulty fundamentals is doomed to failure. If a linebacker does not spend enough time each day on the fundamentals, he will regress.

Try to involve the nontraveling linebackers in the ABC drills. Often coaches exchange the freshmen and assign them to scout team duties directly after stretch. This retards their growth and really hurts their enthusiasm. Sometimes it is simply unavoidable because of the small number of practice bodies available. If possible, however, fight to keep all players involved during the fundamental periods. Over the course of a year it will accelerate their development and bolster their attitude.

Which fundamental drills does a coach use? We expose our linebackers to all the fundamental drill work explained at the ends of chapters 3 through 7 in the spring and again in fall camp. Once we get to the weekly fall practices, we set a routine so that the players recall many of the drills. Rarely, however, do we repeat an ABC drill twice in one week. We introduce few new drills during the season. Teaching many new drills during the fall campaign is distracting and inefficient.

I enjoyed the old Big Eight seasonal format while at Colorado. We played four nonconference opponents and then had a bye week before entering a seven-week league schedule. That open week provided a mental and physical rest. It also permitted an emphasis on training freshmen and a reemphasis on the fundamentals for the varsity. It was a particularly good time to introduce some new and exotic drills.

Techniques

The linebacker coach must next decide how much time to devote to drilling techniques. Usually our goal is to spend 10 minutes per base technique each day in individual time. We have two distinctly different outside linebackers and two different inside linebackers. They are not mirrored positions as in many schemes.

For example, the drop linebacker might require a 10-minute period at 9 technique and the rush linebacker a 10-minute period for wide 5 work. Without a graduate assistant or head coach to help, an outside linebacker coach would require 20 minutes to train one technique to his travelers on a given day.

That is precisely why we limit the number of techniques we ask an athlete to play in our package. If a linebacker routinely aligns in four or five techniques, how can he get sufficient training to master them? Our four linebackers, for nearly 20 years, have each "majored" in one technique and "minored" in another. Seldom would they enter a contest required to perform three techniques well. We don't coach that effectively!

Who is on the demonstration squad during the linebacker drills? Often as I watch other squads practice, I observe the outside or inside linebacker coach teaching the drills each day to new scout-team members. How efficient is that? The same display team should be with a position coach every day so they can learn the drills and get more repetitions. Better yet, don't exchange scout personnel until after the technique work. Now a coach really has a special environment. He will get more snaps and quality hat placement on every read. As a bonus, his young nontravelers will hear his teaching and see the intensity of the drills. They will learn much while serving the upperclass linebackers. In 24 years as an assistant coach, I rarely gave up my scout linebackers to service others until after our individual periods.

When drilling a technique, how many linebackers get the snaps? Usually our staff gives the two deep equal time. When ahead of schedule, a deserving third-unit player may gain some experience, but that is not routine. The first two units need to be focused. The player not getting primary work in the drill should be responding to his key and moving his feet behind his teammate. The third teamer must get "mental reps" and review those tip sheets.

The two deep can experience many snaps in 10 minutes. After a play is executed, the linebacker should run back to read his next key. Often we will challenge the defender by saying, "Give me five perfect reactions and you're done." The intensity picks up and his peers cheer each faultless response. When the player makes an error, we explain the mistake, and he repeats until perfect. We encourage our coaches to reply with, "Great, that's like you!" or "That's not like you! Just press that open seam and it will be perfect."

Remember, men live for encouragement, and great players want to be called to perfection. Tell them that if they wanted to be good they should have gone to the rival school. When they chose this program, they made a decision to be great.

The linebacker coach can make the linebackers much better performers if he can find someone who is willing and able to teach a quality technique period each day. At the high school level perhaps he can enlist a responsible volunteer; at the college level, a graduate assistant or even the head coach. That extra help allows twice as much teaching. Now in 10 minutes, both inside or outside linebackers can work an extra base technique drill.

We began this in 1992 at Illinois and it was not coincidental that the staff generated two Butkus Award winners and four first-team All-Big Ten linebackers in the following four seasons. Think it through. Ten to 20 extra minutes a day developing technique is not a huge deal, but after six weeks it's significant. After two or three years, it can be monumental. As a head coach, I taught 10 to 20 minutes of technique work daily in cooperation with our linebacker coaches. We had to trust one another to teach exactly the same material. It sure gave us an edge on the competition, and our players knew it.

The most efficient teachers of technique know exactly how many looks an opponents' key will give. The coach signals those schemes

Courtesy of Virginia Tech

■ Robert Brown was our scheme's first spectacular rush linebacker. After nearly 20 years, he remains the finest run player we have coached at that position. His quiet, gentlemanly demeanor starkly contrasted with the way he abused tight ends on the field.

to a motivated demonstration squad quickly, and on "Ready, hit" they execute the play. In a 10-minute period, Chris Cosh could get twice as many repetitions as most linebacker coaches. Why? It was not just his energy but the organization of his drill work and the efficiency of the display team. We could wear out the two deep in a high-tempo 10-minute technique period. That should be the goal for both linebacker and coach.

Group Periods

Group periods bring together two or more position coaches to show larger or higher-quality pictures to their players. It may be a teaching drill involving the far 9 technique with the halves corner on routes involving just the two of them. Although they would work it individually, a drill like this confirms the concept that defense is knowing where your help is. Group drills might also cross the line of scrimmage and pull together linebackers and running backs in a one-on-one pass drill. This would have been a lower-intensity drill in individual. Now the one-on-one brings competition and more highly trained opponents.

Some of football's traditional group drills follow. With each, we discuss the management of the drill and the specific handling of the linebackers.

7-on-7

This is perhaps the most commonly used group drill in American football. We describe it generally at the end of chapter 6, but here we analyze it specifically for the linebacker coach.

Position the linebackers together 15 yards behind the line of scrimmage between the offensive huddle and the boundary. That keeps the traveling linebackers together with their coaches and out of the way of the offense. Normally, we travel with a maximum of six inside linebackers and three drop linebackers. Three of those nine will be participating in the drill, so during the season the drill is not cluttered with bodies.

The linebacker coaches should always script the drill so they know the play and the coverage call. The signal caller should signal, not yell, the defense into the huddle. This is excellent practice for game-day signaling. The 7-on-7 pace is usually fast, and the players can test the signals daily in this period, that usually runs 20 minutes.

At the same time, the coach should be telling the linebackers with him the call and the offensive play. Or he can quiz them about the play they expect with a specific formation or about the check they would make. A player who is focused and learning while watching will end up being dependable. He will make those around him more aware.

Once the ball is snapped, the coach and linebackers should focus on their position and the reaction to the key receiver. Before the :25-second clock expires, the coach must give the linebackers comments and issue the next signal. I become frustrated by coaches who are silent during 7-on-7. Some feel that tape review will explain the errors after practice. Immediate review is more effective. The linebacker longs to hear that he's done well or is close to doing it at a championship level.

We believe in rotating our linebackers every four plays to begin 7-on-7s. We do not exceed seven consecutive snaps. We want to foster 93 percent pursuit, discussed in chapter 4, by forcing the defenders to sprint before the ball is thrown on every play. This drill is crucial to creating our pursuit habits.

Tackling is a real bonus in this drill, but many coaches overlook the possibility of drilling it. For 20 minutes, linebackers break to the ball carrier and get to work on open-field tackling. They can see their teammates' pursuit angles and learn where they fit in this coordinated effort to tackle. Once there, the linebacker fronts up the receiver with respect. He should not tackle a teammate to the ground. When he is not the first to contact the ball carrier, he sprints to cover for a missed tackle or to strip a receiver who has been fronted.

During spring practice and fall camp our coaches grade the 7-on-7 drills. Because the players know that the coaches will be evaluating the period, it becomes a higher priority for them. The evaluation also identifies common errors that a linebacker is making that may not be apparent without daily grading.

9-on-7

At Virginia Tech, Bill Dooley called it the middle drill. At Colorado, Bill McCartney termed it the inside drill. At Illinois, John Mackovic referred to it as 9-on-7. Regardless of the terminology, I believe this drill tells a defensive coach more about his unit than any other drill.

I've had defensive teams that have been marginal in their pass coverage or rush yet have been effective defenses. I've never seen a weak interior run defense be part of a successful unit.

The tough run unit also has a mental edge. An offense can drive downfield by throwing, and a defense reacts by feeling that the offense was lucky. A little more rush or tighter coverage, the defense thinks, and they would have had them under control. When, however, an opponent runs the ball right at the gut of a defense and shreds them, the defense can really lose confidence. Luck is not a factor, and the huddle is often full of hollow eyes.

Defensive players and coaches must understand that their future success depends on performing in this drill. Defenders must have the attitude that no one can run through their defense. This drill should always be a highlight of the day's practice (see figure 19.1).

The 9-on-7 drill should be filmed from behind, never from a sideline view. The back view gives the defenders excellent pictures of their alignments and pre-snap factors such as line splits and stances.

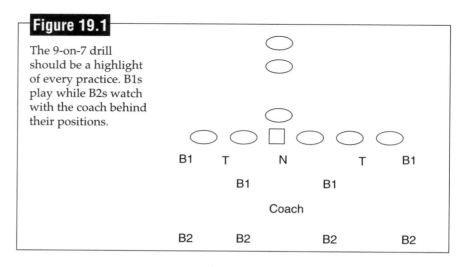

Figure 19.1

The 9-on-7 drill should be a highlight of every practice. B1s play while B2s watch with the coach behind their positions.

Alternate shooting the tape from behind the offense one day and from behind the defense the next. When the defense faces a scout team, the camera should be at its back. It is also an advantage for the linebackers with depth to have yard lines to check their distance from the line of scrimmage.

As with 7-on-7, linebackers should congregate, only now they should be 15 yards behind the defensive side. Each linebacker should hear the call from the script as his coach reads it. The linebacker should then position himself to see his key and monitor the reaction of his peer.

The coach has 25 seconds or less to signal to the huddle and talk to the players surrounding him about the play that will unfold.

The 9-on-7 plays consist of live blocks. The tempo is game speed, except that we tackle the ball carrier high. We instruct defenders never to leave their feet to make a tackle in this drill. We do not want a varsity back getting live rat-a-tat-tats and risking injury.

This is a very natural progression from the technique drills the linebackers do earlier in practice. If he was keying only linemen before, we add backs or vice versa. Before the tempo was softer; now the speed is upgraded. Before the picture was probably incomplete; now all the parts are present.

We normally plan 20 minutes for this drill on both Tuesday and Wednesday during the season. Ideally, one period features a scout team running the opponent's base inside plays. We show every stunt or line movement on cards to the display squad. When they are executing a foreign offense, the scout team should not be surprised by the defense. Sometimes Saturday's opponent has an attack so different from ours that both 10-minute periods are against scouts. We prefer scripting a period on Tuesday or Wednesday versus the varsity offense. It gives both sides a faster look and better execution than the scouts can give. We limit the defensive and offensive calls to those that are similar to schemes of that week's opponent.

Here are some effective variations of the 9-on-7 drill:

- **Challenge 9-on-7:** This is the most competitive form of the drill. We create a scrimmage mentality by permitting defenders to leave their feet to make plays. Any run under three yards is a point for the defense. A run over three yards is a point for the offense. We select an odd number of plays and let them compete.

- **Teaching 9-on-7:** This has less contact than our normal form of the drill. Now we only front up the ball carrier. The blocks at the line are live. Often we use this variation when we lack enough healthy bodies or when we wear shells (helmets and shoulder pads).

- **Pass 9-on-7:** We initiated this variation in 1996 to give our offense a chance to pass protect against full-line twists and blitzes. It has some benefits for defense in timing up those calls and in defending the draw.

Half-Line

This is an outside drill that favors the defense because the defenders always know the direction of the flow. It is an outstanding drill for spring practice and fall camp when teaching the swinging-gate principles (chapter 16). We also feature it when we face teams with superior perimeter attacks, such as wishbone clubs. Half-line permits many snaps in a 10-minute period and can expose a variety of blocking patterns.

Usually we feature two or three perimeter runs along with a play-action pass off one of those actions to both sides of the drill.

Half-line takes a lot of organization, but once set up it moves quickly. Four coaches are required. In figure 19.2, coaches 1 and 2 work with the strong-side offense and defense. They would run play #1 on the script, while the weakside offense and defense huddle to get calls for play #2.

In figure 19.3, coaches 3 and 4 work the boundary-side offense and defense. They would run play #2 on the script, while coaches 1 and 2 organize the strong-side huddles in preparation for play #3 to be run to the field.

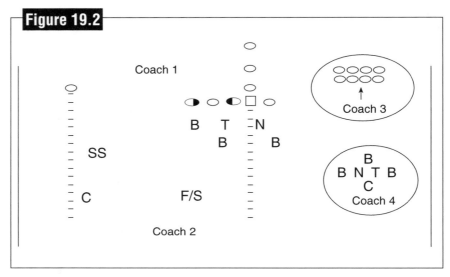

Half-line drill from the right hash working the field side offense and defense. Coaches 3 and 4 huddle with the boundary-side personnel.

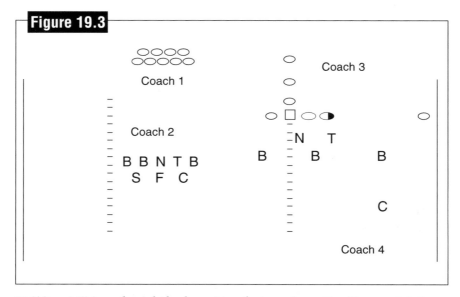

Half-line drill from the right hash working the boundary-side offense and defense. Coaches 1 and 2 huddle with the field-side personnel

The half-line requires more personnel than any other drill work we do. We use 14 defensive players and 17 offensive players, as figures 19.2 and 19.3 indicate. At times during the season finding 17 scout teamers at the needed positions can be a problem.

We spend a complete 10-minute block of time on the right hash one day, and then we run all plays from the left hash the next. Once we organize the drill we usually keep it at that field position. We do not recommend changing hashes within one period.

Plays flow so rapidly that the best coaching does come from tape with this drill. Get the reps and keep the drill moving so the coach can teach from the film.

The tempo of the drill can be live, but usually we liken the tackling to a 7-on-7 pace. We front up the option quarterback or the play-action receiver. All blocks, however, are full go.

Team Periods

A staff must first determine the purpose for their defensive team periods. We always precede team periods with the individual teaching, 9-on-7, and 7-on-7. Because we emphasized the inside runs in 9-on-7, I seldom want to repeat them in team. Because we featured drop-back passes in 7-on-7, we don't run as many of them in team either.

We feel team periods should stress the following points:

- Perimeter plays, especially if half-line drills have not been used. The swinging gate must be tested.
- Play-action pass and bootlegs, that are ineffective in a 7-on-7 setting.
- Special plays run by the opponent such as draws, screens, reverses, and so forth.
- Adjustments to motion, shifts, formation into the boundary, unbalanced lines, and so on.
- Checks to be communicated and reinforced with teammates.

Those five objectives require the lion's share of our attention during team periods. The decisions our players make in this setting tell the staff what kind of teachers we have been. When the outside linebacker immediately recognizes formation into the boundary or unbalanced line, a confidence grows within the whole unit. When the inside linebacker checks instantly to a compelling backfield tendency, his peers gain enthusiasm for the game plan.

During each team period, the linebackers receive signals before each snap. The coach can now introduce alternate or false signals. All nontravelers are with the offensive scout squad. The travelers not in the huddle stay with their position coach, learning from each snap. They should constantly be communicating the checks and adjustments with their mentor.

Our goal is to get 12 to 14 plays run in a 10-minute team period. A dozen should always be possible. If we expect mistakes because of a heavy check emphasis, we design only 12 plays.

How do we divide the repetitions between the first and second units? Normally, we split the plays evenly. There have been years when our first defense was so young that we gave them eight plays and the backups only four. That is not how we prefer to do it. When a second-team linebacker enters the game, we expect him to be accountable for his decisions. That's not possible if he has not had equal practice exposure.

Every practice day the staff met from 1:30 P.M. to 2:15 P.M. to review every practice card for group drills and team periods. This review is essential for developing a good defense. Assistant coaches were usually anxious about this meeting because they had scripted and drawn each card for their assigned periods. Now the whole staff and the head coach scrutinized every line drawn for the scout team. We always found errors and made beneficial changes. Any error not found in this meeting could mean a wasted play in practice. Another payoff of this review was that it gave the coordinator a real pulse for the staff's understanding of the game plan.

At Colorado, we were frustrated initially that our players wore down as practice reached the later team stages. We felt it was more mental than physical fatigue. We needed a jump start as we headed into the team emphasis and came up with an idea we have used consistently since then.

We called it double whistle. When tagged to any team period, it simply meant that we must pursue full speed beyond the whistle. It was overtraining. We blew one whistle when a defender fronted up the runner, but the other 10 pursuers continued until they got to the ball. Once there, they kept their feet moving in place until every teammate reached the pile and the second whistle sounded. Then they jogged back to the huddle.

If one defender did not hustle, the entire unit did grass drills on the spot. All paid a price, just as they would on game day. I do not recommend this adjustment to team during a heavy check period when focus on recognition is intense or when the team may have to repeat plays because of new learning. The peer pressure during a double-whistle period normally increases the unit's energy level dramatically.

Practice Schedules

On the following pages are examples of linebacker practice schedules for spring practice, fall camp, and in-season practices. The examples should help linebackers and coaches understand the practice priorities of each phase of the year. We will review only selected linebacker periods.

Spring Practice #1

This initial practice emphasizes individual teaching (80 minutes), with only one group and two team periods.

We divide the individual time into 30 minutes of fundamentals and 50 minutes of technique work on practice #1.

Table 19.1
SPRING PRACTICE #1—INSIDE LINEBACKERS

Period	Time	Instruction	Comments
1	3:45	Stance Air hit and shed Sled one-step hit and shed	Reviewed stances Used two hit-and-shed drills (see chapter 3)
2	3:55	Crossfield pursuit Confined tackle drill	Spent 5 minutes on pursuit drill (see chapter 4) Spent 5 minutes on tackling drill (see chapter 5)
3	4:05	Hawk technique	Spent 20 minutes on hawk read (see chapter 14) and stunts
4	4:15	(shoot, stunt)	
5	4:25	32 technique	Spent 20 minutes on 32 reads (see chapter 11) and stunts
6	4:35	(nose, shoot stunts)	
7	4:45	Team huddle	Installed huddle as a team
8	4:55	Break	Took 5-minute water break—helps keep players alert
9	5:00	Zone drops versus air drill	Used base zone drill (see chapter 6)
10	5:10	Cover O introduced Key receiver drill	Technique period on Cover O reads
11	5:20	Group undercover drill with OLBs	First group period to work Cover O routes versus whole LB corps
12	5:30	Team pursuit drill	Introduce this fundamental drill early (see chapter 4)

Spring Practice #8

By the end of midpoint of the spring teaching, the amount of individual instruction has decreased significantly. Group work is up from 10 minutes in practice #1 to 50 minutes. Players are now getting a better understanding of where their help is in each front and coverage.

Table 19.2
SPRING PRACTICE #8—INSIDE LINEBACKERS

Period	Time	Instruction	Comments
1	3:45	Cone pursuit drill Column hit-and-shed drill	5 minutes on pursuit drill (see chapter 4) 5 minutes on hit-and-shed drill (see chapter 3)
2	3:55	Eye-opener tackle Bag 45° drops	5 minutes on tackle drill (see chapter 5) 5 minutes on zone drill (see chapter 6)
3	4:05	Man coverage versus RBs	Group challenge versus RBs in man coverage (see chapter 7)
4	4:15	Hawk technique	Key reads (see chapter 14)
5	4:25	32 technique	Key reads (see chapter 11)
6	4:35	9 on 7 (versus split hawk)	Scripted two periods with two different fronts—competitive test will show ILBs progress
7	4:45	9 on 7 (versus tight hawk)	
8	4:55	Break	
9	5:00	7 on 7 (cover 2 emphasis)	20 minutes of group period discussed earlier in this chapter—have a specific purpose scripted for each period
10	5:10	7 on 7 (inside 20-yard line)	
11	5:20	Team versus scouts (versus hash adj.)	Scouts on cards run 12 plays from the hash
12	5:30	Team versus offense (versus middle adj.)	Varsity offense runs from a script of agreed middle-of-the-field plays for more speed and better execution

Fall Camp Practice #3

Now we will examine an early fall practice format for the outside linebackers. This morning session during two-a-day practices picks up after the stretch and kicking work.

Table 19.3
FALL CAMP PRACTICE #3—OUTSIDE LINEBACKERS

Period	Time	Instruction	Comments
1	9:05	Bag pursuit drills Base push-off drill	Both pursuit drills but push-off incorporates tackling (see chapter 4)
2	9:15	Machine gun hit and shed Sideline tackling	See chapters 3 and 5
3	9:25	Zone line drill	Coverage ABC drill (see chapter 6)
4	9:35	Wide 5 technique	Dotted line denotes a split period. Each technique will be worked for 15 minutes (see chapters 16 and 17)
5	9:45	– – – – – – – –	
6	9:55	9 technique	
7	10:05	Cover 4, drop drill	Cover 4 is introduced individually
8	10:15	7 on 7 (cover 4 emphasis)	Group period on cover 4—team still in shorts practice so no 9 on 7 yet
9	10:25	Team versus scout	Usually in shorts this early in camp we choose to emphasize correct alignments and adjustments in team

As with the first spring practice of 1990 outlined earlier for inside linebackers, we use most of the individual time here to teach fundamentals and techniques.

Fall Camp Practice #16

This practice schedule for the outside linebackers is from the middle section of 29 permissible practices in August. In contrast to practice #3, group drills increase as do the team periods. This afternoon practice during double sessions includes a short situational scrimmage. These are vital to a linebacker's development. He needs short, competitive spurts of full-team scrimmage that address a particular situation. On this day it was short yardage.

Table 19.4
FALL CAMP PRACTICE #16—OUTSIDE LINEBACKERS

Period	Time	Instruction	Comments
1	4:10	Tempo	Combine pursuit and tackling (review chapters 4 and 5)
2	4:20	1 on 1 with TEs	OLBs work base and reach blocks with tight ends
3	4:30	Techniques: loose 5 and 9s	Two coaches divide OLBs to double teaching time (see chapters 16 and 17)
4	4:40	9 on 7	Inside drill emphasizing the counter and power plays to the OLBs
5	4:50	Half-line (sweep, option)	OLBs get "swinging gate" work (see chapter 16)
6	5:00	Break	Rush LBs are sent to pass rush, drop LBs to 7 on 7
7	5:05	7 on 7 (versus scouts)	Emphasize two coverages versus scouts and then against the speed of the varsity
8	5:15	7 on 7 (versus offense)	
9	5:25	Team flanker	Scouts run two formations to be emphasized that day
10	5:35	Team 3 WRs	
11	5:45	Scrimmage (short yardage)	A scripted period of 3-1 and 3-2 situations versus the varsity offense

Tuesday Practice #2

This practice schedule is from our in-season preparation for Indiana in October. Chris Cosh designed the periods. We separated the linebackers in period 2 to give them both 15 minutes of concentrated technique work.

Table 19.5
TUESDAY PRACTICE #2—INSIDE LINEBACKERS

Period	Time	Instruction	Comments
1	3:50	Follow-the-leader pursuit Sled approach hit and shed Inside and in front tackling	15 minute fundamental period (see chapters 3-5 for drills)
2	4:05	Technique reads in two groups—ELBs and ILBs	15 minutes of split teaching with two coaches—a great way to double train LBs
3	4:20	9 on 7 versus scouts	An in-season tradition on Tuesday and Wednesday
4	4:30	9 on 7 versus varsity	
5	4:40	7 on 7 versus scouts	Usually two 7 on 7s are standard on Tuesday and Wednesday
6	4:50	7 on 7 versus varsity	
7	5:00	Team double whistle (St-Fd placements)	30 minutes of team versus scouts Period 7 is a double whistle period
8	5:10	Team split placement	Each team period reflects an emphasis for upcoming opponent
9	5:20	Team flanker	

This is a typical Tuesday format that permits adequate time to maintain the fundamentals. We split the technique period to provide quality work on keys and adjustments. Only the two deep get snaps in the group and team periods.

We would view postpractice video on selected plays from periods 3 through 9. The linebackers should have an excellent understanding of the base defense by then.

Chapter 20

Linebacker Grading

I once coached with an old-timer who graded film only because the head coach demanded it. A coach who graded only scrimmages and games, he believed, was like a professor who had only a midterm and a final exam. This coach decided who of his athletes would play by evaluating daily practice situations, not their performance during the limited number of times they were filmed.

If grading is only about who starts or how players rank in the depth chart, then the old-timer may have had a strong point. Grading, however, can be much more than that, especially because the advances in technology have made it so much easier.

When I began coaching in 1967, most college football games were recorded on 16-millimeter film. Filming was costly. The film required processing so we had a definite time lag before we could view it. It wasn't until 1978 at Virginia Tech that I remember seeing practice film of sessions other than a major fall-camp scrimmage. Bill Dooley permitted our staff to shoot a 20-minute team drive period for offense and defense every Wednesday. We would try to capture on film as many checks, adjustments, and new calls as possible so our coaches and players could view it the next day.

By 1990 we were taping with three cameras constantly throughout practice, often capturing drills with both wide and tight shots. The special teams often had a separate camera operator. We copied all tapes for every position coach and were ready for viewing after postpractice showers. Although the switch from 16-millimeter format to video has made filming much easier, the value of video to players and coaches still hinges on how it's used.

Evaluation of tape does much more than establish depth charts. It is central to player understanding and motivation. Done properly, it can identify specific areas in which the linebackers can improve. It often spawns new drills for the coach who is searching for a solution to a poor technique or fundamental.

In spring practice and fall camp we require the position coach to grade all 9-on-7s and many team periods. Why? It motivates the linebackers to perform each day, to be responsible for their daily practice habits. The coach can identify their common errors and reinforce positive reactions.

Grade Work Sheet

This is a form our staff used to grade inside or outside linebackers on daily drills or an entire game. It would normally take me three hours to grade a full game and compile the results in their final form. Usually, I did it alone after church on Sunday mornings. At Virginia Tech, Karen and I graded the films together on Saturday evenings so we could have some family time with Stacy and Matt on Sundays. Karen learned to record on this form. It saved me a lot of writing and gave us something special to share.

Following is a condensed version of the grade work sheet. We wrote on it the name of each player, the date, and on the activity line the opponent (for example, West Virginia) or the drill we were grading (for example, 9-on-7, 7-on-7).

We listed all pursuit errors on the form. We described each pursuit error in section D under technique errors. For example, we might note that LB1 had two pursuit errors from the backside hook-to-curl responsibility, and that he also overran the ball twice in 32 technique, for 6- and 12-yard gains. Those repeated mistakes will get this defense beat if LB1 and his coach do not correct them.

Section B on this form requires a tally for every play that LB1 took during the game. I grade penalty plays if the play was carried to completion. Many coaches disregard them. As long as a staff is consistent it will be fair.

In section B, we separated all plays into four grading groups. The purpose is for the player to recognize that frontside plays carry more weight than plays run away from him. For the coach, it instantly shows how a player performs with run and pass to him (FS) as opposed to plays backside (BS).

GRADING WORK SHEET

Name _LB 1_   **Date** _9/7_   **Activity** _Rutgers game_

Pursuit Errors _////_

Grades

1. Run FS, GA	_//// //// //_		2. Run BS, GA	_//// ////_
	MA	_////_		MA	_///_
3. Pass FS, GA	_//// //// //_		4. Pass BS, GA	_//// ////_
	MA	_////_		MA	_//_

Statistics

Tackles	_//// ////_	Assists	_//_	MTs	_/_
Minus Plays	_-1 yd_	Fumbles Caused	_/_	Fumble Rec	
Sht Yd Stop		PBU		Intercept	
Hurry		Sacks		Other	

Run Technique Errors

Hawk Technique   _32_ Technique   _____ Technique

1. FS, align too wide, poor press	1. BS, overrun ball, +6yds	1.
2. FS, lead draw cut by FB	2. FS, G pull press 5 gap	2.
3. BS, G pulls, false steps f.s.	3. BS, overrun ball, +1 2	3.
4. FS, missed tackle on 1 6G	4.	4.

Pass Technique Errors

_H/C_ Technique   _H/F_ Technique   _Man_ Technique

1. FS, Cover 0 drifting on throw	1. FS, poor G recognition	1. FS, failed to check clamp
2. BS, loaf on throw!	2. FS, 3-1 0, poor depth	2.
3. BS, poor break on ball!	3.	3.
4.	4.	4.

Often a young, talented player will execute well with run to him, yet his poor backside performance will keep him from playing. This grading system will show him that with added discipline on the backside, he can challenge to play. Conversely, we've had some experienced journeymen who provided consistent backside discipline but didn't perform well enough with the ball at them. The journeyman may grade with a high total percentage yet have unacceptable frontside execution.

Section C is synonymous with productivity. It tabulates all the big events that a linebacker engages in during the game. Some defenders just have a penchant for making big plays. Simply take the number of big plays a linebacker makes divided by the snaps he plays to determine his "productivity quotient." The statistician and sports information department seek this kind of information; it's easy to copy this section and give it to them.

Sections D and E are the most important parts of the work sheet. We put this into a more readable format for the linebacker. Ideally, we record here every error in pursuit, in other fundamentals, and in each technique. We list them chronologically (as they occur) on the work sheet, but later we organize the sheet with FS plays first followed by BS plays. Frequent errors or those that particularly concern the staff we indicate with an asterisk. This form is a work copy that no one other than the position coach usually sees.

The grade work sheet must include enough space for the number of techniques that the linebackers use. Rarely do we use more than three run techniques. We do need space to list more than five errors under each technique. The example is abbreviated for display in this book.

Grade Sheet

After we graded the tape, we transferred the work sheet data to the official grade sheet in pencil. Our secretary then typed it on Monday morning so we could pass it out to the linebackers at their position meetings.

A typed copy of that form for player LB1 follows. Notice that we list percentages for run, pass, and the total. The final column on the right is the player's tackle-per-play quotient. Any linebacker over .20 has had an active day. Also note that we list LB1's pursuit grade and big plays on this page for his peers to study.

LINEBACKER GRADE SHEET #1

Name	# plays	Run FS GA-MA	Run BS GA-MA	Run %	Pass FS GA-MA	Pass BS GA-MA	Pass %	Total Grade	Pursuit Grade	Tackles	Assists	MT's	Total tackles	T/P
1. LB1	57	12-4	10-3	76%	12-4	10-2	79%	77%	92.9%	9	2	1	11	.19

BIG PLAYS

1. LB1 caused fumble
2. LB1 made play for minus 1 yd.

This form would list every linebacker who participated in the game. A total grade over 75% is considered a winning performance. A pursuit grade of 93% is challenging, but that is our goal. LB1 had a fine game. His number of assists is low with that many primary hits. He played as well in the passing game as he did versus the run. He was effective frontside. Without the four pursuit errors he would have been quite successful.

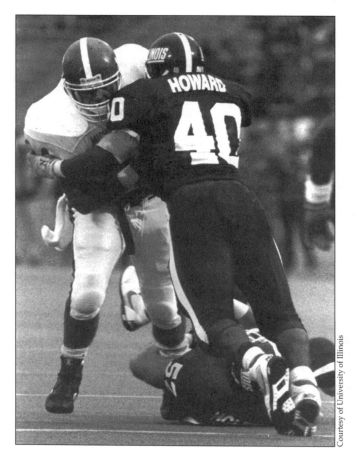

Courtesy of University of Illinois

■ Now playing middle linebacker in the NFL, Dana Howard was perhaps the strongest inside player in my career. His hip and leg strength were legendary in the Big Ten. He was the conference Player of the Year in 1994 and Illinois's first Butkus Award winner.

Seasonal Grade Sheet

Stapled to the grade sheet is a seasonal compilation of every play. The linebacker can compare his most recent game grades with those of past games. After studying this form, we often set goals to improve a particular phase of his game (for example, backside run grade or tackles per play).

A 12-game final-season grade sheet from 1990 follows. Several things are striking about this fine defensive unit.

LINEBACKER GRADE SHEET #2

Name	# Plays	Run FS GA-MA	Run BS GA-MA	Run %	Pass FS GA-MA	Pass BS GA-MA	Pass %	Total Grade	Pursuit Grade	Tackles	Assists	MTs	Total Tackles	T/P
1. Henkel	797	176-68	182-47	76%	140-25	139-20	86%	80%		63	56	27	119	.15
2. Brownlow	758	160-56	176-57	75%	111-32	128-38	77%	76%		105	56	19	161	.21
3. Shelby	79	18-4	12-5	77%	15-4	15-6	75%	76%		7	9	0	16	.20
4. Sidari	26	8-1	2-3	71%	4-2	6-0	83%	77%		5	4	0	9	.35
5. Daniels	22	1-0	1-1	66%	6-2	9-2	79%	77%		3	1	0	3	.14
6. Gretencord	1	0-0	0-0	0%	1-0	0-0	100%	100%		0	0	0	0	.00

LP Pursuit
1. 86.2% (Ariz)
2. 94.2% (CU)
3. 93.4% (SIU)
4. 89.0% (Ohio St)
5. 97.0% (Purdue)
6. 95.2% (MSU)
7. 93.4% (Wisc)
8. 92.1% (Iowa)
9. 92.6% (Mich)
10. 92.0% (Indiana)
11. 93.4% (NW)
12. 92.7% (Clemson)

4th Down Stop
1. Henkel, Purdue
2. Henkel, MSU
3. Brownlow, MSU

PBU
1. Henkel, Ariz
2. Brownlow, SIU
3. Brownlow, SIU
4. Brownlow, OSU
5. Brownlow, Purdue
6. Brownlow, Iowa
7. Henkel, NW

Caused Fumble
1. Brownlow, OSU
2. Brownlow, Purdue
3. Brownlow, Mich

Interception
1. Brownlow, OSU
2. Brownlow, Ind

Recovered Fumble
1. Brownlow, Purdue
2. Henkel, Ind

Sack
1. Brownlow, Wisc
2. Henkel, Wisc
3. Brownlow, Clemson

Pressure
1. Brownlow, Ariz
2. Henkel, OSU
3. Brownlow, Wisc
4. Brownlow, Clemson

Minus Plays
1. Brownlow, CU
2. Brownlow, CU
3. Daniels, SIU
4. Brownlow, Purdue
5. Brownlow, Mich
6. Brownlow, Mich
7. Brownlow, Ind
8. Brownlow, NU
9. Brownlow, Clemson

Short Yardage Stop
1. Brownlow, CU
2. Sidari, SIU
3. Brownlow, Purdue
4. Henkel, MSU
5. Henkel, MSU
6. Brownlow, MSU
7. Brownlow, Mich
8. Brownlow, Mich

- Our starters were healthy. They played much more than their backups. Examine the play number column.
- Both starters performed very well. Brownlow led the Big Ten in tackles and was Big Ten Player of the Year defensively. Henkel was one of only two linebackers I've ever had who graded 80 percent or higher for a whole season. The other was Barry Remington of Colorado in 1985.
- Brownlow made a lot of big plays!

Comment Sheets

Attached to the two grade sheets and three-hole punched with them so the players could keep them in their weekly binder was a comment sheet. This sheet addressed each linebacker about his performance during the week. We even had comments for those who did not play but rendered useful service during practice or on the sideline.

After the linebackers surveyed the numbers on the two grade sheets, they turned to the comment sheets for the coach's interpretation of the numbers. Players admire a good coach. They want to please him, and they respect his opinion because he is knowledgeable and has proven that he cares for them.

A short paragraph usually sums up the linebacker's performance. We also list every error. The linebacker looks for the asterisks that note the mistakes that he must remedy or that have continued to occur and especially concern the coach.

After the linebackers have reviewed every error on paper, they view the tape of the game for nearly 90 minutes with their coach and revisit every snap.

Following is a sample comment sheet for linebacker LB1's game from the fictional contest with Rutgers. It elaborates on errors that we noted in his grading work sheet.

COMMENT SHEET

I. **LB1:** Four pursuit errors stopped you from having a magnificent game. Avoiding any one of them moves you over our 93 percent goal. Those errors are not like you! You had a winning performance, but I am concerned about your overrunning the ball on backside run. This cannot continue! Showed consistent play versus run and pass.

A. Run
    1. Hawk FS, align too wide and don't press 3 gap. Why?
    2. Hawk FS, you recognize lead draw, but cut by FB.
    3. Hawk FS, missed tackle on 16G. Keep head up!
    4. Hawk BS, G pulls and you don't follow. Concentrate.
    5. 32 FS, G pulls and you must accelerate through 5 gap. Too soft.
    6. 32 BS, overrun ball twice (+6 yd., +12 yd.).

B. Pass (H/C= Hook to curl, H/F=Hook to force)
    1. H/C FS, drifting on throw. Pull up with QB.
    *2. H/C BS, twice loafed on throws away. Break before the ball is thrown!
    3. H/F FS, play-action pass and G shows pass. Drop!
    4. H/F FS, third and 10 you were only 6 yd. deep?
    *5. Mental error. Failed to check us to man coverage versus the flat backs. Can we trust you for checks?

Pursuit Forms

In a 10-minute unit meeting before releasing the players with their position coaches to review their grade sheets and game tapes, the coordinator would reflect on the unit's pursuit and our defensive objective chart.

We emphasized pursuit with them in one of two fashions, but we always exposed the pursuit results to the entire unit. We did this for no other individual data from the game. We felt it was important, however, that the unit knew who had committed themselves to our 93 percent pursuit goal.

At times we have simply listed every performer with his pursuit percentage. This may still be the most effective manner to display the efforts. When we expose each player's performance, the mood is serious.

Below is a chart we have used often. This is a reprint of our chart from the 9-7 upset over nationally ranked Arizona. Here we revealed each position as a group. In this particular game, we separated the outside linebackers by rush (RLB) and drop (DLB) and could have just as easily written their names. All four linebacker positions had

ARIZONA PURSUIT GRADES

Position group	Total plays	Correct pursuit	Pursuit %	Comments
Defensive line	218	196	89.9%	Pursuit after pass rush cost us.
Rush LBs	78	73	93.4%	Finished strong.
Drop LBs	80	76	95.0%	Great job!
Inside LBs	160	149	93.1%	Right on target.
Defensive backs	352	334	94.9%	Excellent.
Defensive unit	888	828	93.2%	Keep it up!

outstanding pursuit that day. We usually projected this on a large overhead screen in the meeting room.

Objective Chart

Also in that 10-minute unit meeting before showing the previous game film to the players, the coordinator would review this chart with its seven objectives. The results in this one are also from the Arizona game. We listed pursuit as the second objective. The other columns were items we emphasized as keys to victory each week.

Obviously, column 1 was paramount. But in many victories, only three or four of the other columns would contain a "Yes." We celebrate only when column 1 is a win, but we make it a real celebration. Don't make a victory feel like a loss!

Column 3 indicates our tackling efficiency. Column 4 shows that we gave up no long passes (25 yards or more) and just one long run (15 yards or more). These distances can be massaged to fit the maturity of the team. Moving them both up 5 yards would not be out of line in today's game, especially with a younger defense.

DEFENSIVE OBJECTIVES

#1	#2	#3	#4	#5	#6	#7
Win	Pursuit 93%	Tackling 90%	Control long plays	3rd, 4th down shutdowns	Control sudden change	Control 2 minute

Opponent: Arizona

#1	#2	#3	#4	#5	#6	#7
Yes 9-7	Yes 93.2%	Yes 95.5%	Yes No long pass, 1 run 16 yds	Yes 7/21 (33%)	Yes (None)	Yes Stopped 2 drives

Column 5 speaks to the unit's ability to stop drives and force punts. Column 6 addresses the challenge of stopping an opponent after we have turned the ball over. Versus Arizona, our offense never turned it over except by punting. Column 7 indicates our two-minute performance, that was certainly critical at the end of this close game.

I see football as a living, moving art form that can be evaluated on tape. Grading linebackers is a labor of love. Players and coaches want to know how players perform and improve; game evaluations should accurately measure both. Many coaches don't like grading because it takes time, and because being consistent and fair in grading is hard work. But players appreciate the feedback and will improve because they respect the coach's knowledge and accuracy if he has earned their respect by working diligently in evaluating them.

Index

Note: Page numbers in italics refer to figures.

About the Author

Lou Tepper is one of football's most widely respected defensive coaches. He has coached 20 linebackers who have gone on to play professional football, including three Butkus Award winners—Alfred Williams, Dana Howard, and Kevin Hardy—and one Butkus Award runner-up. He directed nationally ranked defenses at the College of William and Mary, Virginia Tech, the University of Colorado, and the University of Illinois, the last of which became known as "Linebacker University" during his nine-year stay.

After serving as Illinois' defensive coordinator and as assistant head coach to John Mackovic from 1988 to 1991, Tepper was promoted to head coach. In five seasons he guided the Illini to three bowl appearances, including a 30-0 victory in the 1994 Liberty Bowl. During his tenure as head coach at Illinois, 91 percent of the team's seniors graduated. Tepper also developed a racial harmony policy for which he received a Martin Luther King Jr. Award.

Tepper graduated from Rutgers University, where he was a standout defensive back. He went on to assist Jim Root at the University of New Hampshire and the College of William and Mary from 1968 to 1977, Bill Dooley at Virginia Tech from 1978 to 1982, and Bill McCartney at the University of Colorado from 1983 to 1987.

Tepper was named the 1990 Assistant Coach of the Year in the Big Ten Conference by *The Sporting News*. He served as chairman of the Big Ten Head Football Coaches organization in 1996. For three years he was a member of the American Football Coaches Association Ethics Committee, headed by American Football Coaches Association executive director, Grant Teaff. A charter member and chairman of the Illinois State Board of the Fellowship of Christian Athletes (FCA), Tepper is an active speaker for FCA and Promise Keepers, an organization headed by his former coaching colleague Bill McCartney.

Tepper and his wife, Karen, have two children, Matthew and Stacy Ann. His favorite leisure activities include reading, jogging, and racquetball.